THE FALL
RISCA PA
IN WW1

Steve Veysey

Tango Creations Publishers – Wales – UK
www.tangocreations.co.uk

Frist published in the UK by Tango Creations Publishers, Wales UK, 2018-2019
© 2018 - 2019 Steve Veysey & Tango Creations Publishers

Printed and bound by Lulu
Cover Illustration by Martin Sotelano
Photography by: Steven Veysey, Steve Allen, Frederik Sohier, John Hughes, Mick McCann, Steve Lyons and John Rawlings.
Stock photography by Matt Redding, Bruce Mewett and Anja Osenberg, all from Pixabay.
Cover, interior design & landscape images by Martin Sotelano

Steve Veysey asserts the moral right to be identified as the author.
All rights reserved. No part of this book may be reprinted or reproduced or utilized in any form or by any electronic, mechanical, or other means, known or hereafter invented, including photocopying and/or recording, or in any information storage or retrieval system without permission in writing from the publishers.

ISBN: 978-0-244-42820-4

This book is also available in PDF format
First Electronic edition published in the UK by Tango Creations Publishers, Wales, November 2018

As thanks for your purchase of the paperback copy of this book we want to give you the electronic version (Pdf) free (Compatible with any PC, Mobile Phone, Tablet, etc.)
Get your free E-Book copy Now!
Please send an email to info@tangocreations.co.uk attaching the receipt of your purchase. We will send you the link to download the E-Book.

To the memory of

JOHN ARTHUR VEYSEY
2nd Battalion, Monmouthshire Regiment
02/11/1895 - 02/02/1915 (Age 19)
Buried in Strand Military Cemetery, Belgium

JACK VEYSEY
Welsh Guards
27/09/1917 - 15/04/1947 (Age 29)
Buried in Abercarn Cemetery, Wales

Dedication

ROY VEYSEY
Royal Navy
04/08/1928 – 21/07/2019

This book is dedicated to my late father Roy, who gave me the encouragement to write it.

None of our family had ever seen the grave of Uncle Arthur in Belgium and so after we visited it, I decided to research our local war dead and this book is the result.

Also dedicated to my grandchildren, Liam, Kieran, Sophie and Ellie who I hope will never have to see the horrors of war.

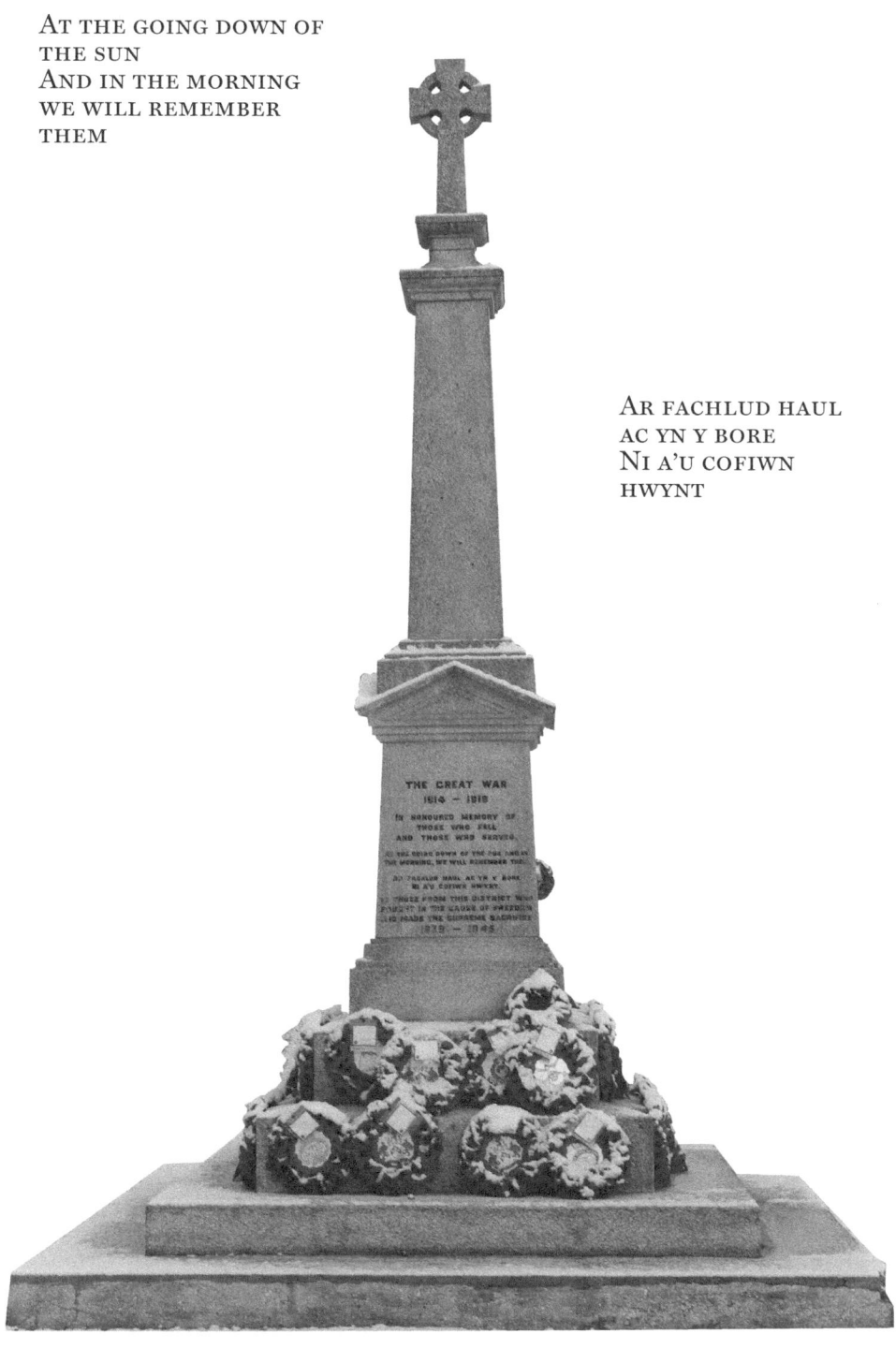

At the going down of
the sun
And in the morning
we will remember
them

Ar fachlud haul
ac yn y bore
Ni a'u cofiwn
hwynt

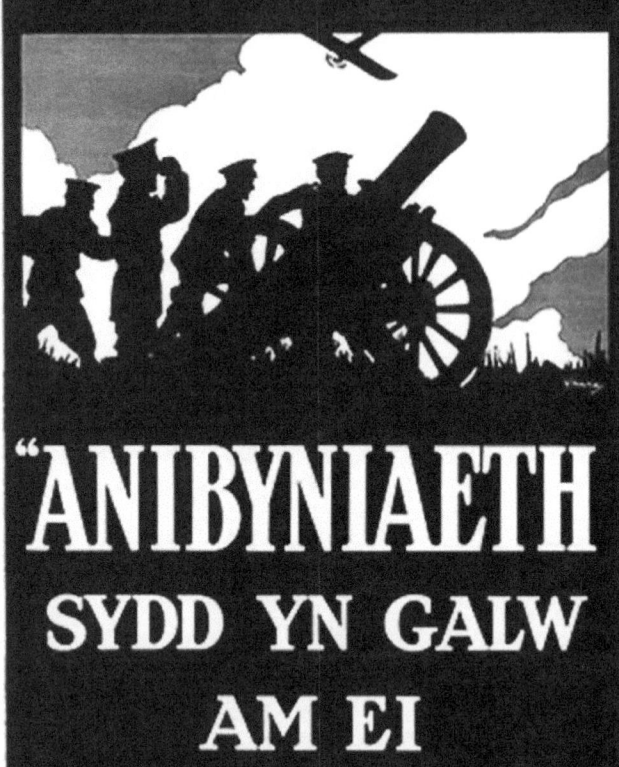

INTRODUCTION

The purpose of this book is to give the reader an opportunity to see the names of the men and women from the parish of Risca, who gave the ultimate sacrifice during World War 1.

I have used the old parish of Risca as my reference area. This starts at the Welsh Oak, Pontymister and extends to Wattsville in the one valley and to Pontywain in the other.

Throughout the parish there are a number of memorials in gardens, cemeteries, churches etc. but none which lists all the names, indeed the War Memorial at St Mary Street, Risca doesn't display any names.

I have endeavoured to list everyone who had a link with the parish but realise that I may have missed some or included people who had a tenuous link at best. Any errors or omissions are due to the author and have been made in good faith. Men and women who were born, lived, taught, worked and are buried in the area are included.

Thanks must be given to a number of people who have helped in my research and allowed me to use their notes and photographs, especially Bernard Osment, who has carried out hours of research on old newspapers and without whose help I would never have started the project. Research was carried out at Newport Reference Library and Gwent Archives using the South Wales and Weekly Argus, the South Wales Daily News and the South Wales Gazette newspapers. Information and photographs have also been supplied by Steve Allen, Frederik Sohier, John Hughes, Mick McCann, Steve Lyons and John Rawlings.

I have also received information from a number of websites including Wikipedia, Newport War Dead, Monmouthshire Warriors, The War Graves Photographic Project, British War Graves, Machen First World War Memorial Site, Commonwealth War Graves Commission and The National Archives.

At this point I must also thank Ray Westlake for producing the books First World War Graves and Memorials in Gwent, which have been a great help in locating some of the memorials shown in this book.

If I have omitted to include anyone who has provided assistance, I apologise, it is not intentional.

If you have any comments please contact me at: risca_ww1@btinternet.com

Steve Veysey
October 2018

About the author

Steve Veysey was born in Llanbadoc, Usk in 1958. After attending Risca Town Junior and Newbridge Grammar Schools he started work for the GPO, later to become BT, in 1974.

His later years with BT were spent as a trainer specialising in the delivery of software training to HM Prison staff and BT engineers. Married with two children and four grandchildren, he is now retired.

He has spent the last five years recording the details of the men and women of the surrounding areas who died in WW1 and WW2 and it is his privilege to keep their memory alive.

Contents

A — 1

ALDER PHILIP	1
ALLEN WINDSOR THISTLE	2
ANDREWS FREDERICK JOHN	2
ANDREWS JOHN	3
ATKINSON ALFRED	3
ATTWELL WILLIAM	4

B — 7

BAKER GEORGE EDWARD	7
BAKER TREVOR	7
BANFIELD JAMES	8
BANWELL FRANCIS GEORGE	9
BARKER ARTHUR JAMES	10
BATEMAN JERVIS	10
BLEWITT FRANK	11
BOOTH JOHN	12
BOOTH LYNDON	13
BRAYSHAW ROBERT HODGSON	14
BRESSINGTON ALFRED WILLIAM	15
BRICE GEORGE ALBERT	15
BRIDGE WILLIAM CHARLES	16
BROWN JAMES ALBERT	17
BROWN OLIVER	18
BRYANT GEORGE CHARLES	19
BUCKLEY JOHN ARTHUR	20
BUDDING WILLIAM JOHN	20
BUDGETT EDWIN GEORGE	21

C — 23

CALLIER ETHEL FANNY MAY CHILTON	23
CARPENTER WILLIAM	23
CARTER SIMEON JOHN	25
CAWLEY FREDERICK	26
CHADWICK WILLIAM JOHN	27
CHICK WILLIAM	28
CLISSOLD CYRIL JAMES	28
CLOTHIER ISAAC	29

COCKELL JOHN GRANT	30
COLES WILLIAM JOHN	31
COMPTON SIDNEY	32
COOK ALFRED JOHN	32
COOPER WILFRED	33
COULSON ANDREW LEWIS	34
CRANE ARTHUR STANLEY	35
CUNNICK WILLIAM HENRY	35

D 37

DANIEL NOEL THOMAS	37
DANIELS WILLIAM JOHN	37
DARBY CHARLES RICHARD	38
DART DAVID WILLIAM BOWEN	39
DART WILLIAM ERNEST	39
DAVIES ARTHUR GEORGE	41
DAVIES GEORGE	42
DAVIES JOHN EMLYN	43
DAVIES MARGARET HANNAH	44
DAVIES OSWALD	44
DAVIS ALBERT REGINALD	45
DAWE ARTHUR HENRY	46
DOBSON WILLIAM	46
DOLLERY FRANK	47
DONOVAN MICHAEL	48
DOWNES ALBERT EDWARD	48
DOWNES CHARLES ARTHUR	49
DUFFIELD WILLIAM EWART	50

E 51

EDWARDS ARTHUR	51
ELLIS FREDERICK WILLIAM	51
EVANS STANLEY	52
EVANS WILLIAM DAVID G	53
EVANS WILLIAM JONES	54
EVERETT SIDNEY CHARLES	55
EVERSON EDWIN	55
EVERSON WILLIAM SAMUEL	56

G 59

GARDNER ALBERT	59
GEEVES WILLIAM CHAPLIN	59
GIBBS CHARLES ARCHIBALD	60

GILES RALPH	61
GILL REGINALD ARTHUR	62
GODDEN JOSEPH EWART	63
GOODING THOMAS JOHN	64
GOUGH MOSTYN GEORGE	65
GREEN WILLIAM JOHN	65
GREENSLADE WILLIAM JOHN	66
GRIFFITHS JOHN	67

H — 69

HALL THOMAS JAMES	69
HANCOCK HUBERT BERTRAM	70
HANN FRANCIS EDGAR GOLDING	70
HARDS WILLIAM JOHN	71
HARDY CECIL JOHN	72
HARPER WILLIAM HUGH	72
HARRIS ARTHUR	73
HARRIS THOMAS	74
HART ERNEST	75
HARTSHORN ARTHUR WILLIAM	76
HATHERALL HENRY JOHN	76
HATTON WILLIAM	77
HAWKINS WILLIAM ISAAC	78
HAYNES HENRY GEORGE	78
HEMMINGS FRANK	79
HERON ALBERT ERNEST	80
HEYWORTH HEYWORTH POTTER LAWRENCE	80
HILEY ANTHONY	81
HODDELL LEONARD	82
HOLLOWAY ELI	83
HOLTHAM THOMAS GEORGE	83
HOPKINS ALFRED	84
HOPKINS IRA	84
HOUGHTON JOHN ALFRED	85
HOWELLS FRED	86
HUMPHRIES GEORGE HENRY	86

I — 89

IVIN JOHN IRA	89

J — 91

JAMES ARTHUR LESLIE	91
JAMES GODFREY GEORGE	91

JAMES JARVIS	92
JAMES NOAH	93
JAMES SAM	93
JAMES THOMAS WILLIAM	94
JAY ALBERT WILLIAM MM	95
JAYNE FREDERICK GEORGE	96
JAYNE WALTER HARVARD JOSEPH	97
JELF ARCHIBALD LEONARD TAYLOR	97
JENKINS ALBERT	98
JENKINS ALBERT EDGAR MM	99
JENKINS ANEURIN	100
JENKINS BENJAMIN	101
JENKINS EDWIN WILLARD	102
JOHNSON GEORGE JAMES	103
JOHNSON WILLIAM HOWARD	103
JONES ALFRED	104
JONES ARTHUR THEOPHILUS SUMPTON	105
JONES EDGAR	105
JONES FREDERICO SALDANHA	106
JONES HERBERT OWEN	107
JONES JOHN	108
JONES RALPH EDWIN	109
JONES RICHARD COBDEN	110
JONES WILLIAM JAMES	110

K — *113*

KEAR ARTHUR WILLIAM	113
KEAR HERBERT STANLEY	113
KENNARD BERTRAM HENRY	114
KENVIN THOMAS	115
KING HERBERT PARRY	116
KIRKPATRICK SAMUEL	117
KNIGHT HUBERT	117
KNIGHT JAMES	118

L — *121*

LEONARD FREDERICK WELLINGTON	121
LEWIS ABNER JOHN	121
LEWIS DAVID	122
LEWIS SIDNEY RALPH	122
LEWIS WILLIAM	123
LIGHT ALBERT THOMAS	124

LLEWELLYN SAMUEL	124
LOTT WILLIAM REES	125

M — 127

MANTLE DAVID JOHN	127
MAYBERRY COURTNEY	127
McGREGOR CHARLES MM	128
MELLISH ALBERT	129
MOGFORD GEORGE	130
MOORE EDWARD	131
MOORE WILLIAM JOHN	132
MORGAN ALFRED	132
MORGAN ARTHUR AUGUSTUS	134
MORGAN CHARLES ERNEST	135
MORGAN JAMES ARTHUR	135
MORGAN JOHN GEORGE	136
MORGAN WILLIAM RICH MC	137
MORRIS EDGAR	137
MORRIS JAMES	138
MORRIS RICHARD	139
MURRAY PHILLIP HENRY	140

N — 141

NICHOLAS TREVOR	141

O — 143

OGBORNE WILLIAM CHARLES	143
ONIONS WILFRED	143
ORMAN REUBEN	144
ORMAN ZEPHANIAH	145
OWEN ALEXANDER PROSSER	146
OWEN JONATHAN	147

P — 149

PARKINS WALTER LEWIS	149
PARSONS GEORGE	149
PEARCE EDWARD	150
PEARSON SYDNEY	151
PERROW WILLIAM	152
PETERSON CHARLES	153
PHILLIPS GODFREY REES	154
PHILLIPS GRIFF	154
POOLE WILLIAM FRANK TREWAVAS	155

POTTER ALBERT HENRY	155
POWELL CHARLES	156
POWELL JOSEPH HENRY	156
POWELL PERCY	158
PRITCHARD CLARENCE HENRY	158
PROTHERO WILLIAM JAMES	159
PROUT CHARLES GEORGE	159
PUGH DAVID JOHN	161

R — *163*

RAFFERTY THOMAS ALFRED	163
RALLISON BERNARD	164
RALLISON VICTOR EDWARD	164
RAWLINGS ARTHUR JOHN	165
RICHARDS GEORGE	166
RICHARDS JOHN READ	167
RICHARDS LEWIS GARFIELD	168
RIDEOUT FRANCIS BENJAMIN	168
ROBATHAN DOUGLAS PARKER	169
ROBBINS HERBERT GEORGE	170
ROBBINS WILLIAM GEORGE	171
ROBERTS ALBERT	172
ROBERTS WILLIAM HENRY	172
ROBINSON FRED	173
ROSE JOHN	173
ROWLANDS DAVID FRANCIS	174

S — *175*

SAGE WILLIAM JAMES	175
SALATHIEL EWART GLADSTONE	176
SHEEHAN DANIEL	176
SHORE JOSEPH	177
SIBLEY JOHN DAVID	178
SKINNER FREDERICK	178
SMITH ERNEST WILLIAM	179
SMITH WILLIAM HENRY	179
STACEY EXTON JAMES	180
STEPHENS RICHARD EVAN	181
STEVENS JOHN MM	181
STEVENS TOM ALBAN	182
STROUD CHARLES HENRY	182
STROUD WILLIAM	184

STROUD WILLIAM JOHN	184
SULLIVAN WALTER ERNEST	185

T — 187

TAYLOR CHARLES	187
TAYLOR JOHN WILLIAM	187
THOMAS EVAN HENRY	188
THOMAS FRANK	189
THOMAS GEORGE DAVID MM	190
THOMAS WILLIAM	190
THOMAS WILLIAM GEORGE	191
TUDOR DOUGLAS	191
TUTTON HARRY	192
TYLER GEORGE EDWARD VICTOR	193

V — 195

VENN WILLIAM GEORGE MM	195

W — 197

WALKER EDWARD JAMES	197
WALLACE JOSEPH	198
WALSH THOMAS	199
WALTERS THOMAS HENRY	199
WARD DANIEL	200
WATKINS HERBERT GEORGE	201
WATTS HERBERT IVOR	202
WATTS PERCY EDWIN	203
WEBB WILLIAM	204
WELCH ERNEST AUGUSTUS	204
WELCH GILBERT GEORGE	205
WEST WILLIAM JAMES	206
WHEELER WILLIAM BERTRAM	207
WHITE EDWIN	208
WIGMORE FRANK HAROLD	208
WILCOX RAYMOND	209
WILDE BENONI REX	209
WILKIE CHARLES JOSEPH	211
WILLIAMS ALBERT STANLEY	212
WILLIAMS EDWARD BOURTON	214
WILLIAMS ISAAC JOHN	214
WILLIAMS OSWALD MORGAN	215
WILLIAMS THOMAS JOHN	215
WILLIAMS WILLIAM JAMES	216

WINSTONE WILLIAM JAMES   216

ROLL OF HONOUR

MEMORIALS   *219*

Cross Keys and Pontywain   *220*
    Gladstone Street, Primitive Methodist Church   220
    Hope Baptist Church   221
    Pontywaun Wesleyan Church & School   222
    St Catherine's Church   223
    Trinity Chapel   224

Risca and Pontymister   *225*
    Bethany Baptist Church   225
    Ebenezer Primitive Methodist Church   226
    Miner's Memorial   227
    Moriah Baptist Church   228
    Pontywaun County School   229
    Risca Workingmen's Club   230
    St John's Church   231
    St Margaret's Church   232
    St Mary's Church   233

Violets
(1915)

By Roland Leighton

Violets from Plug Street Wood,
Sweet, I send you oversea.
(It is strange they should be blue,
Blue, when his soaked blood was red,
For they grew around his head;
It is strange they should be blue.)

Violets from Plug Street Wood-
Think what they have meant to me-
Life and Hope and Love and You
(And you did not see them grow
Where his mangled body lay
Hiding horror from the day;
Sweetest it was better so.)

Violets from oversea,
To your dear, far, forgetting land
These I send in memory,
Knowing You will understand.

CASUALTIES DETAILS IN ALPHABETICAL ORDER

A

ALDER PHILIP
SERGEANT, D COMPANY, 4ᵀᴴ SOUTH WALES BORDERERS
SERVICE No 12501
DIED OF WOUNDS 22 AUGUST 1915, AGE 26
BURIED ALEXANDRIA MILITARY CEMETERY, EGYPT

Philip was born in 1889 in Frome, Somerset, to Joseph and Kate Alder. In 1891 the family were living in Frome with Joseph working as a carter.
Sometime after 1901 Philip moved to Wales working as a miner in 1911 whilst living in 33 Trafalgar Street, Pontymister.
He married Margaret Ann Richards in 1914 and they had a daughter, Phyllis M Alder the following year.
He enlisted in the South Wales Borderers in Newport and at the time of his death he was shown as living at 13 Mill Street Pontymister.
The SWB 4th Battalion landed in Gallipoli on July 15th 1915 with Philip dying of wounds just over a month later after being evacuated to Egypt.
He was entitled to the British War Medal, 1915 Star and the Victory Medal.
The following is taken from the Royal Regiment of Wales Museum fact sheet.
In July 1915, the 13th Division was sent to Gallipoli, together with four other Territorial and New Army Divisions in a final effort to capture the Peninsula. After a fortnight in the line at Cape Helles the Division was landed at Anzac and there took part in a great effort to capture the Sari Bair Ridge in conjunction with a new landing by the other fresh Divisions at Suvla Bay, six miles to the north.
The 40th Brigade was ordered to protect the left flank of the main attack. Its task was to make a night march of two miles northward along the coast, then to wheel half-right, and by a night attack capture Damakjelik Bair, a ridge which formed the lower end of one of the main spurs of Sari Bair.
At 8 p.m. on August 6th 1915 the advance started, the 4th Battalion having the honour of finding the advanced guard. After covering two miles of very broken and difficult ground covered with boulders and prickly scrub the battalion reached the nullah of the Achyl Dere, its deployment position.
Here it was fired on from a trench on the far side, but D Company in the lead dashed across with a cheer and carried the trench with the bayonet. The battalion then crossed, wheeled to its right in the darkness, and by 1.30 a.m. after dealing with several parties of Turks on the way, had secured its objective on Damakjelik Bair, a very fine piece of work.
On August 9th 1915, it met and defeated a most determined counterattack, but in doing so lost Lieutenant Colonel Gillespie, the Commanding Officer who had trained it to such a high standard of efficiency, and who had led it with such skill and resolution in its first action. He was killed early in the attack while directing machine gun fire. By August 22nd, after further heavy fighting, the Battalion had

lost over 400 officers and men out of the 775 who had landed on August 4. Phillip died on August 22nd 1915 and is buried in Alexandria (Chatby) Military Cemetery, Egypt

ALLEN WINDSOR THISTLE
PRIVATE, 2ND/4TH BATTALION
LOYAL NORTH LANCASHIRE REGIMENT
SERVICE No 12501
DIED 3 AUGUST 1917, AGE 20
BURIED DIVISIONAL COLLECTING POST CEMETERY AND EXTENSION, BELGIUM

Windsor, born in 1897 and baptised on February 6th 1898, at St Lythans, Glamorgan, was the son of James and Bessie Allen.
In 1901 the family were living in Llanfrechfa, Pontypool where James was a haulier in the Nut and Bolt Works.
By 1911 they were living in 19 Wellspring Terrace, Risca where James was a foundry worker and Windsor was working on a farm.
He enlisted at Cross Keys as a Private into the York Regiment, Service Number 202545 before transferring later to the 2/4th Battalion, Loyal North Lancashire Regiment.
The 2/4th Battalion was formed at Preston in October 1914 as a second line unit. They moved to Ashford in September 1915 and were placed under the command of 170th Brigade in 57th (2nd West Lancashire) Division. The battalion moved on to Aldershot in July 1916 and then to nearby Blackdown in October. On February 8th 1917 the 2/4th Battalion landed at Le Havre as part of the 170th Brigade in the 57th (2nd West Lancashire) Division. The 57th Division served on the Western Front for the rest of the war.
Windsor was killed on August 3rd 1917 and is buried in Divisional Collecting Post Cemetery and Extension, Belgium.
He was entitled to the British War and Victory medals.

ANDREWS FREDERICK JOHN
GUNNER, 113TH BATTERY 25TH BRIGADE
ROYAL FIELD ARTILLERY
SERVICE No 156885
DIED 27 JUNE 1918, AGE 20
BURIED PERNES BRITISH CEMETERY, FRANCE

Frederick John was one of eight children to John Henry and Sarah Ann Andrews, (nee Gunter).
He was born in 1898 in Cwmbran where his father worked as a shearer in the Iron Works.
By 1901, the family moved from Two Locks road in Cwmbran to Phillip Street, Risca as John Henry was now a coal miner.

Frederick enlisted in Risca and served as a Gunner with 113th Battery, 25 Brigade in the Royal Field Artillery.
He arrived in France sometime after 1915 and died of an illness, age 20, on June 27th 1918.
Frederick is buried in Pernes British Cemetery, France.

ANDREWS JOHN
PRIVATE, 11TH FIELD BAKERY
ARMY SERVICE CORPS
SERVICE NO S/359752
KILLED IN ACTION 22 DECEMBER 1917, AGE 32
BURIED BOULOGNE EASTERN CEMETERY, FRANCE

John was the son of Benjamin and Sarah Andrews. Born in Newport, he was baptised on November 29th 1886 at St Woolos.
John and his family lived in Newport where he was employed as a market gardener alongside his father and brother William. The family lived in Stow Park Gardens and Llandevaud before moving to Bellevue, Cromwell Road, Risca.
He enlisted into the army at Cross Keys, joining the 11th Field Bakery in the Royal Army Service Corps.
I haven't been able to discover much about his time in the Field Bakery Unit, but the following gives an idea of their role.
There is an old adage that an army marches on its stomach, and by 1914 the British Army realised that to fight even a short war in Europe it would have to provide the required infrastructure to feed its troops on campaign. Much of this work was done by the Army Service Corps (ASC) and one of its key units in providing part of the staple diet was the Field Bakery. In 1914 there was one Field Bakery in every infantry division. Staffed by one officer and ninety-two men, it could produce enough bread for more than 20,000 men. Because of the nature of their work they did not set up these bakeries near the front, and many in 1914/15 were based in locations like Rouen and Abbeville, and a little nearer the front in St Omer and Hazebrouck.
John was killed on December 22nd 1917 and is buried in Boulogne Eastern Cemetery.

ATKINSON ALFRED
PRIVATE, 2ND BATTALION
SOUTH WALES BORDERERS
SERVICE NO 14130
KILLED IN ACTION 19 JUNE 1915
REMEMBERED HELLES MEMORIAL, TURKEY

Early records of Alfred are vague, although it is thought he was born in Barrow in Furness, Lancashire between 1876 - 79. His father's name was recorded as William according to one of the military records.

In 1911 he was living in 29 Woodland Terrace, Rogerstone with his wife Mary, (nee Hopkins) and son David age 5.

His occupation is shown as a general labourer in the steel and wire works. They appear to have had two other children, Leonard born 1911 and Vera born in 1912.

Alfred and family had moved to 3 Mill Street, Risca by 1915 and he was now working in Cwmcarn colliery, before he enlisted in the 2nd Battalion, South Wales Borderers.

A newspaper cutting suggests he was in the army previously seeing action in the Boer War and the Indian Frontier.

The 2nd SWB embarked at Avonmouth for Egypt on March 29th 1915 arriving at Alexandria on route to Gallipoli, where they arrived on April 25th at Helles.

The 2nd Battalion landed 3 companies on S Beach on the shores of Morto Bay. In broad daylight on open beaches defended by barbed wire, rifles and machine guns they had 2 officers and 18 men killed or drowned and 2 officers and 40 men wounded.

They saw action throughout the rest of the Gallipoli campaign. In the efforts to advance from Cape Helles in May and June it fought with great determination and stubbornness.

Alfred was killed in action on June 19th 1915 and is remembered on the Helles Memorial.

ATTWELL WILLIAM
PRIVATE, 51ST FIELD AMBULANCE
ROYAL ARMY MEDICAL CORPS
SERVICE NO 78040
KILLED IN ACTION 7 JULY 1916, AGE 29
BURIED GORDON DUMP CEMETERY, OVILLERS-LA BOISSELLE, FRANCE

William was born in 1887 to Francis (Frank) and Margaret Attwell in Cross Keys. Aged 11 years, he was baptised in Risca Parish Church on January 29th 1899. His brother Albert aged 7 and sisters Mary Olive aged 9 and Margaret Anne aged 3 were also baptised at the same time.

In 1891 the family were living in 14 Watts Vale, (Wattsville) Monmouthshire where Frank is shown as employed as a collier. Frank died in 1897 and by 1901 the family have moved to Bright Street, Cross Keys where William 14 and older brother David 17, are themselves now working as miners.

William married Cissie Susannah Leonard on 27th December 1909 in Undy, Monmouthshire, Wales and they lived in 2 Waunfawr Terrace, Cross Keys in 1911. By 1915 William and Cissie had moved to the Causeway, Undy and had an adopted daughter Henrietta Mary aged 9.

He joined the Royal Army Medical Corp at Aldershot on November 2nd 1915 when his service records show he was 5ft 6ins tall and weighed 9 stone. He had an expanded chest measurement of 35½ins and it was noted that he had a scar on his right hand little finger.

His records show he was in the UK from his enlistment until March 15th 1916 when he went overseas. He left Southampton on SS Queen Alexandra arriving in Rouen the next day.

He was posted to the 51st Field Ambulance, part of the 17th (Northern) Division. The Division was involved in fighting at the Bluff (south east of Ypres on the Comines canal), part of a number of engagements officially known as the Actions of Spring 1916.

They also fought in The Battle of Albert in which the Division captured Fricourt and The Battle of Delville Wood. These were both phases of the battles of the Somme 1916.

William, killed on July 7th 1916 is buried in Gordon Dump Cemetery, France.

He was entitled to the British War and Victory medals.

5 QUESTIONS TO MEN WHO HAVE *NOT* ENLISTED

1. If you are physically fit and between 19 and 38 years of age, are you really satisfied with what you are doing to-day?

2. Do you feel happy as you walk along the streets and see <u>other</u> men wearing the King's uniform?

3. What will you say in years to come when people ask you—"Where did <u>you</u> serve in the great War"?

4. What will you answer when your children grow up, and say "Father, why weren't you a soldier, too"?

5. What would happen to the Empire if every man stayed at home?

YOUR KING AND COUNTRY NEED YOU
ENLIST TO-DAY
GOD SAVE THE KING.

B

BAKER GEORGE EDWARD
BOMBARDIER, 412TH HOWITZER BATTERY
ROYAL FIELD ARTILLERY
SERVICE No 13175
DIED OF WOUNDS 22 DECEMBER 1918, AGE 36
BURIED RISCA OLD CEMETERY, RISCA, WALES

George Edward Baker, born in Risca in 1884 was the son of Thomas and Margaret Baker. Originally the family lived in Ty Du Rd, Rogerstone before moving to Risca.
George married Emma Bateman in 1907 and by 1911 they were living with their son Clifford at 5 Gelli Cottages, Risca. George's occupation was shown as an underground colliery worker. He enlisted as a Bombardier into the 412th Howitzer Battery, Royal Field Artillery. At this point there is not much further information regarding his war service apart from him dying in Colchester Military Hospital on December 22nd 1918.
He is buried in Risca Old Cemetery, Cromwell Rd, Risca and commemorated on the memorial in Bethany Church, Risca.

BAKER TREVOR
LANCE CORPORAL, 1ST BATTALION
SOUTH WALES BORDERERS
SERVICE No 7090
KILLED 21 OCTOBER 1914, AGE 40
BURIED PERTH CEMETERY (CHINA WALL), BELGIUM

Trevor was born in Risca in 1885, to parents John and Ann Baker. The family lived in Main Rd, Risca in 1891 and in 1901 at 35 Wood St, Abercarn where John and Trevor were both employed as coal miners. Ann died in 1902 aged 45, with John getting married to Elizabeth Webb in 1903 and by 1911 they were all living in Penrhiwceiber, Glamorgan.
Trevor enlisted in Pontypool into the 1st Battalion South Wales Borderers, and went overseas on August 31st 1914 as part of the British Expeditionary Force.
Battalion War Diary Capt. C.J. Paterson
Wednesday October 21st 1914
   "An early start 4 a.m., marched on towards

BOESINGHE, and it is obvious by the noise that we are in for something very soon. Pass through PILCKEN. Order of March, D, A, B, C. Arrived at LANGEMARCK at about 8 a.m. and halt. C.O. and I sent for the Brigadier and received orders. Queens are to advance and attack POELKAPPELLE soon, whilst S.W.B. attack the same place itself.
In order to do this we have to go very much to the right to connect with the Second Division's left which is on the HAANEBECK stream and this makes our front very large. Start off with D and A in firing line. D on left, A on right. B in support of D, and C in support of A. Come in contact with the enemy at once as soon as we leave the village.
They are in fair strength. We shove them back a bit not much. The breadth we have to cover is too much for one Battalion. News comes from D and A of their casualties, and we hear Curgenven is killed and also young Watkins, who only came out a few days ago. Poor fellows. B Company pushes up in support of D and we hold our own.
The Germans come on in great masses, silly idiots. We are shelled from every side and big coal-boxes are almost more than flesh and blood can bear, though the damage they do is next to nothing unless one lucky shot happens to get in the middle of a mass of men. Towards evening things get a bit quieter and we dig ourselves in. The rolls are called, and we find we have two officers killed, one wounded and missing, and 146 killed and wounded. Not quite as bad as September 26th, but bad enough. And we can't get at most of them.
At last Battalion Headquarters withdraw into the outskirts of the village where we occupy a house of sorts".

Trevor was killed on October 21st 1914, just 2 months after landing in France and is buried in Perth Cemetery, (China Wall), Belgium.

BANFIELD JAMES
SIGNALLER, HMS VIKING
ROYAL NAVAL VOLUNTEER RESERVE
SERVICE NO Z/4591
DIED 5 JULY 1918, AGE 19
BURIED TERLINCTHUN BRITISH CEMETERY, WIMILLE, FRANCE

James, son of Shadrach and Mary Banfield was born May 27th 1899 in Tintern, Mon.
Educated in Pontywaun County School, Risca he left school and became a clerk.
He enlisted on October 2nd 1917 and trained on HMS Victory VI and Victory I training ships before joining HMS Viking on May 1 1918.
In his service record he is described as 5ft 7ins tall with a 34ins chest. He had brown eyes, light brown hair and a fresh complexion with no discernible wounds, scars or marks. He was shown as being of *"Very Good"* character and *"Satisfactory"* ability. James was 'Lost Overboard' on June 22nd 1918 although he wasn't officially declared deceased until July 5th. James' body was recovered some days after being

washed overboard and he was buried at Terlincthun Cemetery, Wimille, near Calais.

James is commemorated on the Pontywaun County School and Moriah Baptist Church memorials.

His parents were sent a letter by Leading Signaller E.W. Griffiths explaining the circumstances of his death.

From the Weekly Argus July 13th 1918.

> *"I will not try to console you with the fact that your son lost his life by accident while 'doing his bit' as I know how futile that would be, having lost my own father by accidental drowning at sea...My greatest regret is that nobody saw him go overboard or else an attempt would have been made to save him had he floated, which is highly improbable. He came on the bridge for duty at 5 p.m. At 5.30 he asked my permission to go and get a bucket for washing his clothes. I let him go down from the bridge at 5.45 which was the last time I saw him......At about 6.10 pm a man picked up a bucket, which was jammed under the guard rail. We do not know how it got there. We can only assume that 'Taff' (as he was affectionately known to us all) reached the deck and a big sea came over him taking him overboard before he had a chance to cling to anything. He probably never knew he went overboard as the suction from the propellers probably drew him under...It greatly upset me as of course, he worked under me. He was just getting used to the ways of the Navy at sea and seemed quite happy. He was only talking to me that evening of what a good time he would spend on his first leave from the Navy and what he would tell you all. He was a very willing lad and a hard worker always trying his hardest to please......assuring you and all his friends of our deep sympathy in your loss. E.W.G.".*

BANWELL FRANCIS GEORGE
PRIVATE, 8TH BATTALION
WELSH REGIMENT
SERVICE NO 19377
DIED 25 APRIL 1916
REMEMBERED BASRA MEMORIAL, IRAQ

Francis (Frank) George was the son of Edwin and Sarah Banwell, (nee Price). Born in 1883 in Pontywain, he grew up in Jamesville, Cwmcarn, firstly in number 51 and then later at number 45. Edwin was a general labourer whilst Frank and three of his brothers worked as coal miners.

He married Clara Ann Pring in 1910 and they moved to Newbridge living in 13 Church Road, Frank was now working as a general labourer.

It appears that they had two children, Hilda born 1913 and Francis G. born in 1915. Frank was living in Llanbradach, Glamorgan when he enlisted in the 8th Battalion, Welsh Regiment serving as Private 19377.

According to his records he landed overseas on October 28th 1915, probably going to Gallipoli where the 8th Battalion were involved in the war against the Turkish army.

On January 7th, after being in action against the Turks at Helles they were evacu-

ated in the following days to Port Said.
They moved to Mesopotamia on February 12th 1916, to join the force being prepared for the relief of the garrison at Kut al Amara, which was under siege.
As part of the Tigris Corps they were unsuccessful in the attempt to relieve Kut. It was during this attempt that Frank was injured and he died of his wounds on April 25th 1916.
Frank is remembered on the Basra Memorial, Iraq.

BARKER ARTHUR JAMES
DRIVER, 63ʳᴰ DIVISION SIGNAL COMPANY
ROYAL ENGINEERS
SERVICE NO 357020
KILLED IN ACTION 30 SEPTEMBER 1918, AGE 27
BURIED ANNEUX BRITISH CEMETERY, FRANCE

Arthur, born in Risca, married Lillian M Cotterell in 1910.
When Arthur enlisted at Edlington, Northumberland, the records show he was living in Doncaster, Yorkshire.
He was in the Royal Engineers Corps of the 63rd (Royal Naval) Divisional Signal Company.
The 63rd (Royal Naval) Division was originally formed as the Royal Naval Division at the outbreak of WW1, from Royal Navy and Royal Marine reservists and volunteers, who were not needed for service at sea.
They saw action at Antwerp in 1914 and at Gallipoli in 1915. After severe losses they were transferred to the British Army in 1916 and designated as the 63rd RN Division, fighting on the Western Front for the remainder of the war.
It is not known when Arthur enlisted but it appears it was after 1915.
In 1918 the Division were involved in a number of battles including St Quentin, Bapaume and Albert.
On September 27th they were part of the Battle of the Canal du Nord in the Nord-Pas-de-Calais region of France.
Arthur was killed in this battle and is buried in Anneux British Cemetery.

BATEMAN JERVIS
PRIVATE, 2ᴺᴰ BATTALION
SOUTH WALES BORDERERS
SERVICE NO 39461
KILLED IN ACTION 27 JANUARY 1917, AGE 35
REMEMBERED THIEPVAL MEMORIAL, FRANCE

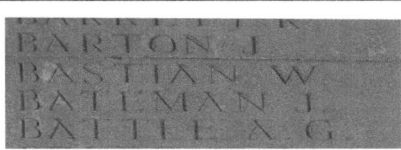

The son of Samuel and Elizabeth, Jervis was born in Risca on December 17th 1881.
His father Samuel ran a greengrocers shop close to the Church in Risca.
He started at Risca School on August 23rd 1886 leaving on July 7th 1888 for the

Mixed Department. After leaving school he joined the family business working in his father's shop as a grocer's assistant.

In 1911 Jervis was lodging with William Sanders and his family at 16 Temperance Hill, Risca before moving to 9 Phillips Terrace, Risca.

His service records have not survived but it is known that he enlisted in Newport and served with the Monmouthshire Regiment, Service Number 3507 before transferring to the 2nd Battalion South Wales Borderers, Service Number 39461. It appears that he enlisted after 1915 as he was only awarded the British War Medal and Victory Medal.

The 2nd Battalion, SWB were heavily involved in the Gallipoli Campaign before arriving in France in March 1916 when it is possible that Jervis joined them at this time.

They were in action at the Battle of the Somme on July 1st 1916 where they lost 11 officers and 235 men killed and missing in the first few minutes, and they had 4 officers and 149 men wounded out of a total of 21 officers and 578 men. Although some of the men made the German wire 300 yards away the Division's attack failed completely.

They fought in various parts along the front line throughout the year and spent the latter part December out of the line at Le Quesnoy training and repairing billets.

Whilst training at Le Quesnoy one of the officers, 2nd Lt. Wardle, had an unfortunate accident. He was throwing bombs when one went off prematurely shattering his right hand and damaging his leg.

The battalion moved on to Carnay Camp then Guillemont before moving into the front line at Morval. The weather was very cold and the conditions underfoot extremely bad. There was 3ins of snow and men were reporting sick with trench foot. They came out of the line on January 20th for two days for rest and treatment of the men's feet.

They returned to the front line carrying out trench repairs and installing duckboards, although the weather was extremely cold and frosty, and the enemy sniping and shelling, this work was carried out with little casualties. Preparations were made over the next few days for an attack on the German front line at Morval. The attack commenced at 05.30 am on January 27th when the battalion moved forward behind the artillery attack. The first objective was easily attained with the capture of 6 officers and 395 German prisoners. Heavy German shelling continued all along the front line and enemy aircraft patrolled the area, although one was shot down with both occupants killed.

It was during this day, January 27th 1917 that Jervis Bateman was killed, his body was never recovered and he is remembered on the Thiepval Memorial.

BLEWITT FRANK
PRIVATE, 2ND BATTALION
MONMOUTHSHIRE REGIMENT
SERVICE No 1905
KILLED IN ACTION 22 JULY 1916, AGE 19
REMEMBERED THIEPVAL MEMORIAL, FRANCE

Frank Blewitt was born in Risca in 1896, second eldest son of Thomas and Elizabeth (nee Davies). The family lived in Danygraig Cottages, Risca in 1901 and Thomas was employed as a colliery labourer.

By 1911 they had moved to 1 Vine Place in Maindee, Newport where Thomas is now a labourer and Frank is a coke and coal haulier.

Frank then moved to live in Pontypool before the war and enlisted in Cwmbran into the 2nd Monmouthshire Regiment. The 2nd Battalion, Monmouthshire Regiment was a unit of the Territorial Force with its HQ in Osbourne Road, Pontypool. It was part of the Welsh Border Infantry Brigade, Welsh Division.

When war was declared in August 1914, they were at once mobilised for war and moved to defend Pembroke Dock. By August 10th they moved to Oswestry and by the beginning of September they were at Northampton.

They proceeded to France on November 7th 1914 landing at Le Havre to join 12th Brigade, 4th Division. They fought in The Second Battle of Ypres, then moved south to the Somme where they were attached to 36th (Ulster) Division, providing instruction to the newly arrived Division. On January 30th 1916 the Battalion left 4th Division and moved to the Lines of Communication. On May 1st 1916 they became a Pioneer Battalion, joining 29th Division who had just arrived from Egypt. In July they went into action in the Battle of the Somme.

As a Pioneer Battalion, the 2nd Mons were responsible for digging the communication trenches and new front line trenches. This work was extremely hazardous as the men would be under constant shelling from the Germans. During July 1916 the battalion were at Mailly Wood where he was killed on the 23rd.

Frank is commemorated on the Thiepval Memorial, France.

BOOTH JOHN
CORPORAL, 1ST BATTALION
WELSH GUARDS
SERVICE NO 338
KILLED IN ACTION 3 SEPTEMBER 1917, AGE 20
BURIED CANADA FARM CEMETERY, BELGIUM

John was born in Pontymister in 1897 to Frederick Charles and Laura Booth, (nee Wallace). In 1901 he was living in 5 Mill Row, Risca with grandparents Joseph and Sarah Booth and three of their children.

Frederick and Laura were living in Cardiff with their other two children, Albert Edward and Florence Hilda. Sadly, Florence died aged 2 in 1902 and Laura, Johns' mother died in 1910 aged 29.

By 1911 Frederick and his two sons, John and Albert living together with Joseph and Sarah in 6 Mill Terrace, Pontymister where John is shown as working in the Tin Mills.

John enlisted in Newport into the Grenadier Guards, Service Number 20077 before transferring to the 1st Battalion, Welsh Guards serving as a Corporal, Service Number 338.

The Welsh Guards were formed on February 26th 1915 and soon recruited about 600 men.

Although many of the recruits were veterans from other Guards regiments, a lot were soldiers who had only joined their regiment the previous month. John's Service Number of 20077 indicates he joined the Grenadier Guards between October 3rd and November 9th 1914, whilst his transfer to the Welsh Guards was between February 27th and March 6th 1915.

The Welsh Guards sailed for France on August 17th 1915 whilst continuing to recruit in Britain.

They landed at Havre on August 18th and joined 3rd Guards Brigade, Guards Division.

They were engaged in various actions on the Western Front including September 27th 1915 - The Battle of Loos, 1916 - The Battle of Flers-Courcelette and The Battle of Morval, 1917 - The German retreat to the Hindenburg Line, The Battle of Pilckem, The Battle of the Menin Road, The Battle of Poelkapelle, The First Battle of Passchendaele and The Battle of Cambrai 1917.

A number of records show he died on September 4th 1917, but the Commonwealth War Graves Commission give the date as September 3rd as does his CWGC headstone. He was entitled to the Victory and British War medals.

He is remembered on his grandparent's headstone at Risca Old Cemetery and Moriah Baptist Church memorial.

John is buried in Canada Farm Cemetery, Ypres, Belgium.

BOOTH LYNDON
Able Seaman, Hawke Battalion,
RN Division
Royal Naval Volunteer Reserve
Service No Z2413
Killed in action 13 November 1916, age 22
Remembered Thiepval Memorial, France

Lyndon John Booth was born in Risca on November 12th 1894 to John and Elizabeth Booth.

In 1901 the family were living in Water Lane, Risca where John is shown as a cast steel and iron cleaner.

By 1911 John is an Inn keeper at the Exchange Inn Risca and Lyndon is a coal picker.

His service records show he enlisted into the Royal Naval Voluntary Reserve on November 15th 1915 and was attached to the 5th Battalion, which was a training battalion at the Royal Naval Depot Crystal Palace.

On February 23rd 1916 he transferred to the 2nd Reserve Battalion in Blandford and then into the 1st Hawke Battalion on July 10th 1916 as a sniper in the British Expeditionary Force.

The Hawke Battalion had become part of the 63rd Royal Naval Division as part of

the British Army.
Battle of the Ancre
The Battle of the Ancre November 13th – 18th, was the final large British attack of the Battle of the Somme in 1916, with the main objective of advancing along the River Ancre to capture Beaucourt.
63rd Division was next to the River Ancre. 189 Brigade had Hawke and Hood Battalions in front of Drake and Nelson Battalions, with 188 Brigade comprising Howe Battalion and 1st Royal Marines in front. To their rear were Anson Battalion and 2nd Royal Marines. At zero hour they all moved forward on the right. Hood and Drake met with heavy machine gun fire but took the German frontlines. Hawke and Nelson Battalion suffered severe losses from heavy machine gun fire.
It was after this assault that Lyndon was reported missing on November 13th 1916 and his death was finally assumed on June 26th 1917.
Lyndon is remembered on the Thiepval Memorial and on the Bethany Church Memorial.

BRAYSHAW ROBERT HODGSON
PRIVATE, 2ND / 5TH BATTALION
ROYAL WELSH FUSILIERS
SERVICE NO 242565
DIED 19 DECEMBER 1917, AGE 37
BURIED CAISTER SEA CEMETERY, GREAT YARMOUTH

Robert, born in 1881, was baptised on January 13th 1884 in St Thomas Church, Lancaster. He was one of seventeen children to Thomas Hodgson and Mary Brayshaw, sadly only five of the children survived.
Named Robert Alfred on earlier records he later used the name Hodgson as his middle name.
The family lived in Lancaster and it was here that Robert worked as an oil cloth painter.
He married Alice Stackhouse on April 14th 1906, the marriage producing two sons, John William born in 1909 and Gordon in 1913.
Robert Hodgson Brayshaw enlisted at Bury, in the 17th Battalion, Lancashire Fusiliers on January 4th 1915.
He was transferred to the 1st Battalion on January 16th 1916 and embarked for France on March 13th.
Robert was admitted to hospital on June 4th 1916 but discharged a week later. He was again admitted on June 17th with Influenza and sent back to England for treatment.
After treatment for Rheumatoid Fever he was discharged and joined the 2nd / 5th Battalion, Royal Welsh Fusiliers on November 11th 1916.
Robert again reported sick on December 12th 1917, being admitted to hospital the following day. It was diagnosed that he was suffering from a cerebral haemorrhage and he died the next day, December 19th 1917.
He was buried in Caister-on-Sea Cemetery, Great Yarmouth.
The only link to the Risca area is the name Robert Brayshaw on the Gladstone

Street Church Memorial.
This is the only Robert Brayshaw who died in WW1, so it is possible that he had relations in the Cross Keys area, who had his name added to the memorial.

BRESSINGTON ALFRED WILLIAM
DRIVER, C BATTERY 61ST BRIGADE
ROYAL FIELD ARTILLERY
SERVICE NO 13908
DIED 3 OCTOBER 1916, AGE 20
BURIED GROVE TOWN CEMETERY,
MEAULTE, FRANCE,

Alfred was born in Bristol in 1896, his parents being Walter and Lilian Bressington. Walter was a builder's labourer in 1911 when the family were living at 13 Pleasant View, Aberaman, Aberdare. Alfred aged 15 was employed as a coal hewer's boy at the colliery. The family then moved to 34 King Street, Cross Keys.
Alfred enlisted at Newport into the Royal Field Artillery, serving as a Driver, 13908 in "C" Battery 61st Brigade. They became part of 11 Corps, 5th Division, arriving in France on September 2nd 1915.
This unit was formed as part of the raising of the First New Army, K1. Sometimes shown as 61 (Howitzer) Brigade RFA, this brigade was originally comprised of numbers 193, 194 and 195 (Howitzer) Batteries RFA and the Brigade Ammunition Column. It was placed under command of the 11th (Northern) Division.
In February 1915 the three six-gun batteries were reorganised to become four four-gun batteries and were titled as A to D.
The brigade left 11th (Northern) Division when that formation was ordered to the Mediterranean in late June 1915. It moved to France and came under orders of the Guards Division on August 24th 1915.
Alfred was wounded and transferred to the 2/2nd London CCS (Casualty Clearing Station) where he died on October 3rd 1916.
He is buried in Grove Town Cemetery, Meaulte, France and commemorated on the Gladstone Street Methodist Church Memorial.

BRICE GEORGE ALBERT
PRIVATE, 1ST BATTALION
WELSH REGIMENT
SERVICE NO 36070
DIED 25 MAY 1915, AGE 32
REMEMBERED YPRES MENIN GATE
MEMORIAL, BELGIUM

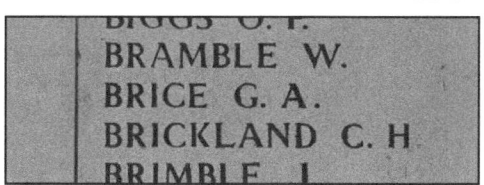

John Brice and Maria English were married in Westbury on Severn district in 1870 before moving to the Midlands where he was employed as a coal miner. George Albert, the youngest of their 5 children, was born in Pelsall, Walsall in 1883.
John died in 1888 and the family were still in the Midlands in 1891. Maria died in

1898 with her death being registered in Chepstow. George was living with his brother Charles and family in 116 Oak Road, West Bromwich in 1901 and was employed in the ironworks.

He married Susannah Mumford in the Parish Church, Walsall on May 4th 1902 before briefly moving to Lydney where his eldest son George William, was born in 1903. They then moved to South Wales where they are shown living in 12 Glan Ebbw Terrace Abertillery in 1911 with their 4 children.

George was living in Pontymister when he enlisted at Newport. Records show that he was originally in the South Wales Borderers, Service Number 18677 before transferring to the Welsh Regiment. He went overseas and landed in France on May 5th 1915, and was reported missing presumed dead just 10 days later.

He has no known grave and is commemorated on the Menin Gate Memorial in Ypres, as well as the Lydney and Pelsall, Staffordshire War memorials.

George was entitled to the British War medal, the Victory medal and the 1915 Star.

BRIDGE WILLIAM CHARLES
LANCE CORPORAL, 24TH BATTALION
ROYAL WELSH FUSILIERS
SERVICE NO 57781
DIED 6 OCTOBER 1918, AGE 18
BURIED LA KREULE MILITARY CEMETERY,
HAZEBROUCK, FRANCE.

William Charles Bridge is probably the youngest person from Risca to go to war. He first enlisted in 1915 giving his age as 19 years and 1 day, when in reality he was 14 years and 11 months old.

Born in Risca on March 13th 1900, William was one of four children to Charles and Elizabeth Bridge (nee Williams).

In 1901, Charles was a colliery labourer and the family lived near the Parish Church in Risca. By 1911 they had moved to 37 Railway Street where the parents and their 3 children are in residence along with Elias Bridge, Charles' brother also working in the colliery.

His service records of his time in the London Regiment have survived and give the details of his enlistment and subsequent discharge.

He travelled to London and enlisted into the 3/2nd Battalion London Regiment, on February 17th 1915 and was given the Service Number 3815. It was recorded he was 5ft 7ins tall with a 35ins chest and vision and physical development was rated 'Good'.

On April 18th 1915 he transferred to the 1/2nd Battalion of London Regiment and leaving from Southampton, went to France as part of the British Expeditionary Force.

A month later on May 28th he was charged with *'Neglect of duty while on sentry in the trenches'*. It was noted that he was sat down whilst carrying out his sentry duties and for this he received 28 days Field Punishment No 1. (Field Punishment Number One, or FP No. 1, involved the offender being bound by his wrists and feet to a fixed object, such as a gun wheel or post, for up to 2 hours per day. It was usually applied in field punishment camps set up for this purpose a few miles behind the front line, but when the unit was on the move it would be carried out by the unit itself).

He was admitted to hospital in France on November 23rd with Erythema Pernio (chilblains) in both feet and then sent back to England four days later.

He went to Wharncliffe War Hospital in Sheffield until he was fit enough to leave on January 13th 1916. He then went to No 8 Hurdcott Camp in Salisbury, Wiltshire and on January 24th he was transferred to 4/2nd Battalion.

On February 25th he was charged with being *"Absent from cookhouse from 09.45 till 10.15 and Insolence to an NCO"* and received a punishment of 7 days *'Confined to Barracks'*.

It was whilst in this camp, his mother sent a letter to the army, explaining that he had joined up aged 15 and against her wishes, and she requested that he be released from the service.

After receiving this letter and a copy of his birth certificate, arrangements were made to discharge him for *"making a mis-statement as to age on enlistment"*.

Despite this, his Commanding Officer Major Filon, wrote that he was *"Honest and steady. Teetotaller. Recommended for employment in a colliery"*. After 1 year and 20 days service he left the army on March 7th 1916.

Sometime later he re-enlisted into the South Wales Borderers as a Private before joining the 24th Battalion Royal Welsh Fusiliers, later becoming a Lance Corporal with them.

He was admitted to the 64th Casualty Clearing Station with a gunshot wound to the head, dying a few days later on October 6th 1918, aged 18 years 7 months.

William is buried in La Kreule Military Cemetery, Hazebrouck, France.

He is commemorated on the St Mary's Church, Risca Memorial.

BROWN JAMES ALBERT
Private, 9th Battalion
Royal Welsh Fusiliers
Service No 19995
Died 23 October 1918, age 33
Remembered Vis-En-Artois Memorial, France

Known as Albert, he was born in Wrexham in 1885 to James Albert and Mary Jane Brown (nee Willding).

He had a brother Joseph baptised on June 29th 1887 in Wrexham.

Sometime after 1901, the brothers moved to south Wales, both working in the local colliery as miners.

Albert married Hilda May Burton in 1907, the marriage producing three children, Albert Reginald born 1908, Norman Joseph born 1909 and Phyllis M born in 1912.

Joseph, Albert's brother, married Sylvia, Hilda's sister also in 1907.

Albert enlisted at Newport in the 9th Battalion Royal Welsh Fusiliers, going overseas on July 19th 1915.

The 9th Battalion RWF, mobilised for war and after landing at Boulogne were en-

gaged in various actions on the Western Front.
Among the many actions, they fought at the Battle of Loos in 1915, the Battle of Albert and the attacks on High Wood in 1916.
They were also heavily involved in the Battles of Messines, Menin Road Ridge and the Battles of Passchendaele in 1917.
On February 4th 1917, Albert was admitted to No 3 Casualty Clearing Station Hospital with indigestion, being discharged on the 19th to 2/1 South Midlands CCS. Both hospitals were in Puchevillers, France.
In 1918 they fought at the Battle of St Quentin, the First Battle of Kemmel Ridge and the Battle of the Aisne before taking part in the Battle of the Selle.
It was during this battle that Albert was killed on October 23rd 1918.
He is remembered on the Vis-En-Artois Memorial.

BROWN OLIVER
LANCE CORPORAL, 86TH COMPANY
MACHINE GUN CORPS (INFANTRY)
SERVICE No 15063
DIED 20 NOVEMBER 1917, AGE 24
BURIED VILLERS PLOUICH COMMUNAL CEMETERY, FRANCE

Oliver, born in Cross Keys on April 21st 1893, was one of three children of Charles Oliver and Emily Brown, (nee Tovey). They lived in Woodland Place, Cross Keys.
He was admitted to Park Street Infants School, Cross Keys on January 12th 1898 and transferred to the Boy's Department August 13th 1900.
Oliver then moved to Waunfawr Junior School on August 19th 1901 leaving on May 11th 1906 to start work.
Oliver's father Charles died in 1901 and his mother married John Leonard in 1906, in 1911 they were living at 11 Gladstone Street, Cross Keys.
Oliver, an underground labourer, enlisted in Newport in the Royal Welsh Fusiliers as Private 17911, later transferring to the 86th Company Machine Gun Corps, serving as a Lance Corporal, 15063.
As a unit of the 29th Division, 86th Coy, MGC took part in the Battles of the Somme, the Battles of Arras, the Battles of Ypres and the Battle of Cambrai.
The Battle of Cambrai started on November 20th 1917 with the 'Tank Attack' in which the Tank Corps deployed its entire strength of 476 machines.
It was on this day, November 20th 1917 age 24, that Oliver was killed in action.
He is buried in Villers-Plouich Communal Cemetery, France.

BRYANT GEORGE CHARLES
Private, 2ND Battalion
Monmouthshire Regiment
Service No 3454
Died 28 January 1917, age 21
Remembered Thiepval Memorial, France

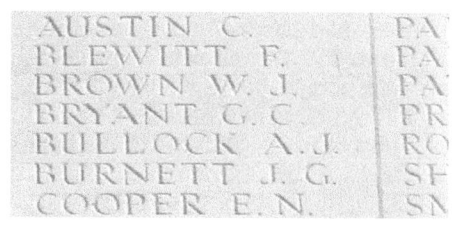

George Charles Bryant was born in Risca between October and December 1895, the only son of Frank and Hannah Bryant.
Frank Bryant was born in Bream, Somerset about 1868 and in 1895, he married Hannah Burchill, daughter of George and Charlotte Burchill of Risca.
In 1901 they lived in 3 Victoria Terrace, Risca, close to Rifleman's Lane and Frank is employed as a coal tipper above ground.
1911 saw them living in 16 Raglan Street, Risca where Frank and George's occupations were both shown as labourer above ground, suggesting they worked in one of the local colleries.
George enlisted in Abertillery into the 2nd Monmouthshire Regiment. Unfortunately his service records have not survived so the exact date cannot be confirmed, but it was about April 14th 1915.
In 1914 the Battalion was very much made up of men from Abercarn, Blaenavon, Crumlin, Cwmbran, Llanhilleth, Monmouth, Usk and Pontypool, with its headquarters at Pontypool. The ages and experiences of the Battalion varied considerably from the boy soldier right through to the veteran of the Boer War.
At the start of the New Year in 1917, the Battalion was at Foudinroy. The History of the Regiment states that *'training was carried out daily, principally on the company attack.'* General de Lisle inspected the Battalion on January 9th and he stated that *'everything was as it should be, and he was proud to have them in his division.'*
On January 20th, 100 men were sent up from each Company to dig a new trench ready for the attack at Le Transloy. The attack on Le Transloy was made on January 27th, with the barrage commencing at 5.30 a.m. After dusk the Battalion was called upon to dig two communication trenches to connect the old front line with the new captured positions. 'B' Company under Captain A L Coppock worked on the right trench and 'C' Company under Captain J T George worked on the left. The completion of the trenches was an amazing achievement as the ground was frozen to a depth of eighteen inches and the men were under hostile fire at close range.
The above account was taken from They Fought with Pride. First World War Experiences of the 2nd Battalion, The Monmouthshire Regiment written by David Nicholas. The 2nd Mons were one of only a small number of Territorial Battalions to have been granted the 1914 Star.
They were mobilised for active service on August 4th 1914 and remained on active service in Germany with the Army of Occupation until May 1919. In November 1914, the Battalion entered the trenches near the Belgian town of Ypres. Large numbers of the soldiers had served underground and it was not long before the

Battalion became well known for its efficiency in trench building.
They had the honour of obtaining the first Distinguished Conduct Medal to be granted to a Territorial Unit. Their honours list is probably as large as any Territorial Battalion.
George is remembered on the Thiepval Memorial, France and in the St John's Church, Risca, Roll of Honour booklet.

BUCKLEY JOHN ARTHUR
CORPORAL, 2ND ROYAL MARINE BATTALION
ROYAL MARINE LIGHT INFANTRY, RN DIVISION
SERVICE NO PLY/782(S)
DIED 27 MARCH 1918, AGE 22
REMEMBERED THIEPVAL MEMORIAL, FRANCE

John Arthur was born September 1st 1895 to Michael and Sarah Matilda Buckley. They had three children but unfortunately Michael died in 1898 and Sarah married John Evans in 1901, moving to Wattsville.
John Arthur attended Waunfawr Infants School and moved up to the Junior School on August 17th 1903.
His school records show that on July 6th 1906 he left the area.
On January 12th 1915, John enlisted as a Private in the 2nd Royal Marines Battalion, Royal Naval Division at Bristol. He gave his trade as a collier and religion as Baptist.
He is described as being 5ft 7ins tall, fresh complexion with grey eyes and light hair. It is also noted that he has a 'Coal mark' on his forehead.
Whilst with the Marines, he sustained a number of injuries and ailments.
John was in the Plymouth Battalion and served as part of the Mediterranean Expeditionary Force, between May 31st 1915 until August 7th 1915, when he suffered a gunshot wound to the head. He re-joined 2nd RM Battalion from September 8th 1915 until September 23rd 1915 when he was treated for Tic Douloureux, (Tic Douloureux or trigeminal neuralgia is a severe, stabbing pain to one side of the face).
He went back to the 2nd RM Battalion from August 21st 1916 to February 7th 1917 when he received an injury to his leg, and caught influenza. He later had a gunshot wound to his left arm. On December 27th 1917 he again rejoined the 2nd Royal Marine Battalion and served with them until his death on March 27th 1918.
He is remembered on the Arras Memorial, France.

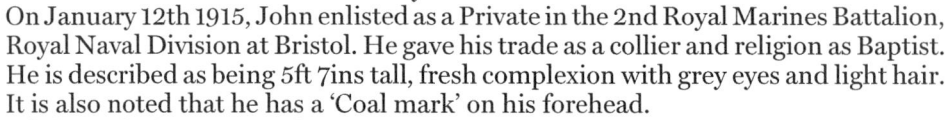

BUDDING WILLIAM JOHN
PRIVATE, 21ST BATTALION
WEST YORKSHIRE REGIMENT (PRINCE OF WALES OWN)
SERVICE NO 58421
DIED 26 APRIL 1918, AGE 39
BURIED GONNEHEM BRITISH CEMETERY, FRANCE

William was born in Risca on January 9th 1879 to Henry and Elizabeth Budding, (nee Willett).

In 1881 the family lived at the "Temple of Fashion" Risca where Henry was a draper and tailor. On the night of the census William was a visitor with his aunt, Anna Maria Willett to The Cross in Llansoy.

They had moved to 67 Richards Terrace, Roath, Cardiff by the following year and William started school on October 31st 1882 at Stacey Road Infants School.

He left on September 24th 1886 and later started working in the family business as an apprentice tailor.

William married Ruth Hannah Williams in 1908 in Cardiff, having a daughter Audrey Ruth born in 1912 and a son Ronald William in 1917.

He enlisted in Cardiff in the Royal Engineers before transferring to the 21st Battalion West Yorkshire Regiment (Prince of Wales Own).

The 21st (Service) Battalion (Wool Textile Pioneers) was formed in Halifax on September 24th 1915 by the Lord Mayor and City of Leeds. They landed in France as a Pioneer Battalion to the 4th Division in June 1916 for service on the Western Front.

As a Pioneer Battalion, its primary role was labouring and construction.

They saw action in the Battle of the Somme in 1916 before moving to Arras for the First and Third Battles of the Scarpe and then later in the Third Battle of Ypres.

The Battalion were then involved in the First Battle of Arras in 1918 before fighting during the Battle of Hazebrouck in which they fought in the Defence of Hinges Ridge, part of the Battle of the Lys.

William was killed in action during the Battle of Lys, and is buried in Gonnehem British Cemetery, France.

BUDGETT EDWIN GEORGE
PRIVATE, 7TH BATTALION
SOUTH WALES BORDERERS
SERVICE NO 3/13455
DIED 18 MARCH 1917, AGE 21
BURIED KARASOULI MILITARY CEMETERY, GREECE

Edwin George, fourth son of Albert and Susan Budgett was born on May 5th 1895 in Nottingham.

Albert was a miner and the family moved to Cross Keys early in Edwin's life living in 15 Provident Terrace.

Edwin attended Park Street Infants School, Cross Keys starting on May 15th 1899. He moved to the Mixed Department on August 19th 1901, leaving school on September 1st 1908.

The family had moved to 31 High Street, Cross Keys by 1911, where he is shown as employed at Nine Mile Point Colliery working as a coal cutter, with his father and three older brothers also working in the pit.

Edwin enlisted on August 18th 1914, and served with the Expeditionary Force in France and Flanders, as a Private in the 7th Service Battalion, South Wales Borderers.

Wounded on May 25th 1916, Edwin was sent home on sick leave. He returned to action on August 16th and went to Salonica where he died of wounds on March 18th 1917. Edwin is buried in Karasouli Military Cemetery, Greece and is remembered on the Trinity Church, Pontywain and Pontywaun Wesleyan Church and School memorials.

C

CALLIER ETHEL FANNY MAY CHILTON
SISTER
QUEEN ALEXANDRA'S IMPERIAL MILITARY NURSING SERVICE No 2/RESERVE/C/3
DIED 22 JUNE 1919, AGE 34
BURIED GREENWICH CEMETERY, LONDON

One of six children, Ethel the daughter of Phillip and Fanny Callier, was born in Tredegar on May 5th 1885. Ethel was a teacher in Risca in 1901, living in 1 Hillside with her sisters Nellie and Gertrude, also teachers. She left teaching and joined the nursing profession at St George's Hospital, London on December 2nd 1912, staying until January 2nd 1917.
She joined the Queen Alexandra's Imperial Military Nursing Service and on April 15th 1918 embarked at Southampton arriving at Basra on June 8th 1918 leaving immediately for Baghdad, arriving 8 days later.
She contracted Tuberculosis and was admitted to the Officers Hospital, Baghdad on September 15th 1918 before being invalided to India on October 20th 1918.
Here she was admitted to Colaba War Hospital and on November 25th 1918 it was decided that she should return to England for treatment and convalescence.
After being sent back to England, she died at Royal Herbert Hospital Woolwich on June 22nd 1919.
Ethel is buried in Greenwich Cemetery, London.

CARPENTER WILLIAM
PRIVATE, 17TH BATTALION
ROYAL WELSH FUSILIERS
SERVICE No 93548
DIED 8 OCTOBER 1918, AGE 24
REMEMBERED VIS-EN-ARTOIS MEMORIAL, FRANCE

William was the son of James and Sarah Jane Carpenter, (nee Powell) who married on May 15th 1883 at Machen Parish Church.
He was born in Cross Keys on February 25th 1894 and started at Waunfawr Infants School on June 29th 1898.
He transferred to the Waunfawr Junior Mixed School on July 19th 1901 where he stayed until February 28th 1908, when he left to start work.
William and his siblings were to lose both parents and stepmother within a few short years.

Living at 39 Tredegar Street, Cross Keys, his mother died age 34 at the beginning of 1899. His father James married Eva Westcott on July 4th 1900 at Bassaleg Parish Church, having a son Ernest from the marriage; James unfortunately died just a few months later on November 22nd 1900.

His step mother Eva then married George James of 57 Tredegar Street, Cross Keys. She died in 1909 leaving George to look after his own son from a previous marriage and his 3 stepsons, Alfred and William, James and Sarah's children and Ernest, James and Eva's child.

In 1911, George, Alfred and William are all employed as coal miners whilst the two youngest boys are still at school.

William was living at 27 Tredegar Street, at the time he enlisted into the South Wales Borderers as Private 58611. He later transferred to the 17th Battalion, Royal Welsh Fusiliers, as Private 93548.

The 13th, 14th, 15th, 16th and 17th Battalion all landed in France as part of the 113th Brigade in the 38th (Welsh) Division in December 1915 for service on the Western Front.

The Division's baptism by fire came in the first days of the Battle of the Somme, where it captured the strongly held Mametz Wood at the loss of nearly 4,000 men. The fight at Mametz Wood in July 1917, saw the destruction of the 13th, 14th, 16th, 17th and 18th Battalions.

This strongly held German position needed to be secured in order to facilitate the next phase of the Somme offensive; the Battle of Bazentin Ridge. Although securing its objective, the division's reputation was adversely affected by miscommunication among senior officers.

A year later it made a successful attack in the Battle of Pilckem Ridge, the opening of the Third Battle of Ypres. This action restored the reputation of the division in the eyes of the upper hierarchy of the British military.

In 1918, during the German Spring Offensive and the subsequent Allied Hundred Days Offensive, the division attacked several fortified German positions. It crossed the Ancre River, broke through the Hindenburg Line and German positions on the River Selle, ended the war on the Belgian frontier, and was considered one of the Army's elite units.

The war diary for the 17th Battalion in October 1918, shows they were at Aubencheul aux Bois, Aisne, France.

> 7 October. Battalion in the line. Casualties nil.
> 8 October. Battalion attacked. Zero 1 A.M. Objective BEAUREVOIR LINE and high ground in front of VILLERS OUTREAUX. All objectives taken.
> About 50 prisoners were taken. Casualties 10 Officers and 120 Other Ranks.

William, along with Edgar Jones of Risca, was one of 39 men killed that day from the 17th Battalion. In all, the Royal Welsh lost 141 from all its Battalions on October 8th.

As he has no known grave William is commemorated on the Vis-En-Artois Memorial, France.

CARTER SIMEON JOHN
Private, 1ST Battalion
Somerset Light Infantry
Service No 7160
Died 26 August 1914, age 27
Remembered La Ferte Sous Jouarre Memorial, France

Simeon, known as Jack, was born in Wellington, Somerset in 1887.
In 1891 he was living in the Workhouse in North Street, Wellington with his mother Sarah Ann, a widow, and his brother Joshua aged 9 months.
Sarah married Samuel Troake in 1897. In 1901 they were living in Westford Higher in Wellington with Samuel's six children and also Sarah's two daughters Martha and Mary.
Jack worked for the Great Western Railway Company initially as a porter, joining in February 1907. He worked first at Ebbw Vale before moving to Cross Keys Station as a signal porter from May 1908 until October 1910. He then worked at Nantyglo Station as a shunter.
In 1911 he was lodging at Station Terrace with the Legge family. He joined the Blaina Branch of the Amalgamated Society of Railway Servants Union on January 29th 1911, later he worked at Llantrissant as a Shunter.
He went back to Taunton and enlisted in the Somerset Light Infantry, serving as Private 7160 in the 1st Battalion.
The following information is taken from the Regimental War Diary.
> The Battalion was mobilised on August 4th. After field training and route marching they moved to Harrow for more training and joined the 4th Division.
> On August 21st they left Harrow and travelled to Southampton Docks for embarkation. Sailing at 8.30 a.m. the following morning, they arrived at Havre Harbour at 7 p.m. but delayed from disembarking due to the tide until midnight. They then marched 6 miles uphill to Rest Camp and arrived about 2 a.m.
> August 24th they detrained at Le Cateau and moved to Briastre. The following morning they moved at 4 a.m. at short notice and marched to Solemnes occupying a position south of the village. Hard heavy firing heard to the North West and about 9 a.m. withdrew to a position North of Viesly. Enemy's cavalry was seen about 6 p.m. south of Solemnes and their position was shelled in a desultory manner.

The following information is taken from Wikipedia.
> The Battle of Le Cateau was fought on August 26th 1914, after the British and French retreated from the Battle of Mons and had set up defensive positions in a fighting withdrawal against the German advance at Le Cateau-Cambrésis.
> On the morning of August 26th, the Germans arrived and attacked II

Corps. Le Cateau was an artilleryman's battle, demonstrating the devastating results which modern quick-firing artillery using shrapnel shells could have on infantry advancing in the open. The British deployed their artillery in the open, about 50–200 metres behind their infantry, while the German artillery used indirect fire from concealed positions. With the guns so close to their infantry, the British had unintentionally increased the effectiveness of the German artillery-fire, because shells aimed at the British infantry could just as easily hit the British artillery.

Holding their ground despite many casualties, the British right and then the left flank began to break around midday, under unrelenting pressure from the Germans. The arrival of the Cavalry Corps (General André Sordet) acted as a shield for the British left flank and supported a highly co-ordinated tactical withdrawal, despite German attempts to infiltrate and outflank the retreating British forces.

That night, the Allies withdrew to Saint-Quentin. Of the 40,000 British troops fighting at Le Cateau, 7,812 British casualties were incurred, including 2,600 taken prisoner. Thirty-eight guns were abandoned, most having their breech blocks removed and sights disabled by the gunners first.

Having arrived in France on August 23rd 1914 Jack was killed just 3 days later during this battle.

A newspaper article stated that whilst in Cross Keys *"he was a zealous worker at the Mission Church and his death will be regretted by a large circle of friends."*

He was awarded the 1914 Star, British and Victory War medals.

As he has no known grave, Jack is remembered on La Ferte-Sous-Jouarre Memorial, France.

CAWLEY FREDERICK
SECOND LIEUTENANT, 35TH TRAINING DEPOT STATION
ROYAL AIR FORCE
DIED 13 OCTOBER 1918, AGE 20
BURIED ST MARY'S CHURCHYARD, MARSHFIELD, WALES

Frederick was born on September 8th 1898 and baptised on October 16th at Marshfield, the youngest of seven children to Alfred and Agnes E Cawley. They lived at Cae Garw Cottages, Marshfield, Alfred is employed as a Domestic Gardener.

Frederick was admitted to Pontywaun County School on May 5th 1913, leaving on March 31st 1915 to start work as a clerk in the Finance Department of Messrs Spillers and Bakers in Cardiff.

He joined the Honourable Artillery Company on November 28th 1916 as Private 9509, being stationed in London. Frederick was commissioned into the Royal Flying Corp as a Temporary 2nd Lieutenant on December 19th 1917.

He was injured in a flying accident on March 4th 1918 but recovered well enough to be described as *"an accomplished pilot"*; being promoted to 2nd Lieutenant on

April 1st 1918, when the RAF came into being.
Frederick was killed in a flying accident at Duxford, Cambridgeshire. The inquest, heard on October 16th 1918, that about 12 noon on Sunday October 13th, Lieutenant Murray RAF observed two machines circling round and apparently about to descend. One landed safely, but the other stalled on a turn and nose-dived to the ground from a height of about 200ft. He ran to the wreck, which was in a field, and saw Lieut. Cawley amongst the wreckage from which he helped to extricate him. Frederick was unconscious and removed to the military hospital.
He was admitted to the hospital at 1.15 p.m. and died at 2.10 p.m., the cause of death being a fracture at the base of his skull.
Frederick age 20, is buried in St Mary Churchyard, Marshfield.

CHADWICK WILLIAM JOHN
SERJEANT 9TH BATTALION
WELSH REGIMENT
SERVICE NO 58099
DIED 7 NOVEMBER 1918, AGE 23
BURIED ETAPLES MILITARY CEMETERY, FRANCE

Born in Blaenrhondda in 1895, William was the son of Mary Chadwick, who married William George Grey in 1899. The 1901 census showed they lived in 52 Brook Street, Blaenrhondda. William Grey was a coal miner but by 1911 had become an assurance agent with his stepson William now employed as a coal miner.
At the time of his enlistment at Cross Keys on December 11th 1915, William's occupation was an insurance agent, living in Bryn Avon, Danygraig Road, Risca.
He was posted initially into the 14th Battalion South Wales Borderers in January 1916 and attended musketry and PT training courses at Kinmel Park, Abergele and Chester where he was promoted to Corporal on July 17th. William became a PT instructor and was promoted to Sergeant on March 24th 1917.
The Battalion went through a number of name changes before becoming the 52nd Graduated Battalion on October 27th 1917.
The conduct sheet which survived with his service papers, shows that whilst at South Lowestoft, on December 6th 1917, he was charged with Irregular Conduct. His offence was *"playing football in the main thoroughfare at corner of Short St and London Rd about 3.50 pm,"* for this misdemeanour he received a reprimand.
On May 1st at Henham Park Camp he forfeited 3 days' pay and was severely reprimanded for being absent without leave.
On May 11th he went to France as part of the British Expeditionary Force and was posted to the 9th Battalion Welsh Regiment on July 4th 1918.
Records show he was wounded in action on November 4th 1918, dying of his wounds a few days later.
A newspaper report stated:
> Mrs Grey of Bryn Avon, Risca, received information on the eve of Armistice Monday that her son, Sergt. W Chadwick, 9th Welsh, had died of wounds at the Etaples Military Hospital, France, three days after receiving a wound in the neck.

Lady May Bradford, who was the letter writer at this hospital, informed the bereaved mother that her son had died peacefully and was carefully nursed to the end – which was a consolation to Mrs Grey. While Sergeant Chadwick was in England he was offered a commission, but he refused, saying he preferred going to France as an NCO and receive a commission afterwards. Sergt. Chadwick was a PT Gym Instructor while in England, and when drilling the lads of 18 he always spoke to them with cheering words, thus encouraging them to be bright and happy while serving their King and country.

He was a Physical Trainer at Kinmel Park, Lowestoft and Yarmouth, and left for France in May 1918. After he reached France he told his mother that he was satisfied now that he had got to that country, but although he was only in France for a short time, his captain said he had proved himself a capable NCO.

William is buried in Etaples Military Cemetery, France.

CHICK WILLIAM
PRIVATE, 1ST BATTALION
ROYAL WELSH FUSILIERS
SERVICE NO 6378
DIED 16 MAY 1915, AGE 43
REMEMBERED LE TOURET MEMORIAL, FRANCE

William, born in North Petherton, Somerset about 1871, married Mary Aish on October 8th 1894 at Bridgwater Registry Office; they went on to have eleven children, three who died in infancy.

While living in Bridgwater, William was a general labourer. Later they moved to 4 Oak Terrace, Cross Keys, where he was now working as a colliery labourer.

He signed up on November 4th 1914 at Newport and stated he had previously served in Royal Welsh Fusiliers before being invalided out. William again joined the 1st Battalion Royal Welsh Fusiliers, serving as Private 6378. He gave his age as 35 years and 4 months, which wasn't correct.

His service records describe him as 5ft 8½ins, 11 stone 11 lbs and a 36ins chest. He had a fresh complexion, grey eyes and dark brown hair.

After training he went to France on April 1st 1915 as part of 22nd Brigade, 7th Division.

William was straight into front line action, fighting in the Battle of Aubers and then the Battle of Festubert, it was during this battle that he was killed in action.

He is remembered on Le Touret Memorial, France.

CLISSOLD CYRIL JAMES
PRIVATE, 8TH BATTALION
KING'S (LIVERPOOL REGIMENT)
SERVICE NO 91016
DIED 31 AUGUST 1918, AGE 19
BURIED QUEBEC CEMETERY, CHERISY, FRANCE

Cyril, born in Risca on December 25th 1898, was the son of Albert William and Gertrude Clissold, (nee James). He was baptised on March 5th 1899 at St Mary's Church, Risca.

They lived at Gladstone Street, Cross Keys when Cyril attended Waunfawr Park School, starting on June 18th 1902. He was only there a matter of months as he left on October 27th when they moved to 'Blenheim', Bridge Street, Risca, he then attended Danygraig School.

An ex pupil of Pontywaun County School from September 19th 1911 until July 23rd 1913, he left to work as a clerk in Lysaght's Newport.

He enlisted at Abertillery in The King's (Liverpool Regiment) serving in the 8th Battalion as Private 91016.

The 8th (Liverpool Irish) Battalion King's (Liverpool) regiment was a Territorial Force unit which had its HQ in Shaw Street, Liverpool. When war was declared in 1914 they had just arrived at their annual summer camp and were quickly recalled home.

They landed in Boulogne, France on May 3rd 1915 being engaged in the defence of Ypres. They saw action at the Battle of Festubert and Givenchy before moving south to the Somme. They were involved at the Battles of Guillemont, Ginchy, Flers-Courcelette and Morval before moving back to Flanders in October 1916.

In 1917 they were in action at Pilckem Ridge and Menin Road Bridge during the Third Battle of Ypres before again moving south to Cambrai where they suffered very heavily during German attacks at the end of November 1917.

During 1918 they were in action during the Second Battle of Arras, Battles of Hindenburg Line and in the capture of Cambrai.

Cyril was killed in action on August 31st 1918 and is buried in Quebec Cemetery, Cherisy, France.

He is remembered on the St Mary's Church and Pontywaun County School memorials.

CLOTHIER ISAAC
DRIVER, 'D' BATTERY, 80TH BRIGADE
ROYAL FIELD ARTILLERY
SERVICE NO 74747
DIED 4 NOVEMBER 1915, AGE 25
BURIED DIVISIONAL CEMETERY, BELGIUM

Isaac was born in Blaenavon in 1889, one of twelve children to Thomas and Ellen Clothier, (nee Skuse).

Living at 1 Station Tump, Blaenavon, Thomas was a coal miner. By 1901 their address had changed to 1 Tump Terrace, although in 1911 it was recorded as Station Terrace. Ellen died and was buried on December 31st 1908 aged 52. Isaac was a driver in the local colliery.

Isaac married Lillian Cole in 1913 and had two children, Elizabeth born 1914 and

Isaac V born in 1916, sadly after his father had been killed.
Isaac and Lillian had moved to Risca by the time he had enlisted at Newport as a Driver in the Royal Field Artillery.
He landed in France with the RFA on July 15th 1915 and was killed just a few months later.
Isaac is buried in the Divisional Cemetery, Belgium.

COCKELL JOHN GRANT
GUNNER, M ANTI-AIRCRAFT BATTERY
ROYAL GARRISON ARTILLERY
SERVICE No 191089
DIED 22 JANUARY 1918, AGE 23
BURIED HAC CEMETERY, ECOUST-ST. MEIN, FRANCE

John, born on January 17th 1895 in Cross Keys, was the son of James and Mary Abraham Cockell, (nee Rodda). They lived at 5 Llanover Street, Cross Keys and John attended Waunfawr Infants School, starting there on March 19th 1901. His father James was a railway signalman, whilst his mother was a dressmaker.
By 1911 the family had moved to 53 Commercial Street, Risca where John worked in the steel mill as an electric engine driver.
On January 5th 1915 he joined at Newport in the Royal Field Artillery serving as Gunner 74417. His service records show his occupation as an electrician, giving his height as 5ft 7ins and weight as 9 stone 8 lbs.
After his initial training John went to France on November 6th 1915, being posted to the 65th Anti-Aircraft Section the following August.
Each anti-aircraft section comprised two lorry mounted guns, two officers, one staff car and one motorcycle. Each gun detachment had a twelve man crew which included the ASC driver. The rest of the team were made up of range finders, fuse setters, height finders, linesman, order board setter, orderly and cook.
On September 17th 1916 John was admitted to 30 Casualty Clearing Station with tonsillitis for 2 weeks. (The Casualty Clearing Station, CCS, was part of the casualty evacuation chain, further back from the front line than the Aid Posts and Field Ambulances. The job of the CCS was to treat a man sufficiently for his return to duty or, in most cases, to enable him to be evacuated to a Base Hospital. It was not a place for a long-term stay).
John was granted leave twice to return to the UK whilst in France, the first time in December 1916 and then the following year on December 25th. When he returned on January 8th he had been transferred to the Royal Garrison Artillery and allocated Service Number 191089. He was killed in action just two weeks later on January 22nd, age 23.
He is buried in H.A.C. Cemetery, Ecoust-St. Mein, France and remembered on the family grave at Risca Old Cemetery, Cromwell Road, although the grave stone is now in disrepair.
His elder brother Harry Grant Cockell was in the Tank Corps, and although wounded in 1915 survived the war.

COLES WILLIAM JOHN
PRIVATE, 6TH BATTALION
SOUTH WALES BORDERERS
SERVICE No 17187
DIED 3 OCTOBER 1915, AGE 37
BURIED HOUPLINES COMMUNAL CEMETERY
EXTENSION, NORD-PAS-DE-CALAIS, FRANCE

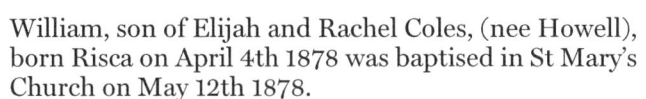

William, son of Elijah and Rachel Coles, (nee Howell), born Risca on April 4th 1878 was baptised in St Mary's Church on May 12th 1878.
In 1881 they lived at William Rossers Row, with William attending Risca Town Infants School from February 27th 1882 until June 17th 1886.
Later moving to Edwards' Cottage, Risca, William was employed in the Tin Works prior to him working as a miner. He later lived at Moriah Cottages.
He enlisted in the South Wales Borderers, serving as Private 17187 in the 6th Battalion.
Landing in France on September 24th 1915, William, operating as a bomb thrower, was killed just over a week later.
The war diary shows that two companies were working West of Le Ruage, when Private Coles of 'C' Company was shot by a sniper and buried at Houplines.
A letter was sent home to his sister Rhoda Bates from Lieut. TG Randolph, 6th Service Battalion, SWB (Pioneers).

"Dear Madam, I beg to tender you my deepest sympathy and to express my own private sorrow in the loss of your brother, Private Coles, 17187, who was most unfortunately killed instantly by a stray enemy bullet, last night, when we were performing our duty by night. He was quite one of the best soldiers in my platoon, and was much respected by the other men of his own section, who undertook today to give him a fitting burial for a noble soldier. If it is in God's providence that we do not come back from this war, none of us could wish for a more noble end than that of your late brother, who died in serving his King and country, for the safety and welfare of all those we have left at home.
His personal belongings are now at our headquarters, and will be sent to you as soon as possible. - Believe me. Yours faithfully". TG Randolph

Another letter from one of William's friends contained graphic details of his death.

"Dear Mr and Mrs Bates, I am very sorry to have to tell you that your brother, Private William John Coles, was killed by a bullet on Sunday night, at 7 p.m. The bullet entered in the neck under the jaw bone and came out on the top of his head so that death was practically instantaneous. We buried him on Monday afternoon about 3.30 in a soldier's grave, not far from the trenches and had a chaplain to read the burial service.
We are all very sorry that it happened and deeply sympathise with you in your loss. William John was one of the best of mates and was well loved by all. He was always cheery and had a smile on his face when he died. It was a

stray bullet that caught him a good distance from the firing line - I remain your sincere friend". Private Fred Moore

A memorial service was held at St Margaret's Church in his honour.
He was killed on October 3rd 1915 and buried in Houplines Communal Cemetery Extension, France.
William is commemorated on the memorial in St Margaret's Church, Risca.

COMPTON SIDNEY
PRIVATE, 6TH BATTALION
SOUTH WALES BORDERERS
SERVICE No 17459
DIED 28 AUGUST 1917, AGE 24
BURIED LIJSSENTHOEK MILITARY CEMETERY, BELGIUM

Sidney was born in 1893 in Warminster, Wiltshire to Edmund John and Thirza Ann Compton, (nee Robbins).
In 1901 the family were living at 6 King Street, Warminster. In 1911 Sidney was boarding at 14 Clyde Street, Risca, working as a smith's helper.
He enlisted at Newport, into the 6th Battalion, South Wales Borderers as a Private, Regimental Number 17459.
The 6th Battalion was raised in south Wales in September 1914. They went to France as the Pioneer Battalion of the 25th Division a year later; Sidney arrived in France on September 24th 1915.
The Battalion spent the winter in the Armentieres sector working in flooded trenches.
They were at Vimy and Neuville St. Vaast in the spring of 1916 consolidating the craters of mines blown under the German lines.
Later they were continuously employed during the Battle of the Somme in the summer of 1916, on one occasion digging a 700 yard communication trench from one captured trench to another under heavy shell fire.
Their next major engagement was at Messines in July 1917, after which they were moved further north in August for the Third Battle of Ypres.
Sidney died of his wounds on August 28th 1917.
He was awarded the Victory, British War medals and the 1914-1915 Star.
Sidney is buried in Lijssenthoek Military Cemetery, Belgium.

COOK ALFRED JOHN
SERJEANT, 4TH BATTALION
SOUTH WALES BORDERERS
SERVICE No 13091
DIED 6 APRIL 1916, AGE 20
REMEMBERED BASRA MEMORIAL, IRAQ

Alfred John, known as John, was born in Draethen, Machen on April 2 1896 to Thomas and Elizabeth Cook.
Living in Draethen, father Thomas was a limestone quarryman.
John attended Rhiwderin Infants School from November 4th 1901 until October 6th 1903 when the family left Machen.
In 1911 they were living in 7 Duffryn Rd, Wattsville and both father and son are working in the colliery, Thomas as a banksman and John as a miner.
He enlisted in Newport and served as a Private in the 4th Battalion, South Wales Borderers.
On June 29th 1915, the 4th Battalion embarked from Avonmouth for Mudros (a small Greek port on the Mediterranean island of Lemnos) arriving on July 12th 1915. On July 15th they landed in Gallipoli and fought through the campaign with distinction until being evacuated to Mudros and then on to Egypt. On February 15th 1916 they left Suez arriving in Basra on March 4th.
As part of the 13th Division, the 4th South Wales Borderers took part in the battles of the spring of 1916 fought by the Mesopotamian Expeditionary Force to relieve Kut. These actions consisted mainly of desperate attacks on strongly entrenched lines carried out in cold, mud and rain with great hardships to the troops.
On April 4th 1916 the British forces attacked the Hanna position. The battalion pushed on through heavy machine gun fire over open ground with little or no cover. Despite severe losses they reached a line about 800 yards from the Turkish trenches.
It was during these daily attacks on the Turkish positions that John was killed.
He has no known grave and is remembered on the Basra Memorial.

COOPER WILFRED
PRIVATE, 5TH BATTALION
SOUTH WALES BORDERERS
SERVICE NO 25718
DIED 7 JUNE 1917, AGE 21
REMEMBERED YPRES MENIN GATE MEMORIAL, BELGIUM

Wilfred, born in Cwmbran on May 6th 1896, was the son of Daniel and Mary Jane Cooper, (nee Gunter). The family lived in Newtown, Cwmbran and he attended St Dials Infants School, Cwmbran leaving on August 24th 1903. They moved to Risca in 1910 living at 10 Mill Street, Pontymister, where Wilfred aged 14 is recorded as being employed as a miner.
He enlisted at Newport as a Private, in the 5th Battalion South Wales Borderers.
Wilfred, as part of the 5th Battalion, landed in France on December 30th 1915.
The 5th Battalion were kept busy in the Loos area throughout the winter repairing roads, constructing tramways, improving trenches, and in mining in close proximity to the enemy.

On March 14th 1916, under a site known as 'Duck's Bill', the Germans exploded a mine which destroyed half the salient. Some volunteers from the battalion rushed across open ground to the Duck's Bill to assist the remaining soldiers in preventing the Germans exploiting the situation.

The battalion lost 220 men during the last ten days of July 1916 in the Battle of the Somme

In March 1917, they moved north to Ypres to prepare for the attack on the Messines Ridge, which was launched on June 7th.

It was during this attack that Wilfred was killed.

He is remembered on the Menin Gate Memorial, Ypres, Belgium and Moriah Church Memorial, Risca.

COULSON ANDREW LEWIS
Lance Corporal, 1st Battalion
Gloucestershire Regiment
Service No 6578
Died 24 November 1914, age 30
Remembered Ypres Menin Gate Memorial, Belgium

Andrew was born in 1884 in South Shields County Durham, to Augustus Edward and possibly Jane Ann Coulson (nee Lewis).

Augustus was born in Sweden and in 1891 was living in Minnie Street, Cathays, Cardiff with Andrew and daughter Malvina Margaretta born January 10th 1890. Augustus is shown as being a widower. A Jane Ann Coulson died in Cardiff, being buried on December 30th 1890 at St Mary's Church, Whitchurch.

Augustus then married Mary Richards in December 1892, moving to Maesmawr Farm, Risca by 1901; where Augustus is a farmer and Andrew is a school teacher. Augustus died on July 27th the following year, being buried in Caersalem Baptist Chapel, St Mellons.

In 1911 Mary and Malvina are living in Maesmawr with Mary's brother William Richards who is now the farmer.

Andrew Lewis Coulson enlisted in Bristol into the 1st Battalion Gloucester Regiment, attaining rank of Lance Corporal, Service Number 6578.

This service number appears to show that he joined the 1st Battalion sometime between April 23rd 1902 and February 9th 1903. The 1st Battalion was part of the Regular Army so he may have signed up, then left and rejoined when war broke out. This appears the most logical explanation as he went to France on 12 September 1914 with them as part of the British Expeditionary Force.

The 1st Battalion was deployed to France in August 1914 and saw action on the Western Front. It suffered its first casualties at Landrecies on August 26th 1914 during the retreat from Mons. More losses were sustained in September during the First Battle of the Aisne. The Battalion entered the First Battle of Ypres on October 19th 1914 with 26 officers and 970 other ranks. It played a pivotal role in the defence of Langemarck, and was called upon several times to counter-attack against enemy breakthroughs and, by the time of its relief four weeks later, had been reduced to 2 officers and 100 other ranks.

Andrew was killed in action on November 24th 1914 and is commemorated on the Menin Gate Memorial, Ypres.
He is commemorated on the Bethany Chapel Memorial, Risca.

CRANE ARTHUR STANLEY
SAPPER, 59TH FIELD COMPANY
ROYAL ENGINEERS
SERVICE NO 11464
DIED 16 OCTOBER 1914, AGE 33
BURIED BETHUNE TOWN CEMETERY, FRANCE

Arthur born in 1881 in Pontypool, was the son of Samuel and Emily Crane (nee Wiltshire).
He served in the Royal Monmouthshire Royal Engineers as 2/Corporal 2172.
Arthur fought in the South Africa campaign in 1901 and 1902 being awarded the South Africa medal with clasps for Transvaal, Orange Free State and Cape Colony.
He married Eliza Abbotson in 1905 in Llanvihangel Pontymoile.
In the 1911 census they were living with their children, Emily, Teresa and Thomas at 141 Islwyn Road, Wattsville where Arthur is shown as being a police constable.
Unfortunately Eliza died in 1913 aged 29 and Arthur married her sister Emma Rose Mattie Abbotson on August 3rd 1914. His address at the time of marriage was 36 Trosnant Street, Pontypool and he was employed as a miner.
The following day, World War 1 broke out and he enlisted into the 59th Field Company of the Royal Engineers.
Arthur went to France on August 18th as part of the 5th Division, British Expeditionary Force, and was killed just 2 months later on October 16th 1914.
He is buried in Bethune Town Cemetery, France.
His son Thomas Arthur Crane died in Italy during WW2.

CUNNICK WILLIAM HENRY
CORPORAL, 5TH BATTALION
KING'S SHROPSHIRE LIGHT INFANTRY
SERVICE NO 15549
DIED 24 AUGUST 1916, AGE 28
REMEMBERED THIEPVAL MEMORIAL, FRANCE

William Henry, born in Cwmaman, Aberdare in 1888, was the youngest of three children to Essex and Martha Cunnick (nee Thomas). His siblings were sister Anne and brother John Thomas.
The family lived at 6 Gooseberry Hill, Godreamon, Aberdare until 1911, with the brothers following their father's employment as coal miners.
In 1914 he went to Newport and enlisted into the 5th (Service) Battalion King's Shropshire Light Infantry. This was a war-raised Service Battalion, formed in Shrewsbury in August 1914 under Lt. Col. HM Smith,

CORPORAL W. H. CUNNICK.

from the mass of enthusiastic volunteers coming forward to enlist. Posted to the 42nd Brigade, 14th Division.

After training around Aldershot, they disembarked at Boulogne on May 20th 1915, first coming under fire at Ypres on May 31st 1915, and then served entirely on the Western Front.

It saw some of the worst fighting of the war in the Ypres Salient in 1915, around Bellewaerde and Hooge and was on the Somme in 1916, seeing particularly heavy action at Delville Wood and Flers-Courcelette.

He married Frances M Garland in early 1916 when home on leave and moved to 4 Tredegar Street, Cross Keys, Newtown.

On Thursday August 24th 1916, the 14th Division was set the task of clearing Delville Wood and the King's Shropshire Light Infantry attacked with 5th Ox and Bucks Light Infantry, 8th and 9th Kings Royal Rifle Corps. The 8th KRRC was stopped at Ale Alley whilst the other Battalions moved through the wood assisted by a creeping barrage.

William was killed during this attack.

His body was not found and he is now remembered on the Thiepval Memorial, France.

D

DANIEL NOEL THOMAS
Gunner, 'B' Battery 87th Brigade
Royal Field Artillery
Service No. 201619
Died 25 April 1918, age 24
Remembered Tyne Cot Memorial, Belgium

Noel Thomas was the eldest son of George and Jane Daniel of Pen-y-dre, Rogerstone. Born in Bassaleg on November 20th 1893, Noel attended Rogerstone Boy's School before moving to Pontywaun County School on September 11th 1905.

When he left in July 1912 he took up a position as an articled solicitor. A keen cricketer, he played for Pontymister 2nd XI.

Noel was the Secretary of Pontywaun County School Old Student's Association. In June of 1915 the Governors and staff of Pontywaun County School, started an appeal for funds for a memorial to be erected at the school.

This was to place on record the esteem and regard that the school and district had for the late Assistant School Master Lieutenant Taylor and old scholars that had lost their lives in the war.

In August of 1915 a letter appeared in the Weekly Argus, from Noel stating that the memorial to Lieutenant Taylor and old students proposed to be erected by their Association had nothing whatever to do with that which the Governors and staff intend setting up.

Noel enlisted at Newport in the Royal Field Artillery as Gunner 201619, in "B" Battery 87th Brigade.

He was killed in France on April 25th 1918 and is remembered on the Tyne Cot Memorial, Belgium.

He is commemorated on the Pontywaun County School Memorial alongside his former School master and fellow pupils.

Noel is remembered on Newport Athletic Club and Rogerstone Library memorials as well as the family grave at St John's Church, Rogerstone.

DANIELS WILLIAM JOHN
Private, 6th Battalion
Machine Gun Corps (Infantry)
Service No. 131162
Died 2 November 1918, age 18
Buried St Sever Cemetery Extension, Rouen, France

William, born about 1900, was the adopted son of Elizabeth Jones of Tyn-y-Pwll Farm, Risca.

He enlisted in the 4th Battalion South Lancashire Regiment serving as 63727. On

December 29th 1917 he transferred to the Machine Gun Corps as Gunner 131162. The 6th MGC took part in the Battles of the Somme, Lys and the Hindenburg Line. William, age 18, died of pneumonia in the General Military Hospital, Rouen, France.
He is buried in St Sever Cemetery Extension, Rouen.
William's headstone bears the inscription 'Greater Love Hath No Man Than This'

DARBY CHARLES RICHARD
CORPORAL, 21ST COMPANY
ROYAL DEFENCE CORPS
SERVICE NO. 16932
DIED 6 JANUARY 1919, AGE 49
BURIED RISCA OLD CEMETERY, RISCA, WALES

Charles Richard, the son of Robert George and Mary Anne, was born in Exeter in 1869 being baptised on September 23rd at St Pauls Church.
The family lived in Exeter where his father was occupied as a paper hanger and Charles was a porter.
Charles had already enrolled in the Western Counties Engineer Volunteers, a local militia group, when he enlisted into the Coldstream Guards on April 12th 1888 for 3 years' service leaving in April 1891.
His records show that he was 5ft 9½ins tall, weighed 9 stone 5 lbs, and had a fresh complexion, blue eyes and brown hair.
On November 30th 1895 he married Sarah Maynard at St David's Parish Church, Exeter. Charles occupation was now a storekeeper.
He was recalled into the army and on October 21st 1899 left for South Africa where he fought in the South Africa Campaigns of 1899 – 1901, earning the South Africa Medal with clasps awarded for Belmont, Modder River, Dreifontein, Johannesburg and Diamond Hill. He returned to England on April 10th 1901 being discharged 6 days later.
He re-enlisted on March 12th 1903 for a further 4 years.
By 1911 they were living in Exeter with their 5 children and Charles was employed as a labourer on the railways. Sometime after this he joined the Royal Defence Corps. It was initially formed by converting the (Home Service) Garrison battalions of line infantry regiments. Garrison battalions were composed of soldiers either too old or medically unfit for active front-line service; the Home Service status indicated they were unable to be transferred overseas.
The role of the corps was to provide troops for security and guard duties inside the United Kingdom; guarding important locations such as ports or bridges. It also provided independent companies for guarding prisoner-of-war camps. The corps was never intended to be employed on overseas service.
Charles had left the Royal Defence Corps at the end of the war and was on the Army Reserve list, finding employment as a Plate layer with the railways in Risca. It was whilst working here that he had an accident and was killed.
He was walking along a line to work when he was struck by a train; the accident

being reported in the Argus on January 11th 1919.

> "Pontymister Man Killed"
> Fearful injuries were sustained by Charles Richard Darby, a platelayer, of Pontymister, on Monday on the railway at Risca. He was knocked down by an up train and terribly mutilated. His coat was found on the engine when it arrived at Newbridge. The injured man was removed to the Royal Gwent Hospital and died the same day. He was 49, an ex soldier and married.
> Dr T Moore, of the resident medical staff, deposed that the man was admitted to the hospital in an unconscious condition. The left leg was nearly amputated; the right leg bone was smashed at the knee; and there were bruises on both hands, back of the head and face.
> It was stated that no one saw the accident and that the train was believed to be a passenger one."

Charles is buried in Risca Old Cemetery, Cromwell Road, Risca.

DART DAVID WILLIAM BOWEN
PRIVATE, 2ND BATTALION
SOUTH WALES BORDERERS
SERVICE NO. 26491
DIED 29 OCTOBER 1916, AGE 29
BURIED ABERCARN CEMETERY, ABERCARN

David, born in Abercarn in 1887, was the eldest son of Tom Walter and Mary Dart, (nee Bowen).
He attended Pontywaun County School in 1899. In 1901 the family lived at 18 Bridge Street, Abercarn, David was employed as an engine fitter's apprentice. In 1911 he was working as a colliery fitter, whilst living at The Mount, Wattstown with his uncle David Livingstone Bowen, who was the local colliery manager.
David had returned from working as an engineer in South Africa to join his three brothers in fighting for the home-land.
He enlisted in Newport in the 2nd Battalion South Wales Borderers serving as Private 26491.
David died of Paratyphoid Fever in the War Hospital, Croydon, on October 29th 1916.
He was buried in Abercarn Cemetery on November 4th.
David is remembered on a number of local memorials including Pontywaun County School, Celynen Collieries Workmen's Institute, Tabernacle Baptist Church Newbridge and Abercarn and Newbridge Cenotaphs.

DART WILLIAM ERNEST
PRIVATE, 2ND BATTALION
SOUTH WALES BORDERERS
SERVICE NO. 14280
DIED 3 OCTOBER 1919, AGE 38
BURIED RISCA OLD CEMETERY, RISCA, WALES

William, born in Torquay on February 6th 1881 was the second son to James and Georgina Emma Dart, (nee Westaway).
Living at 36 Higher Union Street, James was employed as a painter. They later moved to Pimlico, then Temperance Street, Torquay.
William moved to Risca and worked as a collier, living at Park View, Pontymister. He enlisted, at Newport, into the South Wales Borderers on September 1st 1914 having previously served in the Militia with the 2nd Devonshire Regiment until 1903.
His service record shows he was 5ft 4¾ins tall, weighing 9 stone. He had a fresh complexion with brown hair and eyes. William gave his religious denomination as Roman Catholic.
He was posted to the 5th Battalion as Private, 14280 and promoted to Corporal on May 5th 1915.
The South Wales Borderers embarked at Southampton on board the Empress Queen and landed in France on July 17th 1915 in the 38th Brigade as part of the 19th Division. It soon became the Divisional Pioneer Battalion, combining the duties of trench digging and mining with bombing and hard fighting.
After receiving its baptism of fire at Loos in September 1915, the Battalion was kept busy in that area throughout the winter repairing roads, constructing tramways, improving trenches, and in tunnelling in close proximity to the enemy. William was ideally suited to this type of work using his skills acquired as a miner.
He was promoted to Sergeant on December 29th 1915 but the following month he was severely reprimanded for neglect of duty, when in charge of a platoon.
On March 14th 1916, the Germans exploded a mine under a salient in the British line known as the 'Duck's Bill'. Half the salient was destroyed, and most of the garrison, including a working party of the Battalion, were killed or wounded.
During the great Battle of the Somme in 1916 the Battalion had its share of digging, holding trenches, and clearing villages with bomb and bayonet, losing 220 men in the last ten days of July.
William was arrested on October 20th, awaiting trial for being "*Drunk on active service*". He was found guilty and "*reduced to the ranks*" as punishment on November 30th 1916.
On May 10th 1917 he contracted Trench Fever and was admitted to hospital. (Trench fever, also known as "five-day fever", "quintan fever" and "urban trench fever", is a moderately serious disease transmitted by body lice. It infected armies in Flanders, France, Poland, Galicia, Italy, Salonika, Macedonia, Mesopotamia, and Egypt in World War 1).
He left hospital and was granted leave on July 14th 1917 which allowed him to return home and marry Gwendoline May Baker on July 24th 1917 at Risca, rejoining his Battalion on August 9th.
The 5th Battalion were involved at the Third Battle of Ypres and Passchendaele, where the importance of the Pioneers was evident.
During the German attack in March 1918, the Battalion inflicted heavy losses on

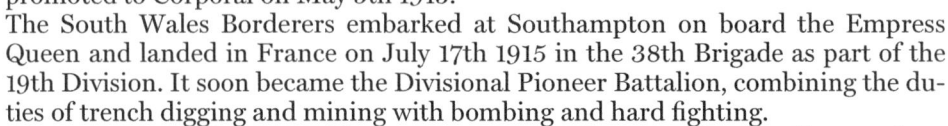

the enemy by determined counter-attacks and steadily withdrawing to previously dug positions. The enemy was stopped at a cost of 150 casualties to the Battalion. The heroic rear-guard fighting continued the following day, with the Battalion making stand after stand.

The Battalion, having been used for the first time as infantry, had proved they could fight as well as dig and wire.

On May 11th 1918 he was again admitted to hospital after being gassed which caused Bronchitis. In mid-August his physical condition was defined as Class B1 (Able to march five miles, and see to shoot with glasses and hear well).

He was compulsorily transferred to the Labour Corps and posted to 88 Labour Company, serving as Private 568202.

William was demobilised at Chiseldon on March 13th 1919 and transferred to the Army Reserve, returning to live at 3 Station Road, Pontymister. His records state that he was still suffering from Bronchitis.

On October 3rd 1919 at 10 Station Road, he died from the effects of gas, aged 38. William is buried in Risca Old Cemetery, Cromwell Road, Risca and commemorated on the Bethany Church Memorial, although he is named as Ernest Dark.

DAVIES ARTHUR GEORGE
PRIVATE, 'D' COMPANY 2ND BATTALION
MONMOUTHSHIRE REGIMENT
SERVICE NO. 1724
DIED 6 DECEMBER 1914, AGE 18
REMEMBERED PLOEGSTEERT MEMORIAL, BELGIUM

Arthur, born in Abercarn in 1896, was the son of Henry and Ellen Davies, living in Mount Pleasant, Abercarn. In 1911, Arthur, a tin plater, was a boarder with his sister and brother in law, Alice and William Thomas. They lived in 77 North Road, Pontywain with their son William. Also living in the house is Darrell Orlando Davies age 4, Arthur and Alice's younger brother, as it appears that both their parents had died; Ellen in 1909 and Henry the following year.

Arthur enlisted on May 20th 1913 in the Monmouthshire Regiment, serving in the 2nd Battalion as Private 1724. He gave his occupation at the time as a collier.

He disembarked in Le Havre with the 2nd Battalion on November 7th 1914.

The 2nd Battalion was posted to the 4th Division, whose 12th Brigade it joined in the trenches near Armentieres before the end of November. In this area it spent the first winter, earning a great name for its capacities in digging and mining. Trench-warfare was active that winter and, if the Armentieres 'Plug Street' area ranked as 'quiet', the 2nd Monmouths' 170 casualties in five months are some indication of what the troops had to go through.

A/Cpl AE Pinchin was awarded the Distinguished Conduct Medal for his act of bravery on 6 December 1914. This is the first fighting decoration ever awarded to a Territorial Soldier. His citation from the London Gazette reads:
> For very gallant conduct in leaving his trench under heavy fire to assist a wounded comrade, and, although himself wounded, remaining with the

man until he died. (London Gazette 16.1.15)
The following interview was given by Pinchin on the incident:
> 'My section was a working party down the left end of our regiment. I had been continually warning the men not to go across some open ground for wood, as we would get the German snipers at the barn. At last about 3 o'clock, about twenty men crossed over, and as I expected, the snipers fired at the barn.
> Lance Corporal Prince and Private Davies were wounded. The former managed to get back, but Davies was dying. I was instructed to go across and get him from there. He was in a dying condition. Sergeant Coombes was with him and between us we did our best for him, but he died trying to say something.
> We could not make out what he said. Another man named Private Roberts was also wounded, and as Private Davies was dead I left him to attend to Private Roberts. When going across to the barn I got hit, and was wounded in the right arm, so that I only had one arm free to work upon Davies and Roberts. I bandaged Roberts up and carried him to a place of safety. I stayed with him until night, as it was not safe to shift him by day. After leaving him in safety I went to see to my own wound. I think Sergeant Coombes acted bravely.'

The above is taken from 'They Fought With Pride' 'First World War Experiences of the 2nd Battalion The Monmouthshire Regiment' by David Nicholas.
Arthur, aged 18, was in France for less than four weeks when he died. He was awarded the British War and Victory medals, along with the 1914 Star and Clasp. As his body was never recovered, he is remembered on the Ploegsteert Memorial, Belgium.

DAVIES GEORGE
PRIVATE, 19TH PIONEER BATTALION
WELSH REGIMENT
SERVICE NO. 31354
DIED 5 JUNE 1917, AGE 41
BURIED FERME OLIVIER CEMETERY, BELGIUM

George, born in Bedwas in 1875, was the son of Richard and Margaret Davies, of Maesycwmmer.
After he married Norah Margaret Griffiths in 1905 they moved to 80 Tredegar Street, Cross Keys. George is shown on the census of 1911 as being employed as a coal miner, they later had three children.
He enlisted in Newport and served as a Private in 19th (Pioneer) Battalion, Welsh Regiment.
The 19th (Service) Battalion (Glamorgan Pioneers) were formed at Colwyn Bay in February 1915 as a Pioneer Battalion. On April 28th 1915 they became part of the 38th (Welsh) Division.
They landed at Le Havre in December 1915, but arrived in France with a poor reputation, seen as a political formation that was ill-trained and poorly led.

The division were heavily involved in the first days of the Battle of the Somme, where it captured the strongly held Mametz Wood at the loss of nearly 4,000 men. This strongly held German position needed to be secured in order to facilitate the next phase of the Somme offensive; the Battle of Bazentin Ridge. Despite securing its objective, the division's reputation was adversely affected by miscommunication among senior officers.

At the end of August 1916, the division was deployed to the Ypres Salient where it remained for the next ten months seeing no major action. The division spent its time rebuilding and consolidating washed out trenches and raiding German positions.

George was killed on June 6th 1917 and is buried in Ferme-Olivier Cemetery, Belgium.

DAVIES JOHN EMLYN
Telegraphist, HMS Victory
Royal Navy
Service No. J/42615
Died 25 May 1918, age 18
Buried Abercarn Cemetery, Abercarn

John Emlyn was born in Newbridge on November 6th 1899 to John and Annie Davies. His father worked as a colliery fireman before becoming a colliery examiner below ground.

An ex-pupil of Pontywaun County School, John Emlyn signed up to the Royal Navy on August 7th 1915 when he was still a schoolboy. From his service record, he was shown as being 5ft 7ins with a 32ins chest, dark brown hair and hazel eyes, with a scar on the back of his head.

Starting as a Boy II he was employed on the Victory I, Impregnable, Ganges and Renown.

He passed for a Telegraphist on October 5th before signing up on November 6th 1917 for a period of 12 years. Whilst employed back on the Victory I he contracted Tuberculosis of the lungs and died in Plymouth hospital on May 25th 1918.

He was brought back to home to Wales and buried in Abercarn cemetery.

The notes below are the recollections of his niece Joan, who knew him as Emlyn.

"Emlyn was very bright, and passed his exams at school. A local solicitor wanted to employ someone and had Emlyn and another boy in mind, but took a long time in deciding. Emlyn got fed up with waiting and went to Newport without his mother's knowledge and enlisted in the Navy. He came home on leave, and was put in the train by his mates at Newport. When the train arrived at Newbridge, the stationmaster who knew him said 'come on Emlyn you get out here' but he was delirious and they had to get a doctor and arrange some conveyance to get him home. Joan says he had double pneumonia. She can remember sitting on his bed while he was ill and him saying 'Hands on the buzzer' (presumably to do with his work). He went back to Portsmouth and sometime later (time unknown) her grandfather received a telegram to say he was very ill. His parents went to Portsmouth

– grandfather went home after a week, but grandmother stayed till he died a week later. Emlyn asked for strawberries and Grandmother looked for them everywhere but unsuccessfully".

Emlyn had full a military funeral in Newbridge, which Joan remembers seeing, saying *"Newbridge had never seen anything like it before"*.

The family were hit by tragedy just a month previous, when John's brother, William Ewart Davies was killed on April 25th 1918. William, a Private with 12th Battalion Gloucestershire Regiment, is commemorated on the Ploegsteert Memorial, Belgium.

John was entitled to the British War Medal and the Victory Medal.

DAVIES MARGARET HANNAH
COOK
QUEEN MARY'S ARMY AUXILIARY CORPS
SERVICE NO. 14857
DIED 13 FEBRUARY 1919, AGE 26
BURIED RISCA OLD CEMETERY, RISCA, WALES

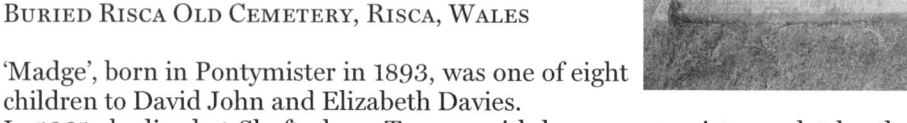

'Madge', born in Pontymister in 1893, was one of eight children to David John and Elizabeth Davies.

In 1901 she lived at Shaftesbury Terrace with her parents, sister and 3 brothers; father David was employed as a steel smelter.

She attended Risca Council School before they moved to 153 Mount Pleasant Road, Ebbw Vale soon after.

Madge and her sister Gladys then attended Pontygof Girls School, Ebbw Vale, both starting on August 21st 1905.

By 1911 the family were back living in 9 Priory St, Risca although Madge was living elsewhere.

She joined Queen Mary's Army Auxiliary Corps with the rank of Worker, Service Number 14858.

Madge died on February 13th 1919 and is buried in Risca Old Cemetery, Cromwell Road, Risca.

DAVIES OSWALD
PRIVATE, 8TH BATTALION
WELSH REGIMENT
SERVICE NO. 11900
DIED 8 AUGUST 1915, AGE 21
COMMEMORATED HELLES MEMORIAL, GALLIPOLI, TURKEY

Oswald, son of William and Rachel Davies, was born in Pontymister in 1893. The family, along with older brother William Charles were living near the New Inn in 1901, father Williams' occupation is shown as a blacksmith.

Rachel died aged 40 in 1907 and William married Alice Hill in late 1910. The family, along with Alice's daughters, were living at the Railway

Tavern in 1911.

William, still a blacksmith, and his two sons, both unmarried labourers, are working in the local tin works.

After the outbreak of war, Oswald signed up with the 8th Battalion the Welsh Regiment at Newport.

The 8th Battalion, formed at Cardiff in August 1914, came under the orders of 40th Brigade in 13th (Western) Division.

They moved to Salisbury Plain and was at Chisledon in October 1914. They went into billets in Bournemouth in December and in January 1915 converted into a Pioneer Battalion to the same Division.

The Battalion moved to Aldershot in February 1915, then embarked at Avonmouth on June 15th 1915 and landed at Alexandria before moving to Mudros, by July 4th to prepare for a landing at Gallipoli. The infantry landed on Cape Helles between July 6th and 16th to relieve the 29th Division. They returned to Mudros at the end of the month, and the entire Division landed at ANZAC Cove between August 3rd and 5th.

Oswald was killed on Sunday August 8th and as he has no known grave, he is commemorated on the Helles Memorial, Gallipoli, Turkey.

DAVIS ALBERT REGINALD
GUNNER, 'B' BATTERY 45TH BRIGADE
ROYAL FIELD ARTILLERY
SERVICE NO. 745347
DIED 21 FEBRUARY 1918, AGE 26
BURIED YPRES RESERVOIR CEMETERY, BELGIUM

Albert Reginald, son of Thomas and Rosina Davis, was born September 24th 1891 and baptized at the Holy Trinity Church, Pillgwenlly, Newport on December 6th.

The family lived at 12 Upper William Street, Pill, 2 Union Terrace and lastly in 1911 at 10 Church Street, Rogerstone.

Reginald was a pupil at Rogerstone Boy's School before attending Pontywaun County School, starting on January 11th 1908 and leaving on September 24th the following year.

In 1911 he is listed as a pupil teacher working for the County Council.

Albert married Gwendolyn S. Howells in late 1917.

He enlisted into the Royal Field Artillery and served as a Gunner in "B" Battery. 45th Brigade.

Age 26, he was killed on February 21st 1918 and buried in Ypres Reservoir Cemetery, Belgium.

Reginald is remembered on the Pontywaun County School and Rogerstone Roll of Honour memorials.

DAWE ARTHUR HENRY
PRIVATE, 2ND BATTALION
GRENADIER GUARDS
SERVICE NO. 15201
DIED 10 NOVEMBER 1914, AGE 28
REMEMBERED YPRES MENIN GATE
MEMORIAL, BELGIUM

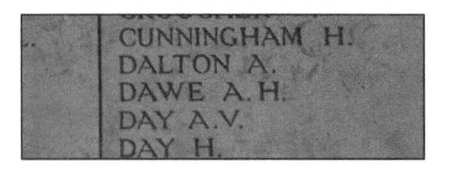

Arthur was the son of George Henry and Mary Ann Dawe, (nee Pritchard). He was born about 1888 in Abercarn according to his army records. In 1891 the family lived in Main Road, Pontywain and then later near the Trinity Church.
On November 28th 1905 he joined the Grenadier Guards at London. His record shows he was 5ft 8¾ins tall and weighed 134 lbs. He had a fresh complexion, blue eyes, brown hair and a large scar on the back of his head.
He gave his address as 1 Primrose Terrace, Pontywain. Arthur was discharged on March 29th 1906 and returned to his previous occupation as a miner, although by 1911 he was again serving with the Grenadier Guards, probably signing up in March of that year.
He went to France on August 31st 1914 landing at Le Havre. The Division engaged in various actions on the Western Front including; The First Battle of Ypres after which only 4 officers and 140 men remained of the Battalion.
Arthur was presumed killed on November 10th 1914 and is commemorated on the Menin Gate Memorial at Ypres, Belgium.

DOBSON WILLIAM
PRIVATE, 11TH BATTALION
SOUTH WALES BORDERERS
SERVICE NO. 22122
DIED 17 MAY 1916, AGE 21
BURIED RISCA OLD CEMETERY, RISCA, WALES

William, eldest son of Thomas and Sarah Ann Dobson was born in Newburn, Northumberland on December 6th 1894.
Thomas was employed as a steel worker and moved to Pontymister working in the steel works.
William attended Pontymister Boys School, before moving up to Pontywaun County School on September 14th 1908. The family at this time lived at 28 Park Place, Pontymister later moving to Moriah Hill, before returning to Park Place, living at number 30.
Leaving school after the summer term in 1910, William worked as an apprentice pattern maker in the Steel Foundry. He enlisted in Newport into the 11th Battalion, South Wales Borderers, serving as a Private.
The 11th (Service) Battalion (2nd Gwent) was raised by the Welsh National

Executive Committee in October 1914. In January 1915 they moved to Colwyn Bay and on April 29th became part of the 115th Brigade, 38th Division. In August 1915 the Battalion moved to Hazeley Down, Southampton in readiness to go to France. They marched from Hazeley Down to Southampton on December 3rd and embarked, arriving in Le Havre on December 4th 1915.

They transferred to Witternesse for Battalion training between December 7th and 18th. The Battalion then moved to Riez du Vinage and carried out trench training before going to the front line on December 28th.

Further training and time in the trenches continued throughout January ending at Neuve Chapelle at the end of the month.

During February, March and April, they were involved at Festubert, Le Touret and Givenchy areas, carrying out front line duties as well as continuing with training.

The battalion then continued in the trenches around Fauquissart, La Gorgue and at Pont du Hem in Northern France.

It was at Pont du Hem that William was severely injured on April 28th 1916 after heavy enemy shelling on the front line and communication trenches. He was sent home to the First Eastern Hospital, Cambridge where he died of his wounds on May17th.

William is buried in Risca Old Cemetery, Cromwell Road, Risca.

He is remembered on the Bethany Chapel and Pontywaun School memorials.

DOLLERY FRANK
PRIVATE, 6TH BATTALION
WILTSHIRE BORDERERS
SERVICE NO. 36403
DIED 29 APRIL 1918, AGE 18
REMEMBERED TYNE COT MEMORIAL, BELGIUM

Frank, born August 1st 1899 in Reading, Berkshire, was the son of George and Lucy Jane Dollery.

In 1901, they lived at 47, Coventry Road, Reading St Giles, Reading and George is employed as a Railway Shunter.

Frank attended New Town Primary School in Reading, starting on October 20th 1902 and leaving a year later, 'until he was older'.

His mother Lucy died in 1903 and was buried on June 27th in London Road Cemetery, Reading.

Now living in 26 School Terrace, Reading, he rejoined on July 11th 1904 and stayed until January 31st 1905 when they moved to Caversham, Reading. In 1908, George moved to south Wales living in 26 Llanarth Street, Newport where Frank and his brothers attended St Woolos Boy's school.

The next move was to 58 George Street, Newport before moving to Bright Street, Cross Keys in February 1911.

Frank's next school was Waunfawr Junior School, Cross Keys leaving in January 1912.

He enlisted at Trowbridge on May 5th 1915, as Private 20674 in 'B' Company, 8th Battalion Wiltshire Regiment.

After just 72 days, Frank was discharged on July 14th 1915 at Bovington Camp,

Wareham as he was only 15 years 11 months old.
He had declared that he was 19 yrs 3 mths old at the time of enlistment, but lied about his age.
Frank's details are shown as 5ft 3ins tall, fresh complexion, brown eyes and fair hair. Although he gave his address at enlistment as 17 Spring Grove, Reading he declared on his discharge he was returning to 34 Wood Street, Cross Keys.
He later enlisted, after 1915, as a Private in 6th Battalion Wiltshire Regiment, Service Number 36403.
The 6th Wiltshire Service Battalion went to France in July 1915 concentrated near St Omer. In 1916 they were in action during the Battle of the Somme, capturing La Boiselle and being involved in the attacks on High Wood, the Battles of Poziers Ridge, the Ancre Heights and Ancre.
In 1917 they were in action in the Battle of Messines and the Third Battle of Ypres. 1918 saw them fighting on the Somme and in the Battle of Lys.
The Battle of Lys, also known as the Fourth Battle of Ypres, the Lys Offensive and the Third Battle of Flanders, was part of the 1918 German Spring Offensive.
This was ordered by General Luderndorff in a final attempt by the Germans to break the Allied lines around Ypres.
It was on April 29th 1918, the last day of the Battle of Lys, that Frank was killed. His body was never recovered and so he is commemorated on the Tyne Cot Memorial.
Frank is remembered on the Hope Baptist Church Memorial, Cross Keys.

DONOVAN MICHAEL
PRIVATE, 1ST BATTALION
ROYAL WELSH FUSILIERS
SERVICE NO. 19155
DIED 11 JUNE 1915
REMEMBERED LE TOURET MEMORIAL, BELGIUM

Early details of Michael, born in Cork, Ireland are uncertain, apart from his father's name was Jeremiah.
In 1911 he lived at 8 Wattsville and was a labourer in the colliery. His sister Annie Hunt lived in 4 Danygraig Cottages, Risca.
Michael enlisted at Newport in the Royal Welsh Fusiliers, serving as Private, 19155, in the 1st Battalion.
Landing in France on May 25th 1915 he was killed less than three weeks later, probably in the Battle of Festubert.
He is remembered on Le Touret Memorial, France.

DOWNES ALBERT EDWARD
2ND CORPORAL, 9TH FIELD COMPANY
3RD DIVISIONAL CANADIAN ENGINEERS
SERVICE NO. 502466
DIED 24 APRIL 1917, AGE 29
BURIED VILLERS STATION CEMETERY, FRANCE

Albert, born in Newport, May 6th 1887, was one of fourteen children to Jesse and Emily Downes, (nee Gay).
Living in Christchurch, Newport in 1891 Jesse was a builder by trade. They moved initially to Pontymister, living in the Commercial Inn, where Jesse is shown as a mason and builder, whilst Albert is a mason's labourer. Later they moved to 26 Bridge Street, Risca.
Albert emigrated to Canada around 1905 living in Regina, Saskatchewan. He married Bertha and they had a child, Henry Munro born 16 August 1910.
On 25 January 1916, Albert enlisted into the Canadian Army at Winnipeg, Manitoba. He served with 9th Field Company, Canadian Engineers. His records state he was 5' 3" tall, had a fair complexion, blue eyes and brown hair.
In April 1917, the 9th Field Company were in Villers-au-Bois, France. They were involved in tunnelling, repairing trenches and roads and making signs. All this work was in advance of the attack and planned capture of Vimy Ridge. Albert was recommended for a Military Medal for his work carried out between April 9th and 17th, tragically he was killed just a few days later.
The War Diary states: '*#502466 2/Cpl Downes Albert Ernest (not Edward) killed by shell fire on the Arras-Lens road in the neighbourhood of Vimy while on duty in charge of a party erecting a camouflage screen over the road. I wish to record the good services rendered by this NCO.*' Major NR Robertson
Albert is buried in Villers Station Cemetery, France.

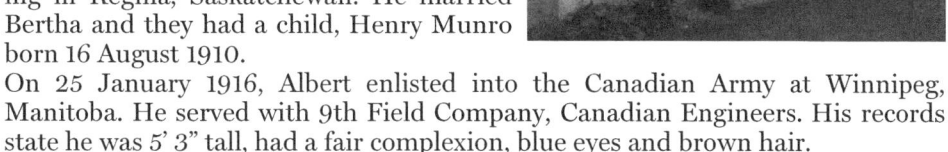

DOWNES CHARLES ARTHUR
LANCE CORPORAL, 1ST BATTALION
SOUTH WALES BORDERERS
SERVICE NO. 18498
DIED 7 JUNE 1915, AGE 18
REMEMBERED LE TOURET MEMORIAL, FRANCE

Charles Arthur, born in Risca in 1896, was the youngest son of Edgar and Elizabeth Ann Downes, (nee Veysey).
Edgar, born in Pontymister was a coal miner, Ann was born in Washfield, Devon.
Charles, employed as a postman in Risca, enlisted at Newport in the South Wales Borderers as Private 18498, later being promoted to Lance Corporal.
He went to France on May 18th 1915 being killed just a few weeks later at Cuinchy on June 7th 1915.
As his body was never recovered, Charles is remembered on Le Touret Memorial, France. He is commemorated on the memorial in Moriah Church, Risca.

DUFFIELD WILLIAM EWART
Private, 2ND Battalion
South Wales Borderers
Service No. 30354
Died 3 December 1917, age 19
Remembered Cambrai Memorial, France

Born in Pontywain on August 26th 1898, William was the son of William Henry and Elizabeth Duffield, (nee Hoskins).
He was baptised, along with his sister Elizabeth Rosine, on September 20th 1898 at Mynyddislwyn Church.
William's father was employed as a helve maker.
In 1901 they lived at Back Lane, Pontywain before moving to 10 Coronation Place by 1911.
William attended Park Street Infants School in Cross Keys, starting on May 12th 1903. He stayed there until August 14th 1905 when he transferred to the Mixed Department.
He enlisted in Abertillery in the 2nd Battalion South Wales Borderers, serving as Private 30354. It is not known when he joined or when he went abroad.
In March 1916, the 2nd Battalion South Wales Borderers, as part of the 29th Division, arrived in France. Its first big action was on July 1st 1916, the opening day of the great Battle of the Somme, when it attacked the impregnable position at Beaumont Hamel. The 2nd Battalion advancing south of the village in the leading line was mown down by machine guns in the first few minutes and lost 11 officers and 235 men killed and missing and 4 officers and 149 men wounded out of a total of 21 officers and 578 men. Some men reached the German wire 300 yards away, but neither here nor at other places did the Division's attack succeed.
The Battalion was reformed and after periods in various parts of the Line fought most gallantly at Monchy Le Preux in April and May 1917.
The 2nd Battalion fought through the desperate Third Battle of Ypres in the summer and autumn of 1917, and then at Cambrai in November and December it earned what is perhaps its greatest honour in the War.
William was reported missing presumed dead on December 3rd 1917 and is commemorated on the Cambrai Memorial at Louverval, France.

E

EDWARDS ARTHUR
Lance Corporal, 9th Battalion
Royal Welsh Fusiliers
Service No. 55403
Died 28 May 1918, age 23
Remembered Soissons Memorial, France

Born in Nantyglo and baptised on May 9th 1895, Arthur was the son of William and Maria Edwards. The family lived in Llanhilleth before moving to 24 Mount Pleasant Terrace, Cross Keys. At this time he worked as a Butcher's assistant before later becoming the manager at Eastman's shop in Cross Keys.
He enlisted at Newport in 9th Battalion Royal Welsh Fusiliers as Private 202859, later serving as 55403.
Arthur arrived in France sometime after 1915.
The 9th (Service) Battalion, Royal Welsh Fusiliers, was raised as part of Kitchener's Second New Army and joined 58th Brigade, 19th (Western) Division. They went to France landing on July 19th 1915 at Boulogne.
Among the many actions, they fought at the Battle of Loos in 1915, the Battle of Albert and the attacks on High Wood in 1916. They were also heavily involved in the Battles of Messines, Menin Road Ridge and the Battles of Passchendaele in 1917.
In 1918 they fought at the Battle of St Quentin, the First Battle of Kemmel Ridge and then the Battle of the Aisne between May 27th and June 6th.
Arthur died May 28th 1918 age 23.
He is remembered on the Soissons Memorial, France as well as the Pontywaun Wesleyan Church and School Memorial.

ELLIS FREDERICK WILLIAM
Private, 1st Battalion
Gloucestershire Regiment
Service No. 1712
Died 30 September 1915, age 19
Buried Chocques Military Cemetery, France

Frederick, born in Cardiff in 1896, was the son of William and Eliza Ellis, (nee Ives).
Originally from Norfolk, William and Eliza moved to Cardiff around 1895, where Frederick and his brother Alvinzie were born. Shortly afterwards they moved to 3 Pleasant Road, Mangotsfield, Gloucestershire, where they were visiting an Albert Hawkins and his family.

By 1911 they were living in their own home in Pleasant Road.
Frederick made blinds in the local window blind factory before enlisting into the 1st Battalion Gloucester Regiment.
The 1st Battalion went to France in August 1914 suffering its first casualties on August 26th during the retreat from Mons.
Frederick joined his regiment in France on November 28th 1914, and fought in the Defence of Festubert in December. January saw them in the Defence of Givenchy.
In May they were at the Battle of Aubers Ridge which was part of the Second Battle of Artois.
The Battle of Loos took place from September 25th until October 8th 1915 in France.
It was the biggest British attack of 1915 and the first time that the British used poison gas.
On September 25th the French and British planned to break through the German defences in Artois and Champagne. Despite improved methods, more ammunition and better equipment, the Franco-British attacks were contained by the German armies.
In many places British artillery had failed to cut the German wire in advance of the attack and British losses were devastating.
When the battle resumed the following day, the Germans had recovered and improved their defensive positions. British attempts to continue the advance with the reserves were repulsed.
Twelve attacking battalions suffered 8,000 casualties out of 10,000 men in four hours.
By September 28th, the British had retreated to their starting positions, having lost over 20,000 casualties, including three major-generals.
Frederick died of his wounds at No 1 Casualty Clearing Station on September 30th and is buried in Chocques Military Cemetery, France.
His parent's address is given in the records as 80 Commercial Street, Pontymister.
Frederick is remembered on the Bethany Chapel Memorial.

EVANS STANLEY
LANCE CORPORAL, 2ND BATTALION
SOUTH WALES BORDERERS
SERVICE NO. 25554
DIED 1 JULY 1916, AGE 21
BURIED HAWTHORN RIDGE CEMETERY No 2, FRANCE

Richard Stanley Evans, commonly known as Stanley was born in Henllys on October 21st 1894 to Llewellyn and Elizabeth Ann Evans, (nee Jones).
The family moved to Risca initially living in Taylorstown.
Stanley attended Risca School, from September 11th 1899 until August 18th 1902 when he transferred to the Mixed Department.
In 1901 the family lived in Clarence Place, Risca before moving to The Gables, Bridge Street by 1911; Stanley, his two

brothers and father were employed as miners.

He enlisted into the South Wales Borderers and went to Gallipoli on November 26th 1915.

The 2nd Battalion South Wales Borderers had already seen action in Gallipoli as part of the 29th Division, suffering many casualties.

In March 1916 the 29th Division arrived in France. Its first major action was on July 1st 1916, the opening day of the great Battle of the Somme, when it attacked the impregnable position at Beaumont Hamel.

The 2nd Battalion, advancing south of the village in the leading line, was mown down by machine guns in the first few minutes and lost 11 officers and 235 men killed and missing and 4 officers and 149 men wounded out of a total of 21 officers and 578 men.

Some of the men managed to reach the German wire 300 yards away, but neither here nor at other places did the Division's attack succeed.

Stanley was killed in this attack and is buried in Hawthorn Ridge Cemetery No 2, Auchonvillers.

He is remembered on the Moriah Chapel Memorial and a family headstone at Zoar Chapel, Castell Y Bwch.

EVANS WILLIAM DAVID G
PRIVATE, 5TH BATTALION
DEVONSHIRE REGIMENT
SERVICE NO. 32452
DIED 29 AUGUST 1918, AGE 17
REMEMBERED VIS-EN-ARTOIS MEMORIAL, FRANCE

Born in Wattsville in 1900, William lived with his grandparents David and Emma Evans in 29 Wattsville before moving to Full Moon Cottage, Cross Keys.

He then lived with his aunt, Mrs Henrietta Morgan in 7 Salisbury Street, Cross Keys. Before joining the army, he worked in the local pit.

William enlisted in Newport into the Cheshire Regiment as Private 52304, later transferring to the Devonshire Regiment, serving as Private 32452 in the 5th Battalion.

The 5th (Prince of Wales) Battalion, Devonshire Regiment was a Territorial Unit headquartered in Plymouth.

As part of the Wessex Division, they were mobilised for war service on August 5th 1914 and sailed on September 9th to India. They left India in spring 1917 going to Egypt for service in Palestine.

In 1918 they moved to the Western Front, landing at Marseille on June 1st joining 185th Brigade, 62nd Division.

They saw action in numerous battles including Tardenois and the Battle of the Scarpe.

It was during this battle that William was killed on August 29th 1918 and is remembered on the Vis-En-Artois Memorial in France.

EVANS WILLIAM JONES
Captain, 5th Battalion
2nd/1st (South Midland) Field Ambulance
Royal Army Medical Corps
Died 13 September 1917, age 27
Buried Vlamertinghe New Military Cemetery, Belgium

William, born at Llangynidr on April 19th 1890, was the only son of the Reverend William and Zillah Evans.
In 1901 they lived at Usk Villa, Llangynidr where his father William was the Baptist Minister.
By 1911 they had moved to 59 Risca Road, Cross Keys where William is now a widower as Zillah had died in 1904. On the census, William junior was shown as a medical student.
The family later lived at 'Tegfryn', Hillside, Risca.
William was engaged to Mabel Russell Benson from Glenside, Waunfawr, she never married and died in 1984 aged 91.
He was educated at Pontywaun County School, at University College of Wales, Cardiff and at the University College Hospital, London.
He took the degrees of Membership of the Royal Colleges of Surgeons and Licentiate of the Royal College of Physicians in 1916, but in the meantime had joined the University of London Officer's Training Corps in October 1914.
As soon as he gained his qualifications, he immediately obtained a commission in the Royal Army Medical Corps and was gazetted as Lieutenant in March 1916.
After a short period of training on Salisbury Plain, he went to France in May, 1916 attached to the 2/1st South Midland Field Ambulance, from which he was later transferred to the Gloucester Regiment.
He became Captain after one year's service.
William was killed in the St Julien sector by the explosion of a shell which wrecked his dug-out while he was ministering to the wounded.
Captain Lander, R.A.M.C., an intimate friend and medical colleague wrote: *"He was of a most generous disposition, always cheerful and warm-hearted..... At his medical work he was keen and up to-date.... I think it might be said without exaggeration that he was one of the most, if not the most, popular medical officers in the division.... It was my privilege to visit him at the advanced aid-post, where he received his mortal wound.*
He was quite calmly doing his duty there, rendering to the wounded the aid they required right in the forward line. I still have a note which he wrote on the day of his death, saying what a rough time he was having and how he had decided to 'stick it out' and not come back to a less exposed position".
William is buried in Vlamertinghe New Military Cemetery, Ypres, Belgium.
He is remembered on the Hope Baptist Church and Pontywaun County School memorials.

EVERETT SIDNEY CHARLES
PRIVATE, 6TH BATTALION
WILTSHIRE REGIMENT
SERVICE NO. 20862
DIED 20 SEPTEMBER 1917, AGE 19
REMEMBERED TYNE COT MEMORIAL, BELGIUM

Sidney, son of John and Emma Everett, (nee Doughty), was born in 1898 in Norton Bavant, Wiltshire.
In 1901, Sidney and his four siblings lived at 28 North Farm, Norton Bavant where his father John is a farm labourer. Sidney's mother Emma died age 43 in 1907. In 1911, John and Sidney were living with Rhoda, Sidney's married sister, and her husband and daughter in Sutton Veny, Wiltshire.
Military records show that Sidney was living in Cross Keys, and travelled to Devizes to enlist in the Wiltshire Regiment, serving as Private 20862 in the 6th Battalion. The war memorial at Sutton Veny, shows Sidney C Everett as serving in the 3rd Battalion but it is assumed this is incorrect.
The 6th (Service) Battalion was raised when there was an overspill of manpower from the creation of the 5th (Service) Battalion.
The 6th Battalion embarked for France in July 1915. Initially in the Laventie and Festubert area, their first attack took place at Loos in September. After this battle they returned to the trenches in the Neuve Chapelle area where they ended the year of 1915.
After April 1916, the Battalion moved to Albert, on the River Somme in preparation for the forthcoming offensive. A week after the start of the Battle of the Somme they took part in the capture of La Boiselle, moving into Mametz Wood shortly after. They suffered 380 casualties in two months.
After spending time near Thiepval, they moved to the Ypres salient in April. They took part in the successful attack on Messines Ridge, gaining all their objectives. A period of trench warfare was followed by heavy fighting on the Passchendaele Ridge. On September 20th they captured and held a position in front of Hollebeke Chateau. Casualties were heavy and the battalion was reinforced by 25 officers and 350 other ranks of the Royal Wiltshire Yeomanry, who had been dismounted.
Sidney was killed in action on September 20th 1917 and as he has no known grave he is commemorated on the Tyne Cot memorial, Belgium.
He is remembered on the village War Memorial and the Roll of Honour in St John's Evangelical Church, Sutton Veny.

EVERSON EDWIN
PRIVATE, 3RD BATTALION
WELSH REGIMENT
SERVICE NO. 60295
DIED 18 OCTOBER 1917, AGE 27
BURIED RISCA OLD CEMETERY, RISCA, WALES

Edwin, son of Edwin and Catherine Ann Everson (nee Hodges) was born in Machen

on October 2nd 1890.
Originally living in Machen they moved to Duffryn Cottage, Mynyddislwyn and then to 135 Islwyn Road, Wattsville.
Edwin attended Waunfawr Junior School on October 6th 1897 leaving on May 3rd 1899 when he started at Ynysddu School.
He left school and worked at the local colliery as did his two brothers and father.
Edwin married Rosina Webb on April 22nd 1912 at Bethesda Chapel, Rogerstone, having a child Katherine born on September 10th 1914.
In 1916 he was living at 12 Rifleman Street, Risca when he went to Cardiff on June 18th 1916 and enlisted in the 3rd Battalion Welsh Regiment serving as Private 60295 in C Company.
The records show he was 5ft 8ins tall with a 36½ins chest.
The 3rd was a reserve battalion and stayed in the UK, firstly at Kinmel Park and then at Redcar.
On October 13th 1917 he was admitted to the Military Hospital, Redcar with Bronchitis, complaining of tightness of chest and difficulty in breathing and pain across his chest. He said he felt ill several days ago.
Over the following days although he said he felt slightly better, his breathing got gradually worse culminating in a decline in his health on October 18th. His death from Bronchial Pneumonia was recorded at 2.15 p.m.
Edwin is buried in Risca Old Cemetery, Cromwell Road, Risca.

EVERSON WILLIAM SAMUEL
BOMBARDIER, 67TH BRIGADE HQ
ROYAL FIELD ARTILLERY
SERVICE NO. 13273
DIED 23 OCTOBER 1916, AGE 20
BURIED LEMBET RD MILITARY CEMETERY, GREECE

William, born in Risca in 1896, was the oldest son of William and Elizabeth Everson, (nee Parnicott).
Living in Ochrwyth, Risca, William senior, worked as a tin sheet roller in the local Tin Plate Works.
William junior, enlisted in Newport in the Royal Field Artillery as Bombardier 13273.
67 Brigade, Royal Field Artillery was originally made up of 211, 212 and 213 Field Batteries RFA and the Brigade Ammunition Column.
The Brigade was assigned to 13 Western Division, a part of General Kitchener's First New Army. The division moved to the Mediterranean Expeditionary Force to reinforce the Gallipoli combatants.
Sailing from Avonmouth on June 15th 1915 they arrived in Alexandria, Egypt on

June 29th. However, instead of going to Gallipoli, they joined the British Salonika Force and transferred to the 10th (Irish) Division, landing in Salonika between October 13th and 17th.

William went abroad on July 1st 1915 and the records show he died in the 29th General Hospital, Salonika and is buried in Lembet Road Military Cemetery, Salonika.

BE READY!

JOIN NOW

G

GARDNER ALBERT
PRIVATE, B COMPANY 17ᵀᴴ BATTALION
ROYAL WELSH FUSILIERS
SERVICE NO. 94240
DIED 29 OCTOBER 1918, AGE 29
BURIED FOREST COMMUNAL CEMETERY, FRANCE

Albert, son of Thomas and Catherine Gardner was born in Chelsea, Middlesex in 1890.
His father Thomas, a railway engine driver was born in Birmingham; his mother Catherine in Risca.
The family lived in 149 Fifth Avenue, London for a number of years before Albert moved to south Wales to find employment as a miner. In 1911 he was living in 3 Glenside, Blackvein with his cousin Joseph Marsh and his family.
He enlisted in Newport in the Monmouthshire Regiment serving as Private 61208, later transferring to B Company 17th Battalion Royal Welsh Fusiliers as Private 94240.
The 17th (2nd North Wales) Battalion, Royal Welsh Fusiliers was raised at Llandudno on February 2nd 1915. After training in Llandudno, they joined 113th Brigade, 38th (Welsh) Division on April 28th 1915. They moved to Windsor in August for their final training before going to France in December.
They saw action on the Somme at Mametz Wood in July 1916, where they suffered severe casualties, resulting in the Division seeing no major action for over twelve months. In 1917 they returned to action at the Third Battle of Ypres, before more fighting in 1918 at the Somme, Hindenburg Line and then the Final Advance in Picardy including the Battle of the Selle, October 17 – 25 1918.
It is assumed he was wounded in this battle as he died whilst in the care of the 130th Field Ambulance on October 29th 1918.
Albert is buried in Forest Communal Cemetery, France.

GEEVES WILLIAM CHAPLIN
PRIVATE, SOUTH WALES BORDERERS
SERVICE NO. 21623
DIED 28 APRIL 1916
BURIED MERVILLE COMMUNAL CEMETERY, FRANCE

William was born William Chaplin in Barking, Essex about 1886.
Not much is known about his early years but in 1891 he was living with his aunts Mary Ann and Sarah Jane Chaplin in Camberwell, London.
In 1911 he appears at the home of Benjamin and Elizabeth Geeves in 18 Fenwick Street, Pontygwaith, Glamorgan. He is show as a visitor but working as a coal miner.
When living in Bedwas he enlisted under the name of William Chaplin Geeves,

joining the 11th Battalion South Wales Borderers in Newport.
On December 4th 1915, William and the 11th Battalion landed at Le Havre, France. They fought alongside the 10th South Wales Borderers on the front line throughout the winter and spring of 1915 - 16.
They saw action at Gorre, Givenchy and Estaires before moving to the Laventie-Fauquissart sector in mid-April.
It was whilst fighting at Fauquissart that William was injured and died of his wounds on April 28th 1916.
He is buried in Merville Communal Cemetery, France.
Army records show that his mother was Mrs E Geeves of Hereford House, 5, Standard Street, Trethomas, Cardiff. It is assumed this is the same Elizabeth Geeves that he was visiting in 1911.
It is possible that he worked in the Risca area as he is remembered on the Risca Workingmen's Club Roll of Honour as well as the Bedwas and Trethomas War Memorials.

GIBBS CHARLES ARCHIBALD
PRIVATE, 1ST / 9TH BATTALION
KINGS (LIVERPOOL REGIMENT)
SERVICE NO. 406608
DIED 20 SEPTEMBER 1917, AGE 29
REMEMBERED TYNE COT MEMORIAL, BELGIUM

Archie, born in Canton, Cardiff in 1888, was the son of James and Clara Gibbs, (nee Jones).
They were living at 120 Pembroke Road, Canton, Cardiff, James is employed as a boilermaker.
It appears that James died before 1901, as Clara married George Thomas that year going to live at 15 The Green, Abertysswg.
Archie, employed as a collier, also lived in Abertysswg for a period before moving back to 60 Pembroke Road.
On July 26th 1905, he signed on for 6 years in the 3rd Welsh Regiment at Cardiff, Service Number 4285.
On his records he was described as 5ft 6¾ins tall, weighed 8 stone 5 lbs, with a pale complexion, brown eyes and brown hair. Archie purchased his discharge after 76 days on May 22nd 1906.
He married Ethel Evans in 1908, having a daughter Cecilia the following year.
At this time he was living at 42 Pleasant View, Wattstown, Pontypridd. He enlisted at Wattstown into the 9th Battalion, Welch Regiment, arriving in France on July 17th 1915.
Sometime later he transferred from the Welch Regiment to The King's (Liverpool) Regiment) 1st/9th Battalion, serving as Private 406608.
Archie was killed on September 20th 1917 during the Battle of Passchendaele in the Vlamertinghe area.
Records show his wife Ethel, now lived in 1 Gelli Cottages, Risca, while George and Clara moved to Australia in 1921.

Archie is commemorated on the Tyne Cot Memorial, Belgium and the Moriah Baptist Church Memorial.

GILES RALPH
Corporal, Auckland Regiment
New Zealand Expeditionary Force
Service No. 12/1637
Died 8 August 1915, age 44
Remembered Chunuk Bair (New Zealand) Memorial, Gallipoli

Ralph, born in 1870 at Tyn y Pwll Farm, Malpas, was a great great grandson of the "Old Squire of Risca", William Phillips of Risca Manor House. Ralph was one of eleven children of George Charles and Ann (nee Rosser) Giles.

The greater part of Ralph's youth was spent in Risca. After leaving school he became a cashier in Pontymister Steel Works and sometime during the late 1800's he emigrated to New Zealand.

When war broke out in 1914, he had been living in Hamilton, New Zealand, for some time. There he enlisted in the army, and so great was his desire to serve his country, that he "put back his age" to secure his entrance. He joined the Auckland Infantry Battalion, giving his next of kin as William Charles Giles (brother) of Tymawr, Pontymister, Wales. (Also known as Risca House and later Giles's Farm)

Some two weeks before his embarkation from Wellington, on February 14th 1915, he wrote his last letter to "My Dear Brother" in Pontymister. In his letter he told of the decision he had made.

> "That up until about five weeks before I had intended to get married in March and return home with my wife. But after mutually considering the matter against the present conditions of affair I considered it necessary to defer the marriage until there is a brighter aspect for our country and empire".

After careful thought he concluded that his country needed what little assistance he could give. He wrote, "The idea was very far from my mind (at least until just lately) that I should ever feel it necessary at my time of life to embark on a mission having its object the protection and safeguarding of our empire, but as there does not appear to be a sufficient number of the younger generation coming forward, it devolves upon us who are older to render what little help our remaining energy will afford in this great struggle for our existence as a nation of liberty, truth and justice".

Several of his friends from the township of Hamilton were in his unit, "A" Company, 3rd. Reinforcements, New Zealand Infantry.

> "The majority of the men have left good positions and sacrificed very much to enter this campaign, and there are several (including my-self) who have reduced their ages to render their aid".

> "Unfortunately (as it always appears to be in the case in the United

Kingdom) there are always those young men who do not and never will realise their duty to their King and Country, as well as the heritage which has been handed down to them by their forefathers for safe keeping, and which has been purchased at enormous sacrifices, so as I have said before, it devolves on us who are older to make up the necessary strength required to overwhelm and utterly defeat a project which can only have for its object the undoing of a century's civilisation, and return to barbarism which England has done so much to eradicate for all time".

He rejoiced that New Zealand and Australia were sending the pick of their manhood, money and other commodities, to assist the mother country to hold the empire together.

"Let us meet her in Empire attitude with the whole of our might, and I am certain that the immediate result will be significant enough to let no doubt remain, even in a German's mind, as to where there position in this world should be for a long time to come".

He concluded his letter with "I have made all arrangements respecting my private affairs, and should anything happen to me, the Defence Department will contact you. In the event of my inability to find time to write to the rest of you will you kindly notify the other members of the family that I have gone to the front. You shall receive another letter from me in a week or two. Hoping you are all well. I remain your affectionate brother. RALPH GILES".

Ralph had hoped their destination was England where he would have taken the opportunity to see his brother, however his regiment was ordered to the Dardanelles where he saw action against the Turks.

He was killed, lost in action on the August 8th 1915 at the battle of Chunuk Bair, Turkey. As if he had a premonition of his fate, before going into the firing line for the last time, he wrote a card to every member of his family.

In late August 1915 William Charles Giles of Ty-mawr Farm, Pontymister, received a telegram from the "Donne, recorder, New Zealand Forces", conveying the news that his brother Ralph Giles of the Auckland Infantry, New Zealand Expeditionary Force, had been killed in action at the Gallipoli Peninsula on August 8th.

GILL REGINALD ARTHUR
PRIVATE, A COMPANY 2ND ROYAL MARINE BATTALION
ROYAL MARINE LIGHT INFANTRY
SERVICE NO. PLY/732/S
DIED 11 NOVEMBER 1918, AGE 22
BURIED NIEDERZWEHREN CEMETERY, CASSEL, GERMANY

Reginald 'Reggie' Gill, born on December 9th 1895 at Tirphil, New Tredegar, was the son of Edward and Annie Elizabeth Gill, nee Ham. He was baptised at Pontlottyn on January 2nd 1896.

His father Edward was a Police Constable stationed at Matthewstown Police Station, Mountain Ash.

Reggie's siblings were Bertie Edward, Willie Douglas and Phyllis. The family moved from Tirphil to 4 Commercial Place, Mountain Ash.

Edward Gill died, aged 39, on July 8th 1902, Annie then married Frederick Brooks in 1905.

In 1911 they were living at 3 Medart Street, Cross Keys. In addition to Reggie, Willie and Phyllis, also living at this address was their son, Donald Brooks and Frederick's brother, Albert.

Frederick, Albert and Reggie were all working as colliers.

Reggie enlisted on December 29th 1914 at Bristol into the Plymouth Battalion. On April 15th 1915 he was drafted onto the Embarkation List (EL) at Gosport, from where he embarked with a draft of reinforcements for Gallipoli (Mediterranean Expeditionary Force) on May 8th. They were landed on May 31st, with Reggie joining Portsmouth Battalion (despite being a Plymouth Division RMLI man) of the Royal Naval Division. The Plymouth (11th) and Portsmouth (10th) Battalions amalgamated in August to form the 2nd Royal Marine Battalion.

In October 1915 Reggie contracted dysentery which caused him to go to hospital. He rejoined the Royal Marines 2nd Battalion on December 22nd.

The Royal Marines left Gallipoli in January 1916 and were posted to serve with the 63rd (Royal Naval) Division in France and Flanders arriving in Marseilles May 12-23 1916, where it remained on the Western Front for the rest of the war.

They took part in The Battle of the Ancre, a phase of the Battles of the Somme, Operations on the Ancre (January-March 1917) and The Second Battle of the Scarpe (April 23-24 1917), a phase of the Arras Offensive, in which the Division captured Gavrelle.

It was during the attack on Gavrelle Windmill, that Reggie was reported missing. He had been taken as a prisoner of war on April 28th at Arras, reportedly suffering wounds to his left arm and loins.

Records show that in June 1917 he was in the hospital of the PoW camp at Langensalza before being transferred to Darmstadt PoW camp.

On August 24th he was moved to Giessen PoW camp until June 27 1918 when he went to Mainz PoW camp.

Whilst he was a Prisoner of War he sent back a horsehair bracelet he had made.

Records show that he had died from 'Flu and Pneumonia' on Armistice Day, and is buried in Niederzwehren Cemetery, Cassel, Germany.

At the time of his death his mother lived at 5 Medart Street, Cross Keys.

Reggie is remembered on the Pontywaun Wesleyan Church and School memorial.

GODDEN JOSEPH EWART
Private, 2nd Battalion
East Lancashire Regiment
Service No. 30939
Died 23 March 1918, age 19
Remembered Pozieres Memorial, France

Joe, son of Joseph and Mary Godden, was born on February 17th 1899 in Todmorden, Yorkshire. Joseph and Mary were born in Dorset but moved to Rhyd y Fraith, Upper Machen where Joseph worked as a farm labourer. The family then moved north to Yorkshire where he was employed as a labourer in a chemical works.

Sometime after 1901 the family moved south again to 5 Duffryn Terrace, Wattsville and Joe was firstly a pupil in Ynysddu Infants School before moving on May 22nd 1905 to Waunfawr Infants School, Cross Keys.

In 1911 they lived at 1 Hillside Terrace, Wattsville. The census records show that Joe was one of 10 children, 3 who had died previously.

He enlisted at Abertillery and served as a Private in the East Lancashire Regiment, South Lancashire Regiment, Lancashire Fusiliers and the Liverpool Regiment.

It was whilst serving with the East Lancashire Regiment that he was killed.

As Joe has no known grave he is commemorated on the Pozieres Memorial, France. He is also remembered on the Pontywaun Wesleyan Church and School Memorial. Joe's brothers George, Trevor, Oliver, William and Vernon also fought during the war but thankfully survived. They are commemorated on the same memorial plaque.

GOODING THOMAS JOHN
PRIVATE, 2ND BATTALION
SOUTH WALES BORDERERS
SERVICE NO. 12502
DIED 21 AUGUST 1915, AGE 29
REMEMBERED HELLES MEMORIAL, TURKEY

Thomas, born in Cwmcarn in 1886, was one of eleven children to Thomas and Mary Ellen Gooding.

Thomas, junior and his brothers followed their father's occupation by working in the local pit.

Whilst living with her family at 10 Pond's Row, Cwmcarn, Mary, aged 43, died in 1905.

He enlisted at Newport into the 2nd Battalion South Wales Borderers, and arrived in Gallipoli on June 14th 1915 where it served throughout the Gallipoli campaign. Great efforts to advance from Cape Helles in May and June saw the battalion fight with great resolve. In August it moved round with the rest of the 29th Division to Suvla Bay.

It was here that a landing by five fresh divisions from England had been brought to a standstill. In a final effort here the 29th put in a most gallant though unsuccessful attack on Scimitar Hill, in which the battalion suffered nearly 300 casualties.

Thomas was killed in action on August 21st 1915 and is remembered on the Helles Memorial, Turkey and on the Risca Workingmen's Club Memorial.

He is listed on the Trinity Church, Pontywain Memorial although he is not shown as being killed on there.

GOUGH MOSTYN GEORGE
PRIVATE, 1ST ROYAL MARINE BATTALION
ROYAL NAVAL DIVISION, ROYAL MARINE LIGHT INFANTRY
SERVICE NO. PLY/16855
DIED 13 NOVEMBER 1916, AGE 20
REMEMBERED THIEPVAL MEMORIAL, FRANCE

Born on July 4th 1896 in Wattsville, Mostyn George was the oldest child of George and Eliza Gough. The family moved around the country, as George who was a coal miner looked for work. His sister Evelyn was born in Cilfynydd, whilst 3 other siblings, Caleb, Willie and Eva were born in Barnsley. Another sister Edith Annie also born in Barnsley in 1900 died aged 1.

In 1901 they lived at 53 Smithies Lane, Barnsley, Yorkshire and by 1911 had moved to 14 Penllwyn Terrace, Cwmfelinfach.

Service records show Mostyn was a miner and a Primitive Methodist. He was 5' 7" tall, dark complexion, brown eyes and black hair and had a mole over his left eye.

Just 7 days after war was declared on Germany on August 4th 1914, he enlisted at Bristol and was attached to the Deal Battalion.

Arriving at Lemnos, Greece on the "Alnwick Castle", Deal Battalion was put under the orders of 1st Royal Naval Brigade and set sail for Egypt. They arrived off Cape Helles at daylight on April 27th 1915. On April 29th Deal and Nelson Battalions, together with Brigade Headquarters landed at Anzac in the evening and moved up through Shrapnel Gully to start their campaign in Gallipoli.

Mostyn remained in Gallipoli until the withdrawal at the end of the year.

The Division was redesignated as the 63rd (Royal Naval) Division on 19th July 1916. The Division moved to France, arriving at Marseilles in May 1916, after which it remained on the Western Front for the rest of the war.

Mostyn was killed on the first day of the Battle of the Ancre on November 13th 1916.

He is commemorated on the Thiepval Memorial and the Celynen Collieries Memorial.

GREEN WILLIAM JOHN
PRIVATE, 13TH BATTALION
WELSH REGIMENT
SERVICE NO. 58285
DIED 22 OCTOBER 1918, AGE 20
BURIED MONTAY-NEUVILLY ROAD CEMETERY, FRANCE

William, born in Cross Keys in 1898, was the son of Charles and Charlotte Green. One of nine children, unfortunately three of his siblings died at an early age. His mother Charlotte died aged 40 in 1910, and his sister Eliza May died in 1915, aged 8.

Living in 22 Bright Street, Cross Keys, his father Charles was a collier, as was

William after he left school.

William enlisted in Newport on September 15th 1916 and was called up on April 24th 1918. He was posted to the 3rd South Wales Borderers before being attached to the 4th Lancashire Fusiliers.

William went to France on September 1st 1918 and transferred to the 13th Battalion Welsh Regiment on the 6th.

He was killed in action on October 22nd 1918 just seven weeks after arriving in France.

William was buried in Montay-Neuvilly Road Cemetery, Montay, France. He is remembered on the Pontywaun Wesleyan Church and School Memorial.

GREENSLADE WILLIAM JOHN
PRIVATE, 1ST BATTALION
MONMOUTHSHIRE REGIMENT
ATTACHED TO 10TH BATTALION SOUTH WALES
BORDERERS
SERVICE No. 226418
DIED 27 AUGUST 1918, AGE 19
BURIED CATERPILLAR VALLEY CEMETERY, FRANCE

Born in Pontywain in 1898, Willie was the third son of George and Sarah Jane Greenslade, (nee Allen).

In 1901 they lived near the Trinity Church, Pontywain, and George is employed as a haulier below ground. By 1911 they had moved to 1 Mount Pleasant Terrace.

Willie enlisted using his middle name John and served as Private 226418 in the 1st Battalion Monmouthshire Regiment attached to 10th Battalion South Wales Borderers.

The 10th Battalion, part of the Welsh Division, took part in the advance across the old Somme battlefield in the British offensive of August/September 1918. In this advance the gallantry and initiative of the junior leaders was conspicuous, NCOs taking over when their officers were hit, and on more than one occasion a platoon was led forward with determination by a private soldier.

The war diary from Tuesday 27th August says –

> *"Near Longuevalle. Battalion holding front line from High Wood to Longuevalle. At about 3.0 pm enemy counter attacked along Delville Wood. Enemy succeeded in getting a Machine Gun into position on right flank and enfilading C Coy who were Right Coy, causing 15 casualties. Right flank curved back to form defensive flank and held up enemy. An American forced to serve in German army gave himself up and volunteered valuable information as to enemy dispositions".*

William John was killed in action during this day and is buried at Caterpillar Valley Cemetery, Longueval, France.

He is remembered on the Cwmcarn Institute and Cwmcarn War memorials.

GRIFFITHS JOHN
Corporal, 'E' Battalion
Tank Corps
Service No. 200968
Died 23 November 1917
Remembered Cambrai Memorial, Louverval, France

Not much is known about John apart from his name, spelt Griffith, appears on the memorial in Bethany Church, Risca.
There was a John Griffiths, born about 1887 in Pentredwr, Denbighshire who enlisted at Cross Keys in the Tank Corps.
This John was living as a boarder in 29 Bloomfield Terrace, Blackwood in 1911, where he gave his occupation as a shop assistant.
He served as a Corporal 200968 in 'E' Battalion.
'E' Battalion deployed 35 tanks at the start of the Battle of Cambrai; by the afternoon of 20th November, 18 had been destroyed or disabled by enemy action, one was ditched and further 9 were unserviceable due to technical difficulties.
29 of the Battalion were dead, 31 were missing and 64 were wounded. No tanks were in action on November 21st and only 11 were used on November 23rd in support of the attack in the area of Moeuvres.
John died on November 23rd 1917 and is commemorated on the Cambrai Memorial, Louverval, France.

"This is not the time to play Games" *(Lord Roberts)*

RUGBY·UNION·FOOTBALLERS are DOING·THEIR·DUTY

over 90% have enlisted

"Every player who represented England in Rugby international matches last year has joined the colours."—Extract from *The Times*, November 30, 1914.

BRITISH ATHLETES!
Will you follow this GLORIOUS EXAMPLE?

H

HALL THOMAS JAMES
Lance Bombardier, 'D' Battery 88th Brigade
Royal Field Artillery
Service No. 4723
Died 21 March 1918, age 23
Remembered Arras Memorial, France

Thomas was born in Pontymister in 1894 the son of William Henry and Mary Ann Hall. Originally from Worcestershire, Thomas had lived in Newport before moving to Risca. The family lived in 10 Machen View, before Mill Street where they lived firstly at 43 and later at 22. William was employed as a bricklayer, an occupation that his father Thomas and his brothers also took up.

Thomas enlisted at Newport in the Royal Field Artillery serving as a Driver, going to France with the RFA on August 22nd 1915. Unfortunately no details of his time in France are available.

On March 21st, 1918, General Erich Ludendorff ordered a massive German attack on the Western Front. Known as the Spring Offensive, it was Germany's attempt to end World War One.

With 500,000 troops moved from the Russian Front added to Germany's strength, Ludendorff was confident of success.

The Germans fired one million artillery shells at the British lines in just five hours, a rate of over 3000 shells fired every minute.

Following the bombardment, the German elite storm troopers attacked. These troops were not burdened with heavy kit, allowing fast hard hitting attacks using weapons such as flame throwers.

21,000 British soldiers had been taken prisoner by the end of the first day of the attack.

The German onslaught had made great advances through the British lines causing the Fifth Army to withdraw. This attack was the biggest breakthrough in three years of warfare on the Western Front.

The Somme region, where so many troops had lost their lives during the great battle of 1916 was now lost. Although they had seized the initiative and had captured a vast amount of ground, the German army struggled to provide support for the forward troops and ultimately the offensive failed.

Between March and April, the Germans suffered 230,000 casualties.

Thomas was killed on the first day of the offensive, March 21st 1918.

His body was never recovered and he is commemorated on the Arras Memorial, France. He is remembered on Risca Bethany Baptist Church Memorial and the family grave at Risca Old Cemetery, Cromwell Road, Risca.

HANCOCK HUBERT BERTRAM
PRIVATE, 11ᵀᴴ BATTALION
SOUTH WALES BORDERERS
SERVICE No. 21892
DIED 4 JUNE 1917, AGE 32
BURIED FERME-OLIVIER CEMETERY, BELGIUM

Born in Risca and baptised on December 13th 1885, Hubert was one of four children to Hubert and Sabine Hancock.
In 1891 they lived near the Brewery at Brynhyfryd, his father Hubert was employed as a groom. They were still at the same address in 1901, Hubert senior is now a mineral water bottler and Hubert junior is employed as a coal miner. Daughter, Sabine Edith is a domestic servant.
Their address in 1911 was 31 Church Road, Risca and Hubert senior is shown as a widower as his wife Sabine had died in 1909.
He is employed as a maltsters' labourer, whilst Hubert junior along with his brother Gilbert are working as coal miners, another brother Robert is a labourer.
Hubert enlisted at Newport and served as a Private in 11th Battalion, South Wales Borderers.
The 11th Battalion (2nd Gwent) was raised in October 1914, as part of the 115th Brigade of the 38th (Welsh) Division, going to France in December 1915.
After spells in the line at Givenchy in the spring of 1916, the Division moved to the River Ancre on July 3rd at the opening of the Battle of the Somme. They had their first real action in the attack on Mametz Wood, where the 11th Battalion lost 220 men.
After a quiet winter in the trenches the Welsh Division had a fairly uneventful period until they attacked the Pilckem Ridge on July 31st 1917, the opening day of the Third Battle of Ypres.
Hubert died of wounds on June 4th 1917 and is buried in Ferme - Olivier Cemetery, Belgium.

HANN FRANCIS EDGAR GOLDING
LANCE CORPORAL, 1ˢᵀ BATTALION
MONMOUTHSHIRE REGIMENT
SERVICE No. 290840
DIED 26 SEPTEMBER 1918, AGE 23
BURIED ROISEL COMMUNAL CEMETERY EXTENSION, FRANCE

Francis, known as Frank, was one of ten children of George and Sarah Hann, (nee Eyears), five of whom died in their early years. Born in Ebbw Vale in 1895, Frank lived with his family at 2 Sychfos, Ebbw Vale.
George was initially a plate layer, later becoming a labourer,

whilst son Frank, along with elder brother William worked as coal miners.
Frank enlisted at Abergavenny into the 3rd Monmouthshire Regiment, as Private 3554, going to France on October 27th 1915.
Sometime later he transferred to the 1st Battalion Monmouthshire Regiment, serving as Private 290840. Early in 1918, Frank married Blodwen Morgan, the marriage producing a daughter Frances.
Frank was killed in action on September 26th 1918 and buried in Roisel Communal Cemetery Extension, France. He is commemorated on St Margaret's Church Memorial, Risca.

HARDS WILLIAM JOHN
Private, 1st Battalion
South Wales Borderers
Service No. 12895
Died 25 July 1916, age 31
Remembered Thiepval Memorial, France

William was born in Risca in 1884, the son of John and Sarah Hards. The family lived in 21 The Copperworks in 1911 and John is employed as a miner. They later moved to 6 Danygraig Road. William aged 16 is also now employed as a miner. In 1906 William married Harriet Hatherall and in 1911 they were living in 5 Machen Street with their children John and Arthur and Sister in Law, Beatrice Hatherall.
He went to Newport and enlisted into the 1st Battalion, South Wales Borderers and landed with them in France on 19th July 1915; he was killed just 6 days later during an attack at Contalmaison. Contalmaison is four miles north east of Albert between La Boiselle and Longueval. North West of Mametz Wood and south of Pozieres, it had a dominant position at the junction of several roads and was surrounded by several redoubts, and defended by the Prussian Guards. (The Imperial Guard of the Royal Prussian Army was considered the premier fighting force of the German Army in the First World War). The following is an extract from the 1st Bn. South Wales Borderers War Diary for July 25th 1916.

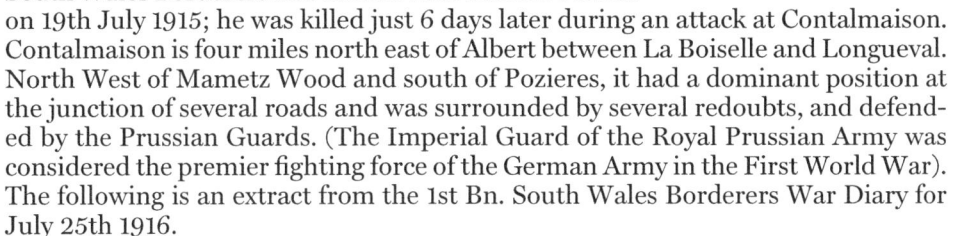

> *"At midnight Coys moved up to their positions for attack and by 2 AM were in two lines of platoons at 50 paces interval and 30 paces distance. A on left, D on right leading, followed by B and C Coys in similar formation. Coys were to remain thus until our artillery fire lifted from MUNSTER ALLEY, when they are to move forward and enter the trench. The Coys moved forward from SUSSEX TRENCH and had barely got into position when hostile machine guns opened a very heavy well directed fire over the whole of the ground between MUNSTER ALLEY and SUSSEX TRENCH. This commenced two or three seconds before our two minute bombardment of MUNSTER ALLEY which commenced at 2 AM. The infantries attack being timed for 2.02 AM. Immediately the platoons moved forward to attack, the Germans opened fire - their MG fire being particularly intense*

and well directed, broke down the attack. All the officers except three became casualties at once. About 2.30 AM, as no information had been received small patrols were sent out and on the Commanding Officer discovering the attack had failed, ordered the companies to withdraw. This was carried out and all the wounded which could be found were brought in before dawn. There were 9 officers wounded and 3 missing, with 10 other ranks killed, 57 wounded and 7 missing".*

William has no known grave and is remembered on the Thiepval Memorial, France.

HARDY CECIL JOHN
Private, 2ND Battalion
South Wales Borderers
Service No. 19593
Died 16 November 1915, age 31
Buried Alexandria Military Cemetery, Egypt

Cecil, born August 31st 1884 at Malvern, Worcestershire, was the son of Robert and Fanny Hardy, (nee Mitchell).
He had a twin brother Robert George as well as at least nine other siblings.
Cecil started school on January 6th 1890 at North Malvern Infants, leaving on July 30th 1891.
In the 1901 census he is shown as a chemist's boy. He married Julia Davis in 1908 moving to Bargoed and then Maesteg.
Julia bore him one daughter and three sons. Cecil worked as a coal miner and prior to the war they moved to Risca where he worked in the local pit.
He enlisted at Newport in the 2nd Battalion, South Wales Borderers, his Service Number of 19593 suggesting that he enlisted between October 1914 and January 1915.
His records show that he arrived in Gallipoli on October 3rd 1915 and was wounded just a month later on November 4th, a few days after his son Reginald was born. Cecil died of his wounds on November 16th 1915 and is buried in Alexandria (Chatby) Military and Memorial Cemetery, Egypt.

The inscription on his headstone reads: "At the going down of the sun and in the morning, we will remember him. Till we meet again".

His widow Julia, returned to live in Henley Place in Malvern, close to her mother's home at Sydenham Place, Newtown Road, remarrying in 1926.
Cecil is commemorated in Holy Trinity Church, North Malvern.

HARPER WILLIAM HUGH
Serjeant, 5TH Battalion
Special Brigade
Service No. 113367
Died 22 September 1916, age 21
Buried Lonsdale Cemetery, Authuile, France

Born in Southampton in 1895, William Hugh was the son of William Norton and Frances Anne Harper. William senior, born in Ripon, Yorkshire was a secondary

school teacher. When the family moved to Risca, they lived firstly in Springfield Villa, Risca and then in 10 York Place by 1911.
At this time William senior was an Assistant School Teacher and a Governor in Pontywaun County School. There were two other sons, James Raymond who was also employed as an Assistant School Teacher and Edwin Frederick who was a colliery clerk. William Hugh was a school boy, later becoming a teacher.
Aged 19, William enlisted on September 18th 1914, originally into the Welsh Regiment, Service Number 15273 before transferring to the Royal Engineers as part of the Special Brigade.
His service record records he was 5ft 8ins tall, 34ins chest and had good physical development.
The Special Companies at the start of the war.
No Special Companies existed in 1914, they were a war time invention. The Great War was the first in which chemical weapons were deployed when Chlorine was released by the Germans against defenceless French troops in the Ypres Salient.
The Special Companies of the Royal Engineers were formed to develop the British response. By 1918, gas was used both offensively and defensively, delivered by a range of sophisticated techniques.
The Special Brigade consisted of Four Special Battalions, each of four Companies, to handle gas discharge from cylinders and smoke from candles; Four Special Companies to handle gas shells fired from 4-inch Stokes mortars. Each Company to have 48 such weapons; Four Special Sections to handle flame projectors (throwers) plus a Headquarters and Depot, making an establishment of 208 officers and 5306 men.
No 5 Battalion was the Stokes mortar unit, and had 3 Companies attached to Fourth Army and 1 to Third Army.
William joined 186 company in 1915 and was admitted to hospital on 5 October 1915 with a facial injury. He was discharged on the 23rd and returned to the Depot before rejoining his unit. Promoted to Corporal on August 29th 1915, he would have taken part in the first British gas attack at Loos on 24th September 1915. He was promoted again to Serjeant on April 20th 1916.
William was killed in action on September 22nd 1916 and is buried in Lonsdale Cemetery, Authuile, France.
He is commemorated on the Pontywaun County School Memorial.

HARRIS ARTHUR
Private, 9th Battalion
Welsh Regiment
Service No. 73185
Died 7 September 1918, age 18
Buried Lapugnoy Military Cemetery, France

Arthur, born 1900 in Babell, Cwmfelinfach, was the son of Henry and Elizabeth Harris.

Living in Babell in 1901, Henry was employed as a coal miner.
In 1911 Henry and Elizabeth lived at Well Cottage, Ynysddu with their son Frank aged 6. Arthur is a patient at Highfield Private Nursing Home, Bassaleg.
Arthur was living in Cross Keys at the time of his enlistment, when he travelled to Cardiff to join the Welsh Regiment, serving as Private 73185 in the 9th Battalion.
The 9th (Service) Battalion, Welsh Regiment was raised at Cardiff on September 9th 1914 as part of Kitchener's Second New Army and joined 58th Brigade, 19th (Western) Division. They trained on Salisbury Plain prior to moving into billets in Basingstoke in November 1914 for the winter. In January they moved to Weston Super Mare and then onto Perham Down in May 1915 for final training.
On July 18th 1915, they embarked the HM Transport Monas Queen and left Southampton, landing at Boulogne with the Division concentrating near St Omer. Their first action was at Pietre, in a diversionary action supporting the Battle of Loos.
In 1916 they were in action during the Battle of the Somme, capturing La Boiselle and being involved in the attacks on High Wood, the Battles of Pozieres Ridge, the Ancre Heights and the Ancre.
1917 saw them in action in the Battle of Messines and the Third Battle of Ypres.
The following year they were again in action on the Somme during the Battle of St Quentin and the Battle of Bapaume. They were also involved in the Battle of Lys at Messines, Bailleul and the First Battle of Kemmel Ridge.
The 9th fought in the Battle of the Aisne and during the Final Advance in Picardy they were in action in the Battle of the Selle, the Battle of the Sambre and the passage of the Grand Honelle.
On September 7th 1918, Arthur, aged 18 died of wounds at the 32nd Casualty Clearing Station located at Lozinghem, France.
In his Will, written in May 1918, he left everything to his mother Elizabeth.
Arthur is buried at Lapugnoy Military Cemetery, France.

HARRIS THOMAS
CORPORAL, 5TH BATTALION
SOUTH WALES BORDERERS
SERVICE NO. 14225
DIED 27 MARCH 1918, AGE 25
BURIED ETAPLES MILITARY CEMETERY, FRANCE

Thomas, one of twelve children born to John and Defina Harris, was born in Mynyddislwyn in 1893. They lived at 17 Thornwood Terrace, Treharris before moving to Henllys. Defina died in 1905 and was buried on June 28th. John and the family later moved to 7 Sansom St, Risca.
Thomas married Mary A Turner in 1915.
He enlisted into 5th Battalion South Wales Borderers as a Private.
The 5th Battalion was formed at Brecon in September 1914 and came under orders of 58th Brigade, 19th (Western) Division. They moved to Park House Camp at Tidworth and was in billets in Basingstoke by December 1914.
On January 10th 1915 they converted into a Pioneer Battalion and moved to billets

in Burnham in January 1915 and then to Bulford in March 1915. They moved again in April 1915 to Perham Down.

After his initial training he arrived at Le Havre, France on July 16th 1915.

The following is taken from a Regimental Museum of the Royal Welsh fact sheet.

> "The 5th Battalion fought with distinction at Loos in September 1915, the Somme 1916 and the Messines Ridge in 1917. During 1917 they were heavily involved in the Third Battle of Ypres and at Passchendaele.
> In the great German attack of March 1918, the battalion was in the Third Army upon which fell a great part of the assault. The battalion fought a memorable action, inflicting heavy losses on the enemy by determined counter attacks and withdrawing steadily to positions which it had dug during the preceding days.
> The Germans were checked in the evening at a cost to the battalion of 150 casualties. Next day the rear guard fighting continued, the battalion making stand after stand and fighting most resolutely.
> This was the first occasion on which the battalion had fought as infantry, and they had shown they could march and shoot as well as dig and wire.
> They had finely upheld the traditions of the Twenty - Fourth in one of the greatest trials to which the British Army has been subjected".

Thomas died of his wounds on March 27th 1918 and is buried in Etaples Military Cemetery, France.

He is remembered on the Risca Workingmen's Club Memorial.

HART ERNEST
DRIVER, 'B' BATTERY 165TH BRIGADE
ROYAL FIELD ARTILLERY
SERVICE NO. 772164
DIED 27 SEPTEMBER 1917, AGE 20
BURIED ROCLINCOURT MILITARY CEMETERY, FRANCE

Ernest, the son of Thomas and Mary Hart, was born in Risca in 1897. Thomas, employed as a collier, and his family, lived at The Bunch, Risca before moving to 35 Mount Pleasant Road.

Mary died in 1910 and Thomas married Catherine Jones the following year.

Ernest enlisted at Risca as a driver in the Royal Field Artillery, serving with "B" Battery. 165th Brigade. The 165th Brigade were part of the 32nd Division, raised by Kitchener early in 1915. In August the Division moved for final training and firing practice at Codford on Salisbury Plain.

In November 1915 the Division received a warning order to prepare to sail for France. The Division was involved in a number of battles including The Battle of the Somme in 1916 and the Operations on the Ancre in 1917.

Ernest was killed in action on September 27th 1917 and is buried in Roclincourt Military Cemetery, France.

HARTSHORN ARTHUR WILLIAM
Lieutenant, 98th Company
Machine Gun Corps
Died 9 January 1918, age 27
Buried Lijssenthoek Military Cemetery, Belgium

Arthur was the son of Theophilus and Ellen Hartshorn, (nee Gregory). Born in Cross Keys in 1890 they lived on the Main Road, Cross Keys where his father was a draper and grocer.
Arthur's elder brother Vernon was a miner who went on to become a Welsh trades unionist and Labour Party politician who served as a Member of Parliament for Ogmore until his death.
They had moved to Twyncarn House, Pontywain by 1901 where Arthur and his sister Emily are living with their parents. In 1911 Ellen is at home in 1 Hartshorn Cottage, Pontywain, whilst Arthur and his father are recorded in Vernon's house in Maesteg.
Prior to joining the army, Arthur assisted Vernon in his work in Maesteg. He joined the Rhondda Battalion, Welsh Regiment, in 1914 as a Second Lieutenant assisting initially in a successful recruiting drive, before going to France on July 27th 1916.
Arthur married Emily G Doughty early in 1916 at Chorlton, Lancashire; a son Donald was born in December 1916.
He later transferred to the Machine Gun Company as a temporary Lieutenant and one newspaper report stated he was attached to the Royal Flying Corps, although no other evidence to support this has been found.
The 98th Company Machine Gun Company, part of the 98th Brigade, 33rd Division were involved in the Battles of the Somme. In 1917 they took part in the Arras Offensive, actions on the Hindenburg Line, and the Third Battle of Ypres.
On February 19th 1918 they joined other Machine Gun Companies of the 33rd Division to become the 33rd Battalion MGC.
It was while serving with these that he died of wounds on January 9th 1918.
His father Theophilus died just a few days later on January 18th.
Arthur is buried in Lijssenthoek Military Cemetery, Poperinge, Belgium.
He is remembered on the family grave at Risca Old Cemetery, Cromwell Road, Risca.

HATHERALL HENRY JOHN
Private, 'B' Company 11th Battalion
South Wales Borderers
Service No. 22343
Died 7 July 1916, age 43
Buried Flatiron Copse Cemetery, Mametz, France

Henry was born in Castleton on October 7th 1873 to William and Mary Ann Hatherall.

William was an agricultural labourer living in Coedkernew in 1881. They later moved to Nettlefolds Terrace in Rogerstone where Henry worked in the local steelworks.
In 1896, Henry married Catherine Jane Hiley and went to live, firstly in Pontypridd and then 45 Hill Street, Pontymister. In the 1911 census Henry and Catherine are living there with their children, Thomas, Emma, Agnes and Katherine.
Henry enlisted at Newport into the 11th (Service) Battalion (2nd Gwent). This was formed in December 1914 at Brecon and joined the 43rd Division (later the 38th) and saw service on the Western Front.
On arrival in France the 11th SWB were stationed at a place called Riez du Venant.
On July 7th 1916 the 11th SWB attacked Mametz Wood from the direction of Marlborough Wood on the right of the Brigade. Starting at 8.24 a.m. the attack encountered much rifle and machine gun fire together with heavy artillery fire. The 11th pushed on but were hit on their flank by machine gun fire from Sabot and Flatiron Copse's and Bazentin le Grande Wood inflicting many casualties and bringing the attack to a halt.
A further attack was attempted at 11.15 a.m. but was again stopped by this machine gun fire. The 10th Battalion was called up to support the attack at 3 p.m. but with no success. By now men were scattered in front of Mametz Wood and soaked by pouring rain. After dark all survivors were withdrawn.
The 11th lost 13 officers and 177 men as casualties with 31 being killed.
Henry was killed during the attack and is buried in Flatiron Copse Cemetery, Mametz.

HATTON WILLIAM
GUNNER, 'D' BATTERY
ROYAL FIELD ARTILLERY
SERVICE NO. 220321
DIED 5 MAY 1917, AGE 24
BURIED RISCA OLD CEMETERY, RISCA, WALES

William was the son of William and Catherine Hatton, (nee Davies). One of six children, he was born in 1892 at Treharris, Glamorgan, growing up in Merthyr Vale.
Like his father and brothers, he worked as a collier underground. At some time the family moved to 27 William Street, Cwmfelinfach.
William enlisted in the Royal Field Artillery serving as a Gunner in "D" Battery. Nothing else is known about his time in the army apart from his death on May 5th 1917.
William is buried in Risca Old Cemetery, Cromwell Road, Risca.

HAWKINS WILLIAM ISAAC
PRIVATE, 15TH BATTALION
MACHINE GUN CORPS
SERVICE NO. 4618
DIED 26 JULY 1918, AGE 33
BURIED ROYALLIEU FRENCH NATIONAL CEMETERY, FRANCE

William, son of Abijah and Hannah Hawkins, (nee Leonard), was born in Soundwell, Gloucestershire in 1884.
Initially living in Gloucestershire, the family moved firstly to 9 Wattsville and then later to 21 Llanarth Terrace, Brynawel.
Abijah, William and his two brothers all worked in the local mines.
William married Bethia Hughes in 1905, the marriage producing two children Abijah and William.
He enlisted at Newport, into the 2nd Battalion South Wales Borderers, going to France sometime after 1915. He later transferred to the 15th Battalion, Machine Gun Corps, who were formed on March 17th, 1918.
They were a unit of the 15th (Scottish) Infantry Division and took part in a number of battles including the Battle of Bapaume and the Battle of Arras in March.
They were later engaged in the Battles of the Marne and between July 23rd and August 2nd, the Battle of the Soissonais and of the Oureq.
It was during this last engagement that William was killed.
He died on July 26th 1918 and is buried in Royallieu French National Cemetery, Compiegne, France.

HAYNES HENRY GEORGE
PRIVATE, 14TH BATTALION
ROYAL WELSH FUSILIERS
SERVICE NO. 31502
DIED 13 SEPTEMBER 1918, AGE 25
BURIED RISCA OLD CEMETERY, RISCA, WALES

Henry, born December 15th 1892 in Risca, was the son of Henry George and Sarah Ann Haynes, (nee George).
He attended Risca School, starting on May 18th 1897 transferring to the Mixed Department on July 31st 1900. The family address was given as 'Near the Longbridge, Risca'.
They later moved to 'The Bunch' and then by 1911 were living at 7 Phillip Street, Risca where Henry is showing as being employed as a miner, as is his elder brother James.

He joined the army on September 4th 1914 at Newport, being posted to 2 Reserve Cavalry on September 7th. He was transferred to the Royal Welsh Fusiliers on June 15th 1915 serving as Signaller 31502.

Henry was posted to the 14th Battalion RWF and arrived in France on February 20th 1916 where he joined the Depot at Etaples. He went to hospital on April 29th 1916 being diagnosed with Rheumatism, he then transferred to the 2 London Casualty Clearing Station, where he was further diagnosed as suffering from Ankylosis of the shoulders. (abnormal stiffening and immobility of a joint due to fusion of the bones).

Henry was sent back to England on May 16th 1916.

He was discharged from the army due to sickness on November 22nd 1917 and awarded the Silver War Badge on November 27th 1917.

Henry died on September 13th the following year.

He is buried in Risca Old Cemetery, Cromwell Rd. and remembered on the Pontywaun Wesleyan Church and School Memorial and Moriah Baptist Church Memorial.

HEMMINGS FRANK
SERJEANT, 11TH BATTALION
SOUTH WALES BORDERERS
SERVICE NO. 21883
DIED 2 DECEMBER 1916, AGE 43
BURIED RISCA OLD CEMETERY, RISCA, WALES

Born in Cross Keys in 1873, Frank, was the son of Joseph and Bridget Hemmings.

Joseph died in the disaster at North Risca Colliery on July 15th 1880, when 120 men and boys perished in a devastating explosion.

Bridget married John Jones in 1889, and was later recorded as living in Full Moon Cottages, Wattsville.

Frank, a miner, enlisted in Newport into the Royal Welsh Fusiliers on April 24th 1894. He was described as 5ft 4ins tall, weighed 8 stone 7 lbs and had a fresh complexion, with brown eyes and brown hair.

He went abroad with the Fusiliers to India, Malta, Crete and Egypt between 1895 and 1898. On December 26th 1898 they went to China until December 1902.

Returning home Frank transferred to the Army Reserve in February 1903. In April 1906 he re-engaged for a further period of 4 years until his discharge on April 23rd 1910.

Frank married Emily Davies on July 8th 1908, having two children, John and Jane. They lived at 28 Church Road, Risca in 1911, later moving to the Albert Hotel, Risca.

He enlisted in Newport in the 11th Battalion South Wales Borderers, serving as Sergeant 21883.

The 10th Battalion (1st Gwent) and 11th Battalion (2nd Gwent) were both raised in October 1914, as part of the 115th Brigade of the 38th (Welsh) Division. In December 1915, they went to France, where their Division was to remain until the end of the

War, winning much glory for Wales.
After spells in the line at Givenchy in the spring of 1916, the Division moved to the River Ancre on July 3rd at the opening of the Battle of the Somme, and both battalions had their first real action in the attack on Mametz Wood. Here they had five days' hard fighting in a thick wood flanked by machine guns. It required skill and determination on the part of all ranks to turn the Germans out, and fine work was done with bomb and bayonet by the courage and initiative of junior leaders. The 10th Battalion lost 180 men and the 11th Battalion, 220.
At some time Frank was injured and returned to England for treatment. He died in hospital at Chatham of his wounds on December 2nd 1916.
He is buried in Risca Old Cemetery, Cromwell Road and commemorated on the memorial in St Mary's Church, Risca.

HERON ALBERT ERNEST
PRIVATE, 6TH BATTALION
CONNAUGHT RANGERS
SERVICE NO. 6475
DIED 21 MARCH 1918, AGE 26
REMEMBERED POZIERES MEMORIAL, FRANCE

Albert, the eldest of five sons of John and Flora Beatrice Heron was born in Risca in 1891. John, born in Grafton, Herefordshire, moved to Risca where he first worked as a brewers' drayman before becoming a colliery timberman.
The family lived in 11 Danygraig Cottages, then moved by 1911 to 8 Temperance Hill, Risca, where Albert is now shown as also working in the colliery as a miner.
He married Mary Ball in 1912, the marriage producing two children, Eileen born in 1913 and Denis born in 1915.
Albert enlisted at Newport into the Connaught Rangers serving as Private 6475, going overseas on November 17th 1915
The 6th (Service) Battalion, formed in County Cork in September 1914, landed at Le Havre as part of the 47th Brigade in the 16th (Irish) Division in December 1915. During the Battle of the Somme in September 1916, they lost 23 officers and 407 other ranks. On March 21st 1918, the same Battalion was *"practically annihilated"* during the German Spring Offensive breakthrough. In one week the battalion lost 2 officers and 618 other ranks.
Because of the severity of the heavy losses, the remaining troops were transferred into the 2nd Battalion, the Leinster Regiment.
It was during this German onslaught that Albert was killed in action. As his body was never recovered he is remembered on the Poziers Memorial.

HEYWORTH HEYWORTH POTTER LAWRENCE
CAPTAIN, 7TH BATTALION
NORTH STAFFORDSHIRE REGIMENT
DIED 6 AUGUST 1915, AGE 37
BURIED SHRAPNEL VALLEY CEMETERY, TURKEY

Heyworth Potter Lawrence Heyworth was born at Waun Fawr, Risca on November 20th 1877 at 9.30 a.m. in the morning, the twin brother of Eanswith Elstrith. Their parents were Lawrence and Rosina Kate Heyworth, (nee Mortimer).

Lawrence was a retired Lt. Colonel with 3rd Battalion Royal Welsh Regiment and a local magistrate. He was also Managing Director of the South Wales Colliery Company and consequently Rose Heyworth, the colliery and district in Abertillery was named after Rosina.

Heyworth and sister Eanswith were baptised on February 4th 1878 at St Mary's Church, Risca.

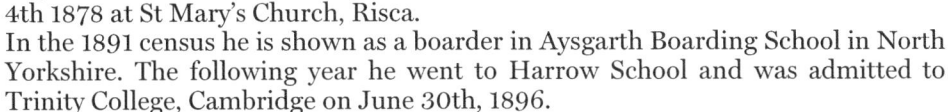

In the 1891 census he is shown as a boarder in Aysgarth Boarding School in North Yorkshire. The following year he went to Harrow School and was admitted to Trinity College, Cambridge on June 30th, 1896.

He enlisted as a 2nd Lieutenant, with the South Wales Borderers in 1900, transferring later that year to North Staffordshire Regiment. In 1901 he was promoted to Lieutenant and became Captain in September 1908. He served in the South African War, between April 21st 1900 and September 14th 1902 on operations in Transvaal, Cape Colony and Orange Free State. He also served in the East Indies from September 1902 until October 2nd 1903. In 1913 he retired on half pay but at the outbreak of war he rejoined his old regiment and was appointed Adjutant of the 7th Battalion, North Staffordshire Regiment in September 1914.

The 7th Battalion embarked for Alexandria on June 19th 1915 moving onto Mudros to prepare for a landing in Gallipoli.

The war diary for the beginning of August describes the action before his death.

> "August 3rd 1915, Embarked at Lemnos in Greece for transport to Gallipoli peninsula.
> 4th. Disembarked at Anzac and marched to Rest Gully. One man wounded.
> 5th. Rest Gully in reserve.
> 6th. Gully heavily shelled for one and a half hours at about 4.30 pm, Captain Heyworth, (Adjutant) Killed by a shell. Lieutenant Menzies wounded and twenty one men killed and wounded".

Heyworth was buried in Shrapnel Valley Cemetery, Turkey and is remembered on the Harrow School Memorial.

HILEY ANTHONY
LANCE CORPORAL, 1ST/1ST BATTALION
MONMOUTHSHIRE REGIMENT
SERVICE NO. 2111
DIED 27 MAY 1915, AGE 24
BURIED NIEDERZWEHREN CEMETERY, GERMANY.

Born in Risca in 1890, Anthony was the second son of James Albert and Elizabeth Hiley, (nee Chubb).

The family lived in 16 Club Row, Pontymister with James working as a labourer in the tin plate works.

Anthony, who followed his brother and father working in the tin works, married Mary Ellen Mullens in 1910. The following year they are shown as living in 29 Brookland Road, Pontymister a few doors away from his parents.

Anthony and Mary had a child, Iris, born in 1914.

He enlisted at Newport in the 1st/1st Battalion Monmouthshire Regiment, a Territorial Force.

The 1st (Rifle) Battalion was created on August 4th 1914 with their Headquarters at Stow Hill, Newport, Monmouthshire as part of South Wales Brigade, Welsh Division. After training they landed in France as part of 84th Brigade, 28th Division on February 13th 1915.

Anthony served as a Lance Corporal, Service Number 2111.

A news report stated that Anthony was severely wounded during fighting in Flanders and was captured by the German Army, becoming a Prisoner of War. He succumbed to his injuries and died on May 27th in Saxony, just 3 months after landing in France.

He was buried originally in Sangerhausen Cemetery, Saxony before being reinterred in Niederzwehren Cemetery, Germany.

HODDELL LEONARD
PIONEER, 333ʳᴰ ROAD CONSTRUCTION COMPANY
ROYAL ENGINEERS
SERVICE NO. 226424
DIED 13 FEBRUARY 1917, AGE 41
BURIED BORDON MILITARY CEMY., HAMPSHIRE, ENGLAND

Leonard, born in 1875 in Rowlstone, Herefordshire, was one of ten children to parents George and Martha Hoddell, (nee Jones).

Leonard moved to Wales and worked on a number of farms including Pontymister Farm, Ochrwyth, Panteg Farm in Machen and Ty Grayn Farm in Bedwas.

In 1917 he was living at Graig Farm, Pontymister, with his father and four of his siblings. His trade was a working farm bailiff but he was unemployed, when he enlisted into the army on March 2nd 1916. He was called up on January 29th 1917, joining the 333rd Road Construction Company of the Royal Engineers as a Pioneer.

According to his service records he was 5ft 4ins tall with a 35ins chest, and weighed 8 stone 12 lbs.

Leonard was found dead on February 16th 1917 in a plantation south of Guadeloupe Barracks, Bordon, Hampshire. At his inquest on February 21st he was believed to have died on February 13th of natural causes. The post mortem examination showed he had died of pneumonia.

He was buried in Bordon Military Cemetery, Whitehill, Hampshire on February 21st 1917.

HOLLOWAY ELI
Private, 21st Battalion
Machine Gun Corps (Infantry)
Service No. 31846
Died 24 August 1918, age 23
Buried Mailly Wood Cemetery, France

Born in Penmaen, Crumlin in 1895, Eli was the second son of Eli and Emma Holloway, (nee Matthews). He had two brothers, Richard and Fred as well as three sisters, Bessie, Edith and Doreen.
The family lived at Ochrwyth before later moving to 9 Wyndham Terrace, Pontymister.
He enlisted in Newport on December 11th 1915 into the 9th Battalion, South Wales Borderers as Private 26631. Eli gave his address as Ochrwyth and occupation as a woodcutter or forester. His height was recorded as 5ft 6ins and religion as Church of England. He weighed 10 stone 4 pounds.
On April 13th 1916, he transferred to the 21st Battalion, Machine Gun Corps serving as Private 31846.
Eli embarked at Folkestone on July 15th 1916 and arrived later that day in Boulogne as part of the British Expeditionary Force.
He was reported missing on March 30th 1918 for a short period of time.
Eli died of wounds on August 24th 1918 and is buried in Mailly Wood Cemetery, Mailly-Maillet, France.

HOLTHAM THOMAS GEORGE
Gunner, 'A' Battery 76th Army Brigade
Royal Field Artillery
Service No. 19795
Died 18 April 1917, age 20
Buried Sucrerie Cemetery, France

Thomas was born in Pontywain on November 11th 1896, his parents were Edward and Naomi Holtham, (nee Paget). Edward, originally from Stratton in Gloucester moved to South Wales, marrying Naomi in 1892 and working in the local mines.
They lived at 5 Mount Pleasant Terrace, Pontywain.
On April 24th 1900, George, as he was known, was admitted to Park Street Infants School, Cross Keys. He left on August 18th 1904 moving up to the Mixed Department.
Thomas enlisted in Newport as a Gunner in 76 Brigade, Royal Field Artillery, arriving in France on September 2nd 1915.
76 Brigade RFA, a new army Brigade, left their base at Rollestone Camp for em-

barking at Southampton on September 2nd 1915. The Brigade embarked on two ships, arriving at Havre on September 3rd 1915 and were firing their guns in anger on the 10th of the month near Haverskerque. On paper each battery A, B, C and D had a full complement of 134 inclusive of 4 Officers and 8 Serjeants, plus 125 horses. They had joined the Guards Division on September 4th 1915 direct from 16 Division.

On September 1st 1916, 76 Brigade marched from Cardonetta to Sailly le Sec during their Somme campaign. There they received orders to relieve gun positions from 108 Brigade. This was carried out on September 5th 1916 and they were positioned between Bernafay Wood and Trones Wood.

76 Brigade remained on the Western Front for the duration of the war.

Thomas was killed on April 18th 1918 and is buried in Sucrerie Cemetery, Ablain-St. Nazaire, France.

He is remembered on the memorial in Cwmcarn Insitute.

HOPKINS ALFRED
PRIVATE, 'A' BATTERY 10ᵀᴴ BATTALION
SOUTH WALES BORDERERS
SERVICE NO. 58303
DIED 8 OCTOBER 1918, AGE 24
BURIED GUIZANCOURT FARM CEMETERY, FRANCE

Alfred was the son of Joseph and Maria Hopkins, (nee Shergold). Born in Abercarn in 1894 the family lived at Colliery Row, Mynyddislwyn. Joseph died in 1897 and Maria married Edgar Thomas in 1899.

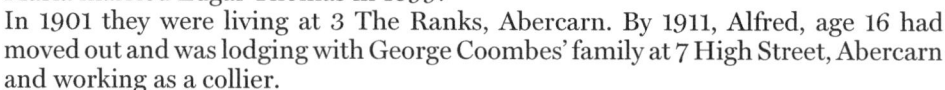

In 1901 they were living at 3 The Ranks, Abercarn. By 1911, Alfred, age 16 had moved out and was lodging with George Coombes' family at 7 High Street, Abercarn and working as a collier.

Alfred married Winifred Drew in the Zion Chapel, Cwmcarn on May 28th 1917; they lived in 2 Coronation Place, Pontywain.

He enlisted at Cross Keys into the 3rd Battalion South Wales Borderers, as Private 58303. Alfred served at home from December 11th 1915 before going to France on September 8th 1918.

Aged 25, he was killed just one month later during an attack near Villers Outreaux, Alfred, one of 36 casualties of the 10th Battalion that day, is buried in Guizancourt Farm Cemetery, Gouy, France.

HOPKINS IRA
PRIVATE, 2ᴺᴰ / 6ᵀᴴ BATTALION
LANCASHIRE FUSILIERS
SERVICE NO. 307498
DIED 21 MARCH 1918, AGE 33
REMEMBERED POZIERES MEMORIAL, FRANCE

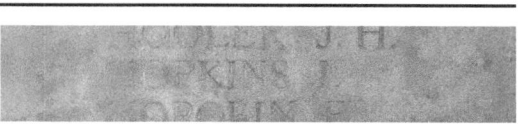

Ira, born in Pontymister in 1894 to John and Mary Hopkins, was the youngest of eleven children.

John, employed as a tin plate doubler, died in 1899. The family lived in 2 Water Lane, Pontymister in 1901, later at 4 Mill Street where Ira was recorded as being employed as a grocer's assistant.
He enlisted in Abertillery into the 2/6th Battalion Lancashire Fusiliers serving as a Private.
The 2/6th Battalion was formed at Mossborough on September 29th 1914 as a home service second line unit.
Attached to 197th Brigade, 66th Division, they moved to Crowborough in May 1915 and later on to Tunbridge Wells and then Colchester in March 1916.
Ordered to go overseas, they landed at Le Havre on February 26th 1917 as part of the British Expeditionary Force.
Ira was killed during the German Offensive launched on March 21st 1918.
His body was never recovered and so he is commemorated on the Poziers Memorial, France.

HOUGHTON JOHN ALFRED
Private, 2ⁿᵈ Battalion
Worcestershire Regiment
Service No. 17806
Died 14 October 1915, age 20
Buried St Sever Cemetery, Rouen, France

John was the son of Allen and Caroline Houghton, (nee Williamson).
He was born in 1895 at Risca and baptised at St Mary's Church on August 4th 1895.
The family moved to Norton Church Lane, Norton, Evesham where they were living in 1901, although John was a visitor to George Griffith's home in Provident Place, Risca during the census.
In 1911 they lived in Harvington near Evesham; John is shown as being a general farm labourer.
John volunteered as soon as war broke out, joining the 2nd Battalion Worcestershire Regiment that became part of 5th Brigade, 2nd Division. He went to France with the Battalion on February 18th 1915.
By 1915, the Western Front had settled down to a long unbroken line of trenches stretching from the Channel to Switzerland.
In what was the first large scale battle of the war, in terms of British forces, it was decided to try to break through the German lines at Loos near Lille.
The battle began September 21st 1915 with an artillery bombardment lasting four days. The first assault troops left their trenches at 06:30 hrs September 25th with 5th Brigade attacking north of a canal towards La Basse.
The attack was a failure and by 09:45 hrs, the men were back in their original trench consolidating their positions, though with the battle continuing to their immediate south, their lives were far from comfortable.
John was shot in the head on September 29th 1915. The 5th Brigade were still holding the same positions that they were 3 days earlier and it is quite likely that he was

wounded while carrying out duties such as reconnaissance or observation of enemy lines. He was moved to hospital in Rouen where he died on October 14th 1915 aged 20.
He is buried in St Sever Cemetery, Rouen, and his name is recorded on a gravestone at St Egwins, Norton, along with that of his brother who died (of natural causes) the previous November.
A memorial service for him was held at Harvington on October 24th 1915.

HOWELLS FRED
PRIVATE, 1ST BATTALION
SOUTH WALES BORDERERS
SERVICE No. 13042
DIED 31 OCTOBER 1914, AGE 32
REMEMBERED YPRES (MENIN GATE) MEMORIAL, BELGIUM

Fred was born in Wiveliscombe, Somerset, son of John and Caroline Howell.
(On censuses he is usually named Howell, on his army records he is called Howells).
In 1891, John was an agricultural labourer living in Church Street, Wiveliscombe. By 1911 Fred was in Risca living at 12 Wellspring Terrace, with his brother Robert's family. Both are working as colliery labourers above ground.
He enlisted at Newport in the 1st Battalion, South Wales Borderers as Private 13042, going to France on September 13th 1914.
The 1st Battalion South Wales Borderers were at the forefront of the action at Gheluvelt where Fred was killed just a few weeks after arriving in France.
Fred is remembered on the Menin Gate Memorial, Ypres, Belgium.

HUMPHRIES GEORGE HENRY
PRIVATE, 1ST BATTALION
SOMERSET LIGHT INFANTRY
SERVICE No. 7469
DIED 12 JUNE 1915, AGE 27
REMEMBERED YPRES (MENIN GATE) MEMORIAL, BELGIUM

George, born 1887 in Tredegar was the son of William and Jane Humphries.
William was a Police Constable and moved around the Monmouthshire area. In 1901 he was stationed in Ebbw Vale along with his wife and two children.
Jane died in 1897 and William married Clara Emma Jones in 1898. By 1901 he was promoted to Sergeant, serving in Risca and living in the Police Station.
In 1911, George is now living with his family in the Police Station, New Tredegar and is employed as a fitter at the colliery.

George married Mary J Rawlings in 1911.
He joined the 1st Battalion, Somerset Light Infantry, arriving in France on August 23rd 1914, being killed just under a year later.
George had transferred to the Royal Engineers a short while before his death.
A newspaper article stated that:

> "He had accidentally drowned in Flanders. He had left the trenches with another Lance Corporal of the company and shortly after entering the water got into difficulties and sank. Brave efforts were made by a soldier of another regiment, and by his friend to save him, but the task was beyond them. Other men in a boat also rendered assistance, but all efforts were in vain, owing to the apparently considerable depth to which he sunk. Although the deceased had been with the company a comparatively short time, the officers add that this loss is keenly felt by many men".

George is commemorated on the Menin Gate Memorial, Ypres, Belgium and the New Tredegar War Memorial.

BRITONS! YOUR COUNTRY NEEDS YOU.

I

IVIN JOHN IRA
PRIVATE, ROYAL ARMY SERVICE CORPS
SERVICE NO. DM2/195223
DIED 20 OCTOBER 1917, AGE 30
REMEMBERED TYNE COT MEMORIAL, BELGIUM

Ira was born in Pontymister in 1887 to Richard and Elizabeth Ivin, (nee Wixcey).
Army records and censuses record him as both Ira and Ivor.
His father Richard died in 1892 and was buried on March 31st.
Elizabeth and her family of four sons and a daughter lived at Shaftsbury Terrace in 1901; Ira is employed as a labourer in the Steel Works.
On February 4th 1904, Ira attested to the South Wales Borderers, stating he was already a member of the 2nd Volunteer Battalion, South Wales Borderers.
He was described as being 5ft 7ins tall, weighing 9 stone with a 32ins chest. He had a sallow complexion, hazel eyes and brown hair and a number of distinctive marks including a scar on the back of his head and tattoos.
Ira only stayed with the SWB for 6 days of drill and bought himself out on February 9th 1904.
A member of Risca RFC, he played with the team in 1910.
Ira is with his family at 37 Trafalgar Street in 1911, working as a blacksmith's striker.
His mother Elizabeth died in 1912 aged 68, being buried on March 11th.
Ira later moved to Hawarden, North Wales and married Catherine Elizabeth Tilley on September 12th 1916 at St. Francis's Church, Sandycroft.
His marriage certificate showed he was a Bachelor and a Soldier, aged 31. It also shows his father Richard was a provision dealer, although it does not show him as deceased.
He enlisted at Flint and was in the Royal Army Service Corps, serving with 594th MT Company, attached to X Corps.
X Corps was formed in France in July 1915 under Thomas Morland. In the autumn of 1916 the Corps took part in the Battle of the Somme where its 36th (Ulster) Division attacked Thiepval.
In 1917, X Corps, formed a part of the Second Army and included the 29th and 30th Divisions followed by others as the Second Army was reinforced for the Flanders operations after the Battle of Arras.
In June 1917 it took part in the Battle of Messines and participated in the Battles of Ypres July 31st to November 10th.
Some records show that he died in France on September 27th 1916, just 15 days after his marriage.

The majority of military records though show him as having died on October 20th the following year, 1917.
Ira is remembered on the Tyne Cot Memorial, Belgium.
He is remembered on the Sandycroft War Memorial in St. Francis's Church and Hawarden War Memorial.

J

JAMES ARTHUR LESLIE
Private, 7th Battalion
Royal Fusiliers
Service No. 9942
Died 16 November 1916, age 20
Buried Contay British Cemetery, France

Arthur was born on September 7th 1896 at Risca, his parents were Thomas and Mary Anne James.
In 1901 they lived at 15 Llanarth Square, Pontymister where Thomas worked in the local tinworks.
Arthur attended Pontymister local school for two years before attending Pontywaun County School, enrolling on September 13th 1909.
In 1911 Arthur was living with his widowed mother and brother David, at 5 Sansom Street, Risca.
After leaving Pontywaun County School in the summer of 1913, he studied at Caerleon College.
Unfortunately his service records have not survived, so although it is known he enlisted in Newport in the 7th Battalion, Royal Fusiliers, it is not known when, although it was after 1916.
In August 1914, the 7th (Extra Reserve) Battalion was embodied at Artillery Place, Finsbury. They stayed there until moving in 1916 to Falmouth, Cornwall on Coastal Defences.
Designated as an (Extra Special Reserve) Battalion they went to France and landed at Le Havre on July 24th 1916 as part of 190th Brigade 63rd Royal Naval Division.
The Battalion was involved in the Battle of Ancre from November 13th to 18th. This was the final large British attack of the Battle of the Somme in 1916.
Arthur was killed on November 16th and is buried in Contay British Cemetery.
He is commemorated on the Moriah Baptist Church and Pontywaun County School memorials.

JAMES GODFREY GEORGE
Serjeant, 10th Battalion
South Wales Borderers
Service No. 21362
Died 4 January 1917, age 41
Buried Bollezeele Communal Cemetery, France

Godfrey, the son of Joseph and Mary James, was born on June 1st 1875 in Cross Keys and baptised at St Mary's Parish Church on August 1st 1875.
Risca Town School records show that he was admitted there on June 24th 1878 whilst living at the Kings Head.

Joseph James was a miner and in the late 1870's the family moved to 8 Nixon Villa, Merthyr Tydfil but had moved back to Woodland Place, Risca by 1891. The family appear to have moved around between the censuses with children being born in Llanhilleth, Troed-yr-rhiw and Tredegar.

Godfrey, now employed as a miner, married Polly Louisa Adcock in the summer of 1899, living in 1901 at Beecher Terrace, Crosskeys.

Godfrey was living with Polly in Aberbeeg, when he went to Crumlin and enlisted into the army joining the 10th (1st Gwent) Battalion, South Wales Borderers.

The 10th (1st Gwent) Battalion, South Wales Borderers, part of the 38th (Welsh) Division, proceeded to France, landing at Le Havre on December 4th 1915.

The Battalion spent time at Givenchy in early 1916 before moving south to the River Ancre in preparation for the Battle of the Somme. Their first action was at the attack on Mametz Wood.

The wood was heavily defended and flanked by machine guns. After five days of extreme fighting the wood was captured at the cost to the battalion of 180 men.

The war diaries show an *'uneventful winter'* especially of the Christmas period where they were in support of the Royal Welsh Fusiliers. On Christmas Day, their day started in support of the 17th RWF with a Church Parade in Battalion Headquarters. Fatigue parties of 2 officers and 80 Other Ranks were sent to the Battalion front line. Although the Germans shelled the support lines in the afternoon there were no casualties reported.

The last days of 1916 were spent in the front line before moving to Bollezeele where they spent their days in *'usual training'*. This included training in musketry, bayonet fighting, Lewis guns and wiring.

It was during this period that Godfrey James became ill and it is recorded in the war diary on January 5th that he died of sickness, although his official date of death is the 4th.

His Medal Index Card shows he was entitled to the Victory and British War Medals along with the 1915 Star.

Godfrey is buried in Bollezeele Communal Cemetery, France.

JAMES JARVIS
PRIVATE, 2ND BATTALION
SOUTH WALES BORDERERS
SERVICE NO. 13324
DIED 26 APRIL 1915, AGE 42
REMEMBERED HELLES MEMORIAL, TURKEY

Jarvis, born in Cross Keys in 1872, was one of nine children to Jarvis and Elizabeth James, (nee Evans). Jarvis senior was an engine fitter and the family lived near the Railway Tavern in 1881. By 1891 they had moved to No. 3 The Copperworks and Jarvis junior, now aged 18, is employed as a miner.

In 1894 he married Sarah Ann Bushell and they went on to have nine children, two of whom died in infancy.

The family lived at Tredegar Cottages, Risca in 1901 with Jarvis working as a coal miner underground.

His wife Sarah Ann died in 1909 and Jarvis was living with five of his children at 20 Raglan Street in 1911.

He enlisted in Newport into 2nd Battalion South Wales Borderers. The 2nd SWB were in Tientsin, Northern China in August 1914 when war was declared. In early August the Japanese entered the war and sent a division to capture the German port of Tsingtao. The Borderers were sent to Tsingtao to take part in the capture and the port fell on November 7th. Tsingtao is a battle honour held by no other British Regiment.

On January 12th, 1915 the Battalion landed at Devonport on its return from China. They then joined the 29th Division billeted around Coventry and local towns until leaving in March for the attack on the Gallipoli Peninsula.

On April 25th the 29th Division made its historic "Landing at Helles" in broad daylight on open beaches defended by barbed wire covered at close range by rifles and machine guns.

On the first day the Battalion lost 2 officers and 44 men killed or drowned and 3 officers and 82 men wounded.

Jarvis was killed just one day later on April 26th, his name recorded on the Helles Memorial, Turkey.

JAMES NOAH
LANCE CORPORAL, 2ND BATTALION
SOUTH WALES BORDERERS
SERVICE NO. 13768
DIED 27 JUNE 1915, AGE 17
BURIED TWELVE TREE COPSE CEMETERY, TURKEY

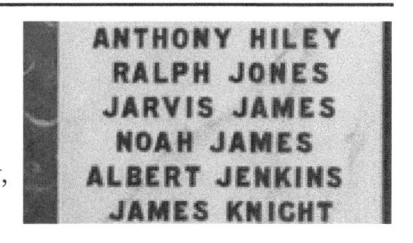

Noah was one of twelve children to James and Elizabeth James. Born in Risca in 1897, he lived at 3 Water Lane, later at 8 Mill Street, Pontymister.

He was employed at this time as a crane boy in the Steelworks.

Noah signed up in Newport to the 2nd Battalion, South Wales Borderers arriving abroad on February 21st 1915.

The South Wales Borderers were heavily involved in the Gallipoli campaign and it was here that Noah died in the 87th Field Ambulance, of wounds received.

He died on June 27th 1915, aged just 17.

Noah is buried at Twelve Tree Copse Cemetery, Gallipoli, Turkey and commemorated on Bethany Church Memorial and in the Welsh National Book of Remembrance.

JAMES SAM
COMPANY SERJEANT MAJOR, 10TH BATTALION
SOUTH WALES BORDERERS
SERVICE NO. 21550
DIED 18 JUNE 1918, AGE 31
BURIED ST. SEVER CEMETERY EXTENSION, ROUEN, FRANCE

Born in Newport in 1886, Sam lived with his uncle John James at 15 Navigation Road, Risca.
In 1911 he is shown as being employed as a colliery labourer.
In 1912 he married Eliza Gwendoline Prout and they had two children, Gwynneth and Kenneth, living in 10 Navigation Road.
He enlisted at Newport, as Private 21550, with the 10th Battalion South Wales Borderers.
Arriving in France on December 4th 1915, the 10th Battalion fought on the front lines at Givenchy, Battle of the Somme, Pilckem Ridge in Third Battle of Ypres and the Battle of Langemarck.
Sam was later promoted to Company Sergeant Major.
He was killed on June 18th 1918 and is buried in St. Sever Cemetery Extension, Rouen, France.

JAMES THOMAS WILLIAM
DRIVER, 'D' BATTERY 312TH BRIGADE
ROYAL FIELD ARTILLERY
SERVICE NO. 190765
DIED 4 NOVEMBER 1918, AGE 19
BURIED RUESNES COMMUNAL CEMETERY, FRANCE

Thomas, born in Bassaleg on February 7th 1899, was the son of Robert George and Margaret James.
In 1901 they were living at Cubillo Cottages, Risca, Robert was employed as a colliery fireman.
Thomas attended Risca School, starting on April 15th 1904 but leaving for 12 months just 3 weeks later. He returned on April 24th the following year staying until August 19th 1907 when he moved to the Mixed Department.
They had moved to 10 Bright Street, Cross Keys by 1911 where Robert is now recorded as a colliery horse keeper below ground. Tommy, is recorded as still at school.
Thomas enlisted in Cardiff in the Royal Field Artillery, serving as a Gunner / Driver in D Battery, 312th Brigade. The 312th Brigade were originally the 2/3 West Riding Brigade RFA. They were a second line territorial brigade formed in 1915 but didn't see action until 1917.
Sailing to France from Southampton on January 7th 1917 they arrived at Le Havre the following day.
They became part of the 62nd Division (2nd West Riding) which was under the command of the 3rd British Army located between the rivers Canche and Authie.
The Division remained on the Western Front in France and Flanders for the rest of the war and took part in numerous engagements:
In 1917 they were in the Arras offensive, the actions on the Hindenburg Line (May 20 – 28) and the Cambrai Operations (Tank attack November 20 – 21 and the capture of Bourlon Wood November 27 – 28). In 1918, they were heavily involved in the Battle of Bapaume (March 25), the First Battle of Arras 1918 (March 28), the First Battles of the Somme 1918, the Second Battles of Arras 1918, the Battles of the

Hindenburg Line and on November 4, the Battle of the Sambre.
This was one of the phases of the Final Advance in Picardy and it was on this day that Thomas was killed.
He is buried in Ruesnes Communal Cemetery, France and is commemorated on the Gladstone Street Church Memorial.

JAY ALBERT WILLIAM MM
CORPORAL, 11TH BATTALION
SOUTH WALES BORDERERS
ATTACHED 115TH TRENCH MORTAR BRIGADE
SERVICE NO. 22188
DIED 31 JULY 1917, AGE 22
REMEMBERED YPRES (MENIN GATE) MEMORIAL, BELGIUM

Albert was born on September 30th 1894 in Norton Canon, Herefordshire, the second eldest son of James and Catherine Jay.
On October 29th 1900 he attended Llanwarne School along with his brother Wilfred. Albert stayed there until September 9th 1907.
James worked as a carter on a farm in Llanwarne, Herefordshire where the family lived. By 1911 Albert had joined him as a farm labourer, as did his younger brother Ivor. Albert, who moved to live in New Hall, Pencoyd a few miles away had served with the Army Service Corps, Territorial Army for 2 years, when he joined the police force.
He joined them on February 3rd 1914 as a 3rd Class Constable, before being promoted to 2nd Class Constable on February 2nd 1915. His police records describe him as 5ft 9ins tall with a 36 1/2ins chest. He had a fair complexion, blue eyes and light brown hair.
Albert was stationed at Police Headquarters until March 30th 1914 when he transferred to Risca Police Station.
His police record shows that on April 15th 1915, Albert resigned from the police to join the Welsh Guards. Military records though, show that he served with the 11th Battalion, South Wales Borderers as a Corporal.
Albert went to France with the 11th Battalion, landing on December 4th 1915. At some stage he was attached to the 115th Trench Mortar Brigade but it isn't known which date or what actions he was involved in, whilst attached to them. He won the Military Medal in 1917, the recognition being recorded in the London Gazette Supplement of July 18th 1917.
The 11th were involved in the attack on Mametz Wood during the Battle of the Somme, where they lost 220 men. The following year on July 31st 1917, they were engaged in the capture of Pilckem Ridge on the opening day of the Third Battle of Ypres. As the 115th was the Reserve Brigade, they began their advance 100 minutes after the two lead brigades set off. The advance went well, and Pilckem was taken. The 115th troops then had to move onto Iron Cross Ridge, and down towards the Steenbeeke stream as their objective. They were hampered by increasing rain, and the resistance of numerous concrete pillboxes and strongpoints, though these were eventually captured and the stream was crossed.

During this attack, Sergeant Ivor Rees of the 11th SWB, gained the Victoria Cross for his attack on a German machine gun position.
He rushed the post, shooting one defender, bayonetted another and silencing the machine gun. He then bombed the adjacent pillbox killing five of its defenders and capturing two officers and thirty men.
The enemy then prepared to counter-attack, and the 11th SWB were only just able to hold them off, part of the force having to retire back across the Steenbeeke.
At the end of the action about 50 per cent losses were suffered, including 4 officers and 116 men dead or missing
Albert was killed in action during the day of July 31st 1917.
As his body was never recovered he is remembered on the Ypres (Menin Gate) Memorial in Ypres, Belgium.
(There is a James Jay recorded on the memorial in St Margaret's Church, Risca but no James died in the war. It is possible it was supposed to be for Albert).

JAYNE FREDERICK GEORGE
SERJEANT, 1ST / 4TH BATTALION
WELSH REGIMENT
SERVICE NO. 22188
DIED 11 AUGUST 1915, AGE 31
REMEMBERED HELLES MEMORIAL, TURKEY

Frederick was born in Risca in 1883, the son of Frederick William and Sarah Ann Jayne.
He was baptised February 6th 1886 along with his sister Jane and brother William in St Mary's Church, Risca.
In 1891 the family lived at Foundry Cottage, Risca, father Frederick was employed as an iron moulder.
In 1911 they were living at 56 Coleshill Terrace, Llanelli, Carmarthen and Frederick was employed as a steel moulder and his father as a foreman steel moulder.
Frederick married Sarah Giles in 1912 in Llanelli, living at 7, Birdin Terrace, Felinfoel, Carmarthen.
He enlisted at Llanelli into the Welsh Regiment serving in the 1st/4th Battalion as a Serjeant, 4438.
The 1/4th (Carmarthenshire) Battalion raised on August 4th 1914 was part of the South Wales Infantry Brigade. On July 19th 1915 they embarked on SS Huntsend from Devonport for Mudros, on the Greek island of Lemnos, arriving there August 5th 1915.
On August 9th they landed at Suvla Bay and Frederick was wounded during the Battle of Sari Bair and died just two days later.
He is remembered on the Helles Memorial in Turkey.
Frederick is remembered on the Llanelli and Felinfoel memorials and a family grave in Layton Cemetery, Blackpool.
His brother Walter Harvard Joseph Jayne was killed on March 21st 1918.

JAYNE WALTER HARVARD JOSEPH
Lance Corporal, 11ᵗʰ Battalion
Leicestershire Regiment
Service No. 46589
Died 21 March 1918, age 24
Remembered Arras Memorial, France

Joseph as he was known, was born in Pontymister in 1892, the son of Frederick William and Sarah Ann Jayne. They had seven children, one of whom, William died in infancy. Joseph was baptised in St Mary's Church, Risca on February 5th 1893.

Fred, originally from Liverpool, married Sarah and moved to live in Foundry Cottage, Risca and later at Millbrook Cottages, Pontymister.

By 1911 they had moved to 56 Coleshill Terrace, Llanelli, in Carmarthenshire where Fred worked as a foreman steel moulder in the local iron foundry. His sons Fred and James also worked as steel moulders, whilst Joseph was employed in the iron foundry as a pattern maker.

While still living in Llanelli, Joseph travelled to Lancashire and enrolled in the Royal Engineers as Private 242488. He later transferred to the 11th Battalion Leicestershire Regiment, serving as Lance Corporal 46589.

The 11th (Service) Battalion, known as the Midland Pioneers, were formed at Leicester in October 1915 by the Mayor and local committee. In March 1916 they landed in France and came under the orders of 6th Division as a Pioneer Battalion on April 1st.

As a Pioneer Battalion they were intended to assist the Royal Engineers, with skilled labour and to relieve the infantry from some of its non-combatant duties. Pioneers wired, dug and revetted in all weathers and in all terrain. On many occasions they abandoned their working tools and fought alongside the infantry in repelling enemy attacks.

The 11th Leicester's were part of the defence against the Great Spring Offensive on the Somme, which was launched on March 21st 1918. They took part in the Battle of St Quentin, and it was on this day that Joseph was killed.

Having no known grave he is commemorated on the Arras Memorial. He is remembered on the family grave in Layton Cemetery, Blackpool.

His brother Frederick George Jayne also fell in the war on August 11th 1915.

JELF ARCHIBALD LEONARD TAYLOR
Private, 1ˢᵗ Battalion
Gordon Highlanders
Service No. 11155
Died 25 September 1915, age 26
Remembered Ypres (Menin Gate) Memorial, Belgium

Archibald, born in Abergavenny on December 23rd 1889, was the second son of Walter and Selina Eliza R Jelf, (nee Price), of 56 Park Street, Abergavenny. He was baptised in St Mary's Church, Abergavenny on January 19th 1890.

In 1891 they lived at 65 Park Street; Walter wes employed as a Contractor's Clerk.

By 1901 the family had moved to the Bridge End Hotel in Risca, Walter is now the licensed victualler. Archibald attended Pontywaun County School, Risca and was also a member of Risca Wednesday's football team.

The family were still there in 1911 when Archibald was employed as an Auctioneer's Clerk. He was articled to Mr Pearce Pope, auctioneer, Gloucester, for three years later setting up his own business at Risca.

Selina died on December 2nd 1911 at the Bridge End and was buried at Risca Old Cemetery, Cromwell Road, Risca

Archibald and Walter moved to Hasfield, Gloucester early in 1912 where Walter took up farming.

He enlisted at Gloucester into the 1st (Royal) Dragoons) and was shortly afterwards drafted into the Royal Scots Greys (2nd Dragoons). Cavalry being of little use in the war, he was, in the first week of July, attached to the 1st Battalion Gordon Highlanders, and towards the end of the month left for France landing there on July 27th 1915.

He was an excellent shot and was soon made a sniper, continuing in this way until he volunteered and was accepted for the bomb section of his Brigade

It was as a bomb thrower that Private Jelf met his death. He had had one or two narrow escapes before this. On one occasion he had a tin of jam smashed in his hand by shell fire, and on another later occasion he was posted all night with other bombers in a large shell crater, ten yards from a German communication trench, when a star shell revealed their presence. Bombs were thrown, by two Germans ten yards away, but one failed to explode, thereby saving his life.

He was offered his discharge on two occasions owing to ill health, but preferred to remain in the Army.

Archibald was killed in action at Hooge on September 25th and is commemorated on the Menin Gate Memorial at Ypres, Belgium.

He is remembered on his mother's grave at Risca and the Pontywaun County School Memorial.

JENKINS ALBERT
Private, 10th Battalion
South Wales Borderers
Service No. 21942
Died 15 June 1918, age 24
Buried Englebelmer Communal Cemetery Ext., France

Albert, born in Risca in 1894, was the son of Alexander and Elizabeth Jenkins, of 3, Llanarth Square, Pontymister.

He worked as a galvanised sheet marker in the local tin

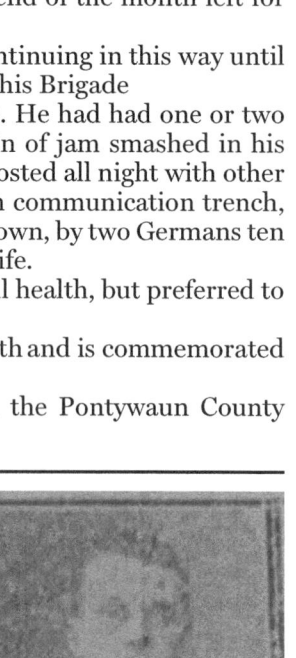

plate works, his father and six brothers were also employed in the same place.
In 1911 the family lived at 3 Llanarth Square, Pontymister.
Albert enlisted in Newport and served as Private, 21942, in 10th Battalion South Wales Borderers and arrived in France on December 4th 1915.
The 10th Battalion had fought on the front lines at Givenchy, Battle of the Somme, Pilckem Ridge in the Third Battle of Ypres and the Battle of Langemarck.
On June 15th 1918, the war diary states, *"Battalion in Reserve to 113th Brigade. Usual training carried out in addition to working parties found for wiring etc. Baths at Forceville were allotted to this unit and much appreciated. Day passed off quietly, the enemy making no attack, as was expected. Casualties 2 Other Ranks Killed"*.
Albert is buried in Englebelmer Communal Cemetery Extension, France and remembered on the Bethany Baptist Church Memorial.

JENKINS ALBERT EDGAR MM
PRIVATE, 2ND BATTALION
ROYAL WELSH FUSILIERS
SERVICE NO. 8813
DIED 23 APRIL 1917, AGE 27
BURIED WANCOURT BRITISH CEMETERY, FRANCE

Albert was born on August 22nd 1889 to Joseph Thomas and Selina Jenkins, (nee Whitfield) and was baptised at St Luke's Church, Cheltenham on August 2nd 1891.
At this time the family were living at 23 Hermitage Street, Cheltenham and Joseph was working as a labourer.

A. E. JENKINS, porter, Traffic Department, Risca.

On March 5th 1904 Albert started work as a cleaner at Worcester Railway Station, leaving on July 22nd 1905. It is probable that he served in the 2nd Battalion Royal Welsh Fusiliers as his Service Number of 8813 indicates a July 1905 enlistment.
Albert rejoined the railway company on December 23rd 1913 working as a porter at Risca, where he was paid a wage of 20/- a week (£1). He joined the National Union of Railwaymen on April 12th 1914.
He left on August 5th 1914 to join the 2nd Battalion Royal Welsh Fusiliers landing at Rouen, France on August 13th 1914 as part of the British Expeditionary Force.
It was then they took on the duties of lines of communication troops. The Battalion transferred to the 6th Division on October 12th 1914 before moving to other divisions during 1915 and 16. They were in action at the Somme in 1916 before moving to Arras, the Hindenburg Line and later at the Third Battle of Ypres.
Albert was awarded the Military Medal in 1916, the award being announced in the London Gazette on September 1st 1916.
The Arras Offensive was fought from April 9th until May 16th 1917.
The British army were supporting a larger French attack at the Battles of the Chemin des Dames and in the hills of Champagne. The army were encouraged in the opening attacks at Vimy and the Scarpe and made good advances. Unfortunately

the German defences recovered and the conflict turned into a war of attrition.
The Second Battle of the Scarpe started on April 23rd 1917 and it was during this first day that Albert was killed.
Initially buried in Fontaine Road, British Cemetery, Heninel, his body was exhumed along with eleven 2nd Bn. RWF comrades and reburied at Wancourt British Cemetery, France.

JENKINS ANEURIN
LANCE CORPORAL, 2ND BATTALION
MONMOUTHSHIRE REGIMENT
SERVICE NO. 2519
DIED 13 MAY 1915, AGE 24
BURIED BOULOGNE EASTERN CEMETERY, FRANCE

Aneurin, born in Pontywain on August 5th 1890, was the son of Aneurin and Lydia Jenkins.
Their early addresses were Old Lane and Back Lane, Risca. His father and brothers, James and Taliesin worked in the local pit as coal miners, a career that Aneurin followed when he left school.
He started at the Infants school in Park Street, Cross Keys on April 1st 1895.
His father, Aneurin died in 1904; by 1911 the family were living in 75 North Road, Pontywain where Aneurin is the oldest son living with his mother, aunt Eliza and niece Lydia.
He married Sylvia May Edwards towards the end of 1911, the marriage apparently producing two sons, James A, born 1912 and Aneurin WC Jenkins born 1914. Sadly Aneurin died just after his first birthday.
Aneurin enlisted in Pontypool in the 2nd Monmouthshire Regiment as Private 2519, later gaining promotion in France as a Lance Corporal.
His number suggests he was an early recruit and he went to France on November 7th 1914, landing at Le Havre as part of 12th Brigade, 4th Division. On November 20th 1914 they moved to Le Bixet.
The Battalion was posted to the 4th Division, whose 12th Brigade it joined in the trenches near Armentieres before the end of November. In this area it spent the first winter, digging and mining. Throughout the winter the Battalion were involved in trench warfare around the Armentieres *'Plug Street'* area. *'Plug Street'* was the name given by the troops for Ploegsteert. This was known as a *'quiet area'*, although the 2nd Monmouths' had 170 casualties in five months.
At the end of April the Fourth Division left Plug Street, and went straight into the thick of the fighting around Ypres, where the first German gas attack of April 22nd 1915, had just added a new terrible dimension to war. The 2nd Monmouths found themselves fighting alongside their other two Battalions, the 1st and 3rd Monmouthshires.
All three Battalions came in for very severe fighting throughout May.
It appears that Aneurin was taken to Boulogne Hospital and died there on May 13th 1915, as he is buried in Boulogne Eastern Cemetery, France.
He is commemorated on the Trinity Church, Pontywain Memorial.

JENKINS BENJAMIN
Corporal, 1st Battalion
South Wales Borderers
Service No. 13730
Died 19 November 1917, age 28
Buried Lijssenthoek Military Cemetery, Belgium

Benjamin, born in Llansamlet, Glamorgan in 1890 was the son of Griffith and Mary Jenkins.

They lived at Nantyffyn Road, Llansamlet Higher, Swansea before another son, Lewis Tudor was born in 1892. The family then moved to 32 Hoo Street, Briton Ferry. By 1911 Benjamin was living as a Boarder with Mary Davies at 13 Maryland Road, Pontymister. He was employed as a shorthand clerk at the Monmouthshire Steel and Tin Plate Works, Pontymister.

He enlisted at Newport in the 1st Battalion, South Wales Borderers serving as Corporal 13730.

The 1st Battalion fought at the Battle of the Aisne and Gheluvelt in 1914. Just before Christmas they were called up to recover trenches close to the town of Festubert. Due to the water logged mud flats they could do little more than re-establish a line round Festubert and remained in the area for the first five months of 1915. It was into this area that Benjamin arrived on January 11th 1915.

The Kaiser's Birthday attack on Givenchy on January 25th was successfully repulsed before the attack on May 9th by the First Division against the virtually impregnable German breastworks along the Rue du Bois.

After May 9th it shifted across the La Bassee Canal to relieve the French, and from then till the battle of Loos was in and out of the different sectors of the British right. During the three weeks' fighting of Loos (September 25th – October 13th 1915), the battalion was in reserve for the original attack but had plenty of fighting, making one gallant but unsuccessful attempt against Hulluch, beating off several counter-attacks; one on September 26th being in considerable force, and adding nearly another 200 casualties to its list.

They spent the winter of 1915-16 in the salient created by the Loos fighting or in the adjacent sectors taken over early in 1916 from the French.

In the middle of July 1916 the 1st Battalion had its first turn in the long drawn out struggle on the Somme. It was here that it had three turns, near Contalmaison in the middle of July 1916, near High Wood in the second half of August and near Fiers at the end of September.

The winter, where the weather defied description and the conditions were atrocious, was spent mainly on the Somme battlefield or just south of it, in sectors recently taken over from the French.

In March 1917, the First Division found itself detailed for a spell of road-making. Not till the very end of 1917, when it was employed in the closing stages of Third

Ypres, was the 1st SWB again in action, and then the main difficulty was that of movement, of reaching the Germans rather than of defeating them. Mud foiled the attack of November 10th 1917, along the Goudberg Spur.
Benjamin suffered severe injuries to his head, arm and leg and on November 11th was removed to a clearing station.
He died there of his wounds on November 19th 1917 and was buried in Lijssenthoek Military Cemetery, Belgium.
His headstone inscription reads *"Until The Day Dawns And The Shadows Flee Away"*.

JENKINS EDWIN WILLARD
PRIVATE, 8TH BATTALION
GLOUCESTERSHIRE REGIMENT
SERVICE NO. 38587
DIED 20 SEPTEMBER 1917, AGE 19
REMEMBERED TYNE COT MEMORIAL, BELGIUM

Edwin, one of fourteen children, was the son of Daniel and Anne Jenkins, (nee Richards).
Born in Mynyddislwyn on March 12th 1898, Edwin and his family lived in Ty Llwydd Farm, Mynyddislwyn. Daniel worked as a farmer whilst the sons either worked in the colliery or helped on the farm.
He attended Ynysddu School before going on to Pontywaun County School in Risca, starting on October 9th 1911 and leaving on September 23rd 1913, working as a clerk in a solicitor's office.
Edwin enlisted in Abertillery in the South Wales Borderers as Private 46022, later transferring to the 8th Service Battalion, Gloucester Regiment.
The 8th (Service) Battalion, formed in Bristol in September 1914 and under the command of 57th Brigade in 19th (Western) Division, landed in France on July 18th 1915.
The 19th Division concentrating near St Omer, saw their first action at Pietre in a diversionary action, supporting the Battle of Loos. The following year they fought in the Battle of the Somme and were involved in the attacks on High Wood, and the Battles of Pozieres Ridge, Ancre Heights and the Ancre.
In 1917 they were again involved in heavy fighting, this time in the Battle of Messines and later at the Third Battle of Ypres.
The Third Battle of Ypres, also known as the Battle of Passchendaele, took place on the Western Front from July 31st to November 10th 1917, for control of the ridges south and east of the Belgian city of Ypres in West Flanders.
It was during this battle that Edwin was killed in action on September 20th 1917.
As his body was never recovered he is commemorated on the Tyne Cot Memorial.
He is remembered on a family grave at Risca Old Cemetery, Cromwell Road, Risca.

JOHNSON GEORGE JAMES
Lance Corporal, 1st Battalion
South Wales Borderers
Service No. 18829
Died 16 January 1916, age 25
Buried Lapugnoy Military Cemetery, France

George, a native of Bristol was born in 1886 to James and Isabella Johnson. They also had two other children, Edwin and Elsie.
The family lived at 42 High Street, Abercarn, where both father and son were employed as colliers in the pit, before moving to 12 Salisbury St, Cross Keys.
George enlisted into the army at Newport joining the 1st Battalion South Wales Borderers as a Private, landing in France on May 2nd 1915 with the SWB.
On May 9th, they were involved in attacks along the Rue de Bois against strong German opposition before moving across the La Bassee Canal to relieve the French. They were used in different sectors of the British front line until the Battle of Loos, September 25th until October 13th 1915.
At Loos, it was in reserve for the first attack but saw plenty of fighting, making one gallant but unsuccessful attempt against Hulluch, beating off several counter attacks; one on September 26th being in considerable force and adding another 200 casualties to its list.
The Battalion spent the winter of 1915 – 16 in the salient created by the fighting at Loos or in the adjacent sectors taken over in early 1916 from the French. 'Trench warfare' that winter tended to be aggressively conducted by both sides and the fighting was often fierce and the result very costly, and it was during this period on the Somme that George was killed.
He is buried in Lapugnoy Military Cemetery.

JOHNSON WILLIAM HOWARD
Private 648th Motor Transport Company
Army Service Corps
Service No. M/287424
Died 4 November 1918, age 26
Buried Dar Es Salaam Cemetery, Tanzania

William, who sometimes went by his middle name, was born December 19th 1892 in Risca. His parents were William Edmund and Eliza Johnson, (nee Summers).
He went to Risca School initially from January 28th 1896 until February 20th 1896. He was then readmitted on September 7th 1896 until July 31st 1900 when he moved to the Mixed School.
In 1901 the family lived in Burlington House, 76 St Mary Street, Risca, father William was employed as a butcher. Eliza died in in 1905 aged just 39.
After leaving school, Howard worked alongside his father and brother as a butcher's assistant, later going to work as a munitions worker.
He enlisted in the Motor Transport Company at Abertillery on December 9th 1915.

He was recorded as being 5ft 4 3/4ins tall, and weighing 112 lbs. At that time he went on the Army Reserve being called up on February 5th 1917 serving as a learner fitter.
On June 9th 1917 he embarked for East Africa arriving at Dar-es-Salaam on the 17th, now as a driver with the motor transport group.
Howard was admitted to the 84th General Hospital, with malaria on October 26th 1918. He died from influenza a few days later on November 4th.
He is buried in the Dar-es-Salaam (Upanga Road) Cemetery, East Africa.

JONES ALFRED
LANCE CORPORAL, 10TH BATTALION
SOUTH WALES BORDERERS
SERVICE NO. 30352
DIED 31 AUGUST 1918, AGE 25
BURIED GUARDS' CEMETERY, LESBOEUFS, FRANCE

Alfred, son of David and Margaret Jones was born on October 3rd 1893 at Risca.
David employed as a brick maker, lived with his family at Darran Lane, Risca.
Alfred attended Risca School and was admitted on May 3rd 1897, then transferred to the Mixed Department on July 31st 1900.
In 1911 their address was given as 15 Mountain View, Darran Lane.
David was now a coal miner and Alfred iwas a colliery lamp man.
Alfred enlisted at Cross Keys into the South Wales Borderers, sometime after 1915, serving as Private 30352 in the 10th Battalion.
The 10th Battalion, part of the Welsh Division, took part in its victorious advance across the old Somme battlefield in the great British offensive of August/September 1918. In this advance the gallantry and initiative of the junior leaders was conspicuous, NCOs taking over when their officers were hit, and on more than one occasion a platoon was led forward with determination by a private soldier.
The war diary on Saturday August 31st 1918 reports -

> *"All Companies spent a good day in Les Bouefs. B Company very comfortable, situated in deep dugouts.*
> *Advance temporarily held up by machine gun nest East of the village.*
> *2/Lt Jewell killed by shell. Only a few casualties among Other Ranks.*
> *Men rested and moral very high.*
> *2/Lt Roberts took over duties of Intelligence Officer".*

Alfred was killed on August 31st 1918 and is buried in Guards' Cemetery, Lesboeufs, France.
He is remembered on the Ebenezer Primitive Methodist Church Memorial, Risca.

JONES ARTHUR THEOPHILUS SUMPTON
2ND ENGINEER, S.S. LORLE (WEST HARTLEPOOL)
MERCANTILE MARINE
DIED 11 JUNE 1918, AGE 50
REMEMBERED TOWER HILL MEMORIAL, ENGLAND

Born in Newport and baptised on November 11th 1867, Arthur Theophilus Sumpton was the son of John Henry Sumpton and Eliza Ann Jones.
When Arthur married Elizabeth Annie Lillie Walsh in 1893, her address was given as "Craganour," St. Mary St., Risca.
Arthur served as a 2nd Engineer in the Merchant Navy aboard SS Lorle a steam cargo ship.
The Lorle was sunk on June 11th 1918 by a torpedo fired by German submarine UB-103 approximately 12 nautical miles South-South-West of The Lizard. She was en route from Bilbao to Heysham with a cargo of ore.
Arthur was drowned as a result of the attack and is remembered on the Tower Hill Memorial, London.

JONES EDGAR
PRIVATE, 17TH BATTALION
ROYAL WELSH FUSILIERS
SERVICE No 93865
DIED 8 OCTOBER 1918, AGE 19
BURIED BOIS-DES-ANGLES BRITISH CEMETERY,
CREVECOEUR-SUR-L'ESCAUT, FRANCE

Edgar, born in Montgomery, the son of Edgar and Mary Jane Jones, was baptised on August 6th 1899 at Montgomery Parish Church.
Edgar and Mary who had 15 children, 6 of whom died in childhood, lived in Montgomery before moving to 86 Grove Road, Risca by 1917.
He enlisted at Newport on February 10th 1917, when he was sent to the Army Reserve. He gave his age as 17 years 11 months and occupation as a collier. His records show he was 5ft 3ins tall with a 33ins chest. He weighed 109 lbs, had light hair and a fresh complexion.
He was mobilised on April 10th 1918 and posted to the 3rd Battalion, South Wales Borderers as Private 32170.
On July 26th 1918 he was awarded 5 days Field Punishment Number 2 for being *'Absent off draft leave from Reveille until July 30th 1918.'*
(Field Punishment Number 1 consisted of the convicted man being shackled in irons and secured to a fixed object, often a gun wheel or similar. He could only be fixed like this for up to 2 hours in 24, and not for more than 3 days in 4, or for more than 21 days in his sentence. This punishment was often known as 'crucifixion' and

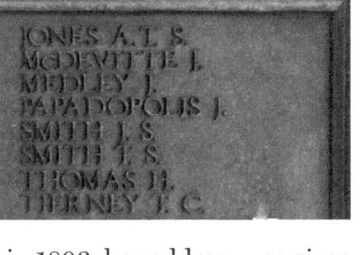

due to its humiliating nature was viewed by many Tommies as unfair. Field Punishment Number 2 was similar except the man was shackled but not fixed to anything. Both forms were carried out by the office of the Provost-Marshal, unless his unit was officially on the move when it would be carried out regimentally i.e. by his own unit).

On July 31st he was posted to the 15th Battalion South Wales Borderers.

After training, he arrived in France on September 17th 1918, transferring to the 17th Battalion, Royal Welsh Fusiliers on September 30th.

The war diary for the 17th Battalion for September 30th 1918, shows they were at SORELLE GRANDE, France undergoing training in throwing German stick bombs.

The beginning of October saw them continue their training in bomb throwing and Lewis Gun instruction. They marched to LEMPRIE on the 3rd arriving at 7pm.

The next day the Battalion marched into the line at BONY and relieved the King's Own Yorkshire Light Infantry. The Battalion then moved into the line at LE CATALET. A and B companies were in the front line with C and D companies in support. Casualties - 6 Other Ranks wounded.

On October 5th the Battalion advanced to a line near AUBENCHEUL AUX BOIS with no casualties.

The 6th and 7th saw them still in the line with 1 Officer and 23 Other Ranks wounded.

The Battalion attacked on the 8th October at 01:00 A.M. Their objective was the BEAUREVOIR LINE and high ground in front of VILLERS OUTREAUX. All objectives were taken with about 50 prisoners captured. Casualties 10 Officers and 120 Other Ranks.

Edgar, along with William Carpenter of Cross Keys, was one of 39 men killed that day from the 17th Battalion. In all, the Royal Welsh lost 141 from all its battalions on October 8th.

He was in France for just three weeks before being killed. Edgar is buried in Bois-des-Angles British Cemetery, Crevecoeur-Sur-L'escaut, France.

JONES FREDERICO SALDANHA
6TH ENGINEER, SS DRINA (BELFAST)
MERCANTILE MARINE
DIED 1 MARCH 1917, AGE 22
REMEMBERED TOWER HILL MEMORIAL, ENGLAND

Frederico, born in Rio de Janeiro on January 19th 1896 was the second son of Richard Morris and Kathleen Jones, (nee Lloyd).

Richard was a seaman who worked his way up from Second Mate to Captain making trips between Britain and Rio de Janeiro, Brazil. He later became Marine Superintendent in Rio.

Their first child, Herbert Morris Rio Jones was born in Cardiff on February 4th 1893. Census records indicate that he died but no death record can be found, it may be that he died in Rio when Kathleen visited her husband.

Frederico and Kathleen returned to the family home in Merthyr where they are

recorded with her father Herbert Lloyd in 1901.
Frederico attended Georgetown School, Merthyr Tydfil starting on May 29th 1899, Herbert Lloyd is shown as his guardian. In 1902 his father is shown as Morris and then in 1907 his parent is Cath.
It is believed that his father David died in Rio between 1911 and 1913, but again no record has been found.
Kathleen Jones married Jonathan Hughes in 1913 in the Merthyr district, at some time the family moved to 7 Gelli Crescent, Risca.
Frederico joined the Merchant Navy and served aboard SS Drina as an engineer.
The SS Drina was an Ocean Liner of 11,483 tons and was carrying 4,000 tons of cargo when she was sunk by a mine laid by German submarine UC-65 on March 1st 1917. The Drina was enroute from Buenos Aires to Liverpool. She sank approximately 2 nautical miles west of Skokholm Island, Milford Haven with the loss of 15 lives.
Frederico is remembered on the Tower Hill Memorial, London.

JONES HERBERT OWEN
Assistant Paymaster, HMS India
Royal Naval Reserve
Died 8 August 1915, age 17
Buried Narvick Old Cemetery, Norway

Herbert, born on June 9th 1898 in Risca, was the son of Richard and Sarah Jane Jones.
In 1901 they lived at 4 Church Terrace, Risca where Richard is shown as being employed as a locomotive engine driver.
He attended Risca Town School from October 17th 1901 until transferring to the Mixed Department on August 13th 1906.
In 1911 the family of 2 adults and 5 children lived at 12 Railway Street, Risca, the census shows that three other children had died.
Herbert joined the Royal Naval Reserve and served as an Assistant Paymaster aboard HMS India.
The India, with attached hired trawlers Saxon and Newland, was on patrol off the Norwegian coast to intercept iron ore carriers sailing from Narvik to Germany via Rotterdam. When the Swedish ship, SS Gloria was sighted at 08:30, India intercepted, boarded and searched her, and details of Gloria were radioed in.
Other ships were sighted and followed. At noon, India was ordered to send Gloria into Kirkwall, and proceeded to search for her. At 17:40, the alarm gong sounded, and a torpedo track was seen approaching. It could not be avoided and struck the starboard side aft near No.3 gun.
The torpedo was fired by German U Boat U-22 commanded by Bruno Hoppe. The ship immediately started to settle by the stern. Of the four starboard and three port life boats kept lowered for such an emergency, six were successfully manned.
Unfortunately, with the ship still moving forward, a port life boat capsized and on the starboard side the life boats were fouled or stove in.

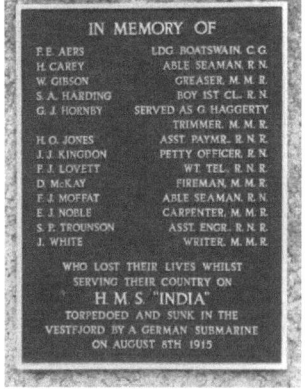

The ship sank in five minutes, 6-7 miles NNW of Heligver Light near Bodo, Norway. 121 lives were lost - 11 officers, 53 ratings including some Royal Marines and 57 Merchant seaman.
Some survivors from HMS India were taken ashore to Narvik by the Swedish ship Gotaland.
8 officers, 52 men and 7 dead were picked up by the armed trawler HMS Saxon, and landed at Narvik.
According to the rules, the men landed by the Gotaland were allowed back to Britain, but the rest were interned.
HMS Saxon, again by the rules, was allowed to stay a maximum of 24 hours in a neutral port. She left within that time, but without the men from the India, as she would have been too overcrowded.
Commander Kennedy of the India was offered the chance to sail with her, but decided to stay with his men.
Herbert, age just 17 and the rest of his dead comrades, were buried with full ceremony in Narvik cemetery.

JONES JOHN
Driver, Royal Field Artillery
53rd Welch Division
Service No. 305
Died 12 August 1915, age 18
Buried Risca Old Cemetery, Wales

John, born in Pontymister, was the only boy out of six children to John and Mary Ann Jones.
Father John, born in Lyonshall, Hereford was a foundry labourer. Their address in 1911 was given as 'Near the Foundry', Pontymister, later they moved to 23 Wellspring Terrace, Pontymister where John's occupation was a groom.
On January 7th 1915 he enlisted at Newport in the Royal Field Artillery, 4th Welsh Brigade serving as a Groom / Driver, Service Number 1320. John was underage when enlisting, giving his age as 19.
He transferred to 53rd Welsh Division on June 4th 1915, having a new Service Number, 305.
John was admitted to hospital on August 8th 1915 after being kicked in the stomach by a mule, causing a ruptured intestine. Although surgery was carried out, he died five days later from peritonitis.
At an inquest held at Bedford Hospital into his death, Lieutenant Godfrey Parsons, said that on August 6th he was observing some men grooming mules which were tied to trees. John Jones was grooming his mule's hindquarters when he saw a kick coming and endeavoured to get out of the way. He was caught by the full swing of the near hind leg. He staggered away and fell. Lieutenant Parsons examined him and found a large bruise to the centre of his abdomen.
A local newspaper described the funeral.
> "His body was brought from Bedford County Hospital and was conveyed on a gun carriage to the railway station. On arrival at Risca the body was

conveyed to the deceased mother's residence, from where it was interred at Risca Cemetery on Monday afternoon. About 40 soldiers were present. The coffin was of unpolished oak with heavy brass mountings and was covered with the Union Jack. The greatest sympathy is felt for Mrs John Jones. Only recently she lost her husband in a fatal accident".
John is buried in Risca Old Cemetery, Cromwell Road, Risca.

JONES RALPH EDWIN
SERJEANT, 'C' COMPANY 6TH BATTALION
SOUTH WALES BORDERERS
SERVICE NO. 17455
DIED 30 MAY 1918, AGE 23
REMEMBERED SOISSONS MEMORIAL, FRANCE

Ralph was born in Pontymister on July 2nd 1895, the son of William and Helen Rosina Jones. He was baptised at St Mary's Church on September 11th 1895. The family lived at this time in Tydu Road, Risca, before moving to 77 Commercial Street, Pontymister.
He joined Pontymister Boys School, before attending Pontywaun County School on September 14th 1908 leaving on July 25th 1909 to become a carpenter's apprentice.
Ralph enlisted at Newport as a Private in C Company, 6th Battalion, South Wales Borderers.
The 6th Battalion was raised in South Wales in September 1914. They went to France as the Pioneer Battalion of the 25th Division on September 23rd 1915, spending the winter in the Armentieres sector working in flooded trenches.
They were at Vimy and Neuville St. Vaast in the spring of 1916 consolidating the craters of mines blown under the German lines.
The Battalion were continuously employed during the Battle of the Somme in the summer of 1916, on one occasion digging a 700 yard communication trench from one captured trench to another under heavy shell fire.
Their next major engagement was at Messines in July 1917. They were moved further north in August for the Third Battle of Ypres. The winter of 1917 was spent digging reserve lines and in March 1918 the 5th and 6th Battalions fought against the German drive on Amiens. This meant 6 days of hard digging and stubborn fighting in which the high qualities of the Battalion were magnificently displayed.
Moved up north after this trying experience the 6th along with 2nd and 5th Battalions met the full force of the new German offensive on the Lys, where they sought to exploit the limited success gained in the drive on Amiens. On April 10th the Battalion lost 80 killed and wounded in a gallant attack on Ploegsteert village.
Ralph was killed on May 30th 1918 and is remembered on the Soissons Memorial, France.
He is remembered on the Pontywaun County School and Bethany Church Memorials.

JONES RICHARD COBDEN
PRIVATE, 19ᵀᴴ BATTALION
KING'S (LIVERPOOL REGIMENT)
TRANSFERRED TO 738ᵀᴴ AREA EMPLOYMENT COMPANY
SERVICE NO. 74703
DIED 13 FEBRUARY 1919, AGE 30
BURIED COLOGNE SOUTHERN CEMETERY, GERMANY

Richard was born in Brynmawr in 1888, one of eight children to Thomas James and Caroline Maud Jones.
Living in the Old Castle Inn, Beaufort Street, Llanelly Caroline was a licensed inn keeper
He was baptised April 30th 1895 along with his brothers, William Albany, his twin, and Horace Powell.
By 1901 he had moved with his four brothers to Abercarn and was living at 2 Islwyn Street, with his Aunt Elizabeth Richards.
Richard attended Pontywaun County School.
In 1911 he was living in 44 Oakfield Street, Cardiff with his mother, sister and brothers and was working as a clerk in a colliery company.
He enlisted after 1915 into the 19th Battalion, King's Liverpool Regiment before later transferring to the 738th Area Employment Company in the Labour Corps.
His service records have not survived so unfortunately very little is known about his war service.
Richard was admitted to the 64th Casualty Clearing Station in Cologne but died of his wounds on February 13th 1919 and is buried in Cologne South Cemetery, Germany.
He is commemorated on the Pontywaun County School Memorial.

JONES WILLIAM JAMES
PRIVATE, 2ᴺᴰ BATTALION
SOUTH WALES BORDERERS
SERVICE NO. 33260
DIED 28 JANUARY 1917, AGE 23
BURIED A.I.F. BURIAL GROUND, FLERS, FRANCE

William was born on March 30th 1893 at Bucklands Buildings, Woodcroft, Gloucestershire, the son of Warren and Emily Jones. On May 14th, William was baptised at St Luke's, Tidenham, Warren was described as a quarryman.
In a later census whilst living at 4 Penmoel Rd, Tutshill he was employed as a carter in a farm, later becoming a general labourer.
In 1911 William, his sister Ellenor and parents lived in 15 Railway Street, Risca. William aged 18 and Warren are both general labourers.
As with so many soldiers in WW1 his service records have not survived but it is known he enlisted into the 2nd Battalion South Wales Borderers at Abertillery, allocated Service Number 33260.

It appears that he enlisted after 1915 as he was only awarded the British War Medal and Victory Medal.

The 2nd Battalion was involved at the Gallipoli campaign before going to France in the spring of 1916.

Its first big action was on July 1st 1916, the opening day of the great Battle of the Somme, when it attacked the impregnable position at Beaumont Hamel.

In the first few minutes of the attack, the 2nd Battalion advancing in the leading line was mown down by machine guns and lost 11 officers and 235 men killed and missing and 4 officers and 149 men wounded, out of a total of 21 officers and 578 men.

In January 1917 they were attacking the German front line at Morval when William was killed.

He is buried in AIF Cemetery, Flers, France.

COLD-BLOODED MURDER!

REMEMBER
GERMANY'S CROWNING INFAMY
THE SINKING OF THE LUSITANIA, WITH HUNDREDS OF WOMEN & CHILDREN

Germans have wantonly sacked Cities and Holy Places.

Germans have murdered thousands of innocent Civilians.

Germans have flung vitriol and blazing petrol on the Allied Troops.

Germans have killed our Fisherfolk and deserted the drowning.

Germans have inflicted unspeakable torture by poison gases on our brave Troops at Ypres.

Germans have poisoned wells in South Africa.

Germans have ill-treated British Prisoners.

Germans have assassinated our Wounded.

THESE CRIMES AGAINST GOD AND MAN ARE COMMITTED TO TRY AND MAKE YOU AFRAID OF THESE GERMAN BARBARIANS

The place to give your answer is
THE NEAREST RECRUITING OFFICE

ENLIST TO-DAY

K

KEAR ARTHUR WILLIAM
Private, 11th Battalion
South Wales Borderers
Service No. 21931
Died 8 June 1917, age 38
Buried Ferme-Olivier Cemetery, France

Arthur was born in 1879 at Pontrilas, Hereford, his parents were Richard and Mary Kear. They lived in Monmouth until Arthur left and moved to Pontymister, lodging at 6 Foundry Row. He was employed as a mason's labourer.
He married Martha Annie Rowlands in 1902 and they lived in 4 Hill Street, Pontymister where they brought up four children, Kate, Audrey, Arthur and Francis, who sadly died aboard SS Lerwick in WW2.
Arthur enlisted at Newport and served as Private, 21931, in the 11th South Wales Borderers.
As part of the 115th Brigade of the 38th (Welsh) Division they landed in France on December 4th 1915.
After spells in the line at Givenchy in the spring of 1916, the Division moved to the River Ancre on July 3rd.
It was at the opening of the Battle of the Somme where they had their first real action in the attack on Mametz Wood, where the 11th Battalion lost 220 men.
Arthur was killed on June 8th 1917 and is buried in Ferme-Olivier Cemetery, Belgium.

KEAR HERBERT STANLEY
Private, 11th Battalion
South Wales Borderers
Service No. 22112
Died 16 October 1917, age 23
Buried Erquinghem-Lys Churchyard Ext., France

Herbert born in Oldcroft, Gloucestershire in 1894, was the son of Francis and Elizabeth Ann Kear, (nee James). They lived in the Barracks, West Dean before moving to Wales to live in 11 Llanarth Street, Wattsville. The census shows that he was one of eleven children although three had died by 1911.
He enlisted at Newport into the 11th Battalion, South Wales Borderers serving as Private 22112.
The 11th Battalion (2nd Gwent) was raised in October 1914, as part of the 115th

Brigade of the 38th (Welsh) Division.
The Battalion went abroad on December 4th 1915 landing at Le Havre.
After spells in the Line at Givenchy in the spring of 1916 the Division moved to the River Ancre on July 3rd at the opening of the Battle of the Somme, and the Battalion had their first real action in the attack on Mametz Wood. Here they had five days' hard fighting in a thick wood flanked by machine guns. In achieving their objectives, the 11th Battalion lost 220 men.
After an uneventful winter in the trenches the Welsh Division found itself attacking the Pilckem Ridge on July 31st 1917, the opening day of the Third Battle of Ypres. The two leading Brigades were to capture, as their three objectives, the German line east of the Ypres Canal, the German second line on the Pilckem Ridge, and a further ridge east of Pilckem known as Iron Cross Ridge. By the third day they had gone straight through to its final objective, had consolidated the ground won, and had smashed up the famous German 3rd Guards Division. The 11th Battalion had lost 350 of all ranks.
After taking part in the battle of Langemarck in the latter half of August, in which the 11th lost nearly 100 men, the Welsh Division was relieved and sent down to the Armentieres sector where they again distinguished themselves.
The war diary shows that on October 16th 1917 they were in the L'Epinette Sub Sector, Armentieres Section.

> "16.10.1917
> Enemy quiet throughout the day. Two of our patrols were in NO MANS LAND during the night".

Herbert was killed on October 16th 1917. A newspaper report says he died in the act of rescue. It is possible that he died whilst on patrol in No Man's Land.
He is buried in Erquinghem-Lys Churchyard Extension, France.

KENNARD BERTRAM HENRY
LANCE CORPORAL, 'C' COMPANY 58TH BATTALION
MACHINE GUN CORPS (INFANTRY)
SERVICE NO. 10292
DIED 11 AUGUST 1918, AGE 22
REMEMBERED VIS-EN-ARTOIS MEMORIAL, FRANCE

Bertram, son of Henry and Annie Kennard, (nee Hall) was born in Risca and baptised March 11th 1896 at St Mary's Church, Risca.
Henry was a journeyman baker, and the family had moved to 4 Kirkham Villas, Bromyard, Herefordshire by 1901.
In 1911 they are living in Sherford Street, Bromyard, and Bertram is shown as an ironmonger's apprentice.
He enlisted in Worcester into the Worcester Regiment as Private, 25120, later transferring to the Machine Gun Corps, and serving with 'C' Company of 58th Battalion as Lance Corporal, 10292.
The 58th Machine Gun Company disembarked at Le Havre on February 9th 1916 and joined the 19th (Western) Infantry Division on February 14th 1916.

As a unit of the Division, it will have taken part in the battles of the Somme in 1916, and in 1917, Messines and Ypres.

On February 14th 1918, it was amalgamated with the 56th, 57th and 246th Machine Gun Companies to form No. 19 Battalion, Machine Gun Corps. They were involved in the battles of the Somme and Lys. The last action Bertram would have been involved with, was the Advance to Victory. This began on August 8th 1918 with the Battle of Amiens.

Allied forces advanced over 7 miles on the first day, one of the greatest advances of the war, with the British Fourth Army playing the decisive role. The battle is also notable for its effects on the morale of both sides, and the large number of German forces that surrendered. This led Erich Ludendorff to describe the first day of the battle as *"the black day of the German Army"*.

Bertram was killed in action during this battle on August 11th 1918 and is commemorated on the Vis-en-Artois Memorial, France.

He is remembered on the Bromyard War Memorial.

KENVIN THOMAS
PRIVATE, 6TH BATTALION
YORK AND LANCASTER REGIMENT
SERVICE NO. 11690
DIED 10 AUGUST 1915, AGE 50
REMEMBERED HELLES MEMORIAL, TURKEY

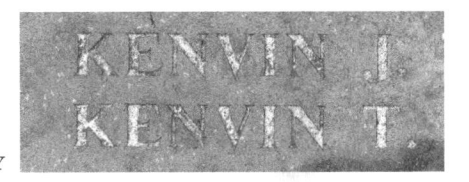

Thomas was born in Risca in 1871, to Isaac and Hannah Kenvin, (nee Brittain). Isaac, who was born in Rudry, was a coal miner and the family lived in Mill Road, Pontymister. In 1881 the family were living with Hannah's father, George Brittain, in Haines Row, Abercarn. There were now three daughters and two sons, Thomas and Joseph.

He moved away from the family and worked in the Rhondda as a coal miner in 1891. In 1895 he married Rhoda Maria James, born in Coleford, Gloucestershire and they moved to Jarrow where Thomas was now employed in the shipyard. They had a son Gwilliam born in 1890 and daughter Gwendoline in 1891.

The family moved back to Wales in the early 1900's and records show that Rhoda died in 1907 in the Bedwellty district. By 1911 Thomas was living in New Tredegar working as a coal miner and the children were living with their Grandmother in Scwrfa, Tredegar.

At some stage Thomas moved north again as he enlisted into the 6th Battalion York and Lancaster Regiment at Barnsley.

The 6th (Service) Battalion, York & Lancaster Regiment was raised at Pontefract in August 1914 as part of Kitchener's First New Army.

They joined 32nd Brigade, 11th (Northern) Division and after initial training in the Pontefract area moved to Belton Park, Grantham to train with the other infantry units of the Division. They moved to Witley in April 1915 for final training and at 1.30pm on July 3rd 1915 sailed from Liverpool in HMT Aquitania, having embarked the previous morning. They arrived at Mudros on July 10th and disembarked the following day.

They then sailed and landed on "B" Beach by 10pm on the August 6th near Lala

Baba at Suvla Bay. The troops landing on "B" Beach had a long march to Yilghin Burnu via the cut and Hill 10. They also went around the salt lake. This route was apparently to help the inexperienced troops of the Division as Yilghin Burnu was supposed to be heavily fortified. Although further to march it was allegedly an easier attack at the end.

The Turkish enemy were first engaged on Lala Baba but in order not to alert the Turks inland, it was bayonets only. Many officers and men became casualties and once the Hill was taken, the men could not fire at the retreating Turks. The 6th Yorkshires led the attack and once finished were too tired to carry on to the meet up with troops from 'A' beach. The 6th Yorks therefore fought the first engagement of the landings. Lala Baba was renamed York Hill in recognition of the attack and Thomas would have fought with the bayonet on the 7th.

Thomas was killed in action on August 10th 1915 at Gallipoli.

He is commemorated at Helles Memorial, Gallipoli and is remembered on Tredegar Memorial along with a J Kenvin. It is possible it is his brother Joseph, but no WW1 death for a J Kenvin can be found.

KING HERBERT PARRY
PRIVATE, 13ᵀᴴ BATTALION
WELSH REGIMENT
SERVICE NO. 58333
DIED 18 SEPTEMBER 1918, AGE 20
REMEMBERED VIS-EN-ARTOIS MEMORIAL, FRANCE

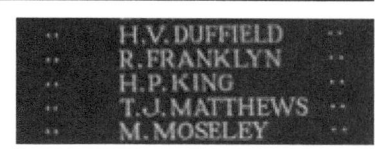

Herbert, born in Risca on October 19th 1897, was the eldest son of James Nathaniel and Hannah King, (nee Parry).

On March 13th 1901 he started at Park Street Infants School, before transferring to the Mixed Department at Waunfawr School, then leaving on September 19th 1910. In 1901, the family, with youngest son Ivor, lived in Western Terrace, Cross Keys; James was employed as a coalminer. They had moved to 3 Llanover Street by 1904 and then by 1911, they were living at 50 Gladstone Street, Cross Keys. James was now a green grocer and general dealer, Herbert and Hannah were recorded as assisting in the business.

He married Phyllis C Davies in 1916, later moving to Cwmcarn. Herbert enlisted in Cross Keys into the South Wales Borderers later transferring to the Welsh Regiment serving as Private 58333 in the 13th Battalion.

The 13th Battalion Welsh Regiment were part of the 114th Brigade, 38th (Welsh) Division. They landed in Le Havre, France in December 1915. They were heavily involved in the action at Mametz Wood, Somme in July 1916. The Division didn't return to major action for more than 12 months when in 1917 they were in action in the Third Battle of Ypres. The following year they were again in action on the Somme, in the Battles of the Hindenburg Line and then the final advance in Picardy. He was reported as missing at Gouzeaucourt on September 13th 1918 and officially declared missing on the 18th, just a few weeks before his 21st birthday.

Herbert is commemorated on the Vis-en-Artois Memorial, France.

He is remembered on the Pontywaun Wesleyan Church and School, Cwmcarn Institute and Cwmcarn War Memorials.

KIRKPATRICK SAMUEL
PRIVATE, 2ND BATTALION
WELSH REGIMENT
SERVICE NO. 9017
DIED 26 SEPTEMBER 1914, AGE 27
REMEMBERED LA FERTE-SOUS-JOUARRE MEMORIAL, FRANCE

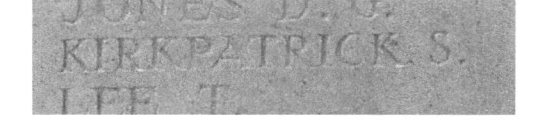

Samuel was born in 1887 at Pontymister, the son of Samuel and Margaret Kirkpatrick, (nee Jones).
In 1891 they lived at Mill Pond Cottage, Risca and Samuel was employed as a labourer. By 1901 they had moved to near the New Inn and Samuel senior was a labourer at the furnace and his son a labourer in the iron foundry.
Samuel joined the militia, signing up to the 3rd Welsh Regiment on May 14th 1906 at Cardiff for 6 years.
The record shows his height was 5ft 8¾ins and he weighed 9 stone 5 lbs, he had a fresh complexion, blue eyes and brown hair.
Samuel was in Cairo with the 1st Battalion Welch Regiment in 1911, stationed at the Main Barracks, Abbassia, Cairo.
He had joined the 2nd Battalion by the outbreak of war and was with them when they landed at Le Havre on August 13th 1914.
They fought on the Western Front throughout the war, taking part in a number of the major actions.
In the first year of the war, they fought at the Battle of Mons and the subsequent retreat, the Battle of the Marne, the Battle of the Aisne and the First Battle of Ypres.
Samuel was killed in action on September 20th 1914 and is remembered on the La Ferte-Sous-Jouarre Memorial.

KNIGHT HUBERT
PRIVATE, 11TH BATTALION
SOUTH WALES BORDERERS
SERVICE NO. 21924
DIED 13 JULY 1916, AGE 18
BURIED DAOURS COMMUNAL CEMETERY EXTN., FRANCE

Hubert 'Bert' Knight, one of nine children to John and Ann Knight, was born in Risca in 1897.
In 1901 they lived at Cae Moises, Risca before moving to 15 Malvern Terrace by 1911. Bert was one of six surviving children and was a schoolboy at the time of the census.
His father was employed in the tinworks as a tinplate roller, his brother Mark as a 'catcher' in the same works.
He joined the 11th (Service) Battalion (2nd Gwent) South Wales Borderers at Newport, and landed in Le Havre, France on December 4th 1915. The SWB 11th Battalion served with the 38th (Welsh) Division in France from the end of 1915. After spells in the line at Givenchy in the spring of 1916, the Division moved to the

River Ancre on 3rd July at the opening of the Battle of the Somme.
The 11th Battalion arrived in their billets at Buire Sur L'Ancre at 02:15, where they rested until July 5th. They then marched to Carnoy and onto Caterpillar Wood arriving at 02:30. At 08:24 they attacked Mametz Wood in conjunction with the Cardiff City Battalion.
The attack failed and after reforming they attacked again at about 11:00. This attack also failed with 1 officer killed, 8 injured and 120 Other Ranks killed.
Over the following days the companies of the 11th Battalion were fighting in Caterpillar Wood, Marlboro Wood and Mametz Wood.
On July 12th they went back to Carnoy resting.
During the 5 days hard fighting in the thick wood the 11th Battalion lost 220 men.
Bert died of his wounds on July 13th and is buried in Daours Communal Cemetery Extension, France.
He is remembered on the Bethany Church Memorial.

KNIGHT JAMES
PRIVATE, 2ND BATTALION
LANCASHIRE FUSILIERS
SERVICE NO. 307499
DIED 2 SEPTEMBER 1918, AGE 34
REMEMBERED VIS-EN-ARTOIS MEMORIAL, FRANCE

James was born in Pontymister in 1884, son of William and Sarah Ann Knight. He was one of seven surviving children of ten born to the couple.
In 1891 they lived in 1 Clyde Terrace, Pontymister and William was employed as a contractor. They later moved to Kensington Place and William, James and his elder brother Arthur are all employed as tin workers.
By 1911 they had moved to 11 Coronation Street, Pontymister. William was now a mason's labourer whilst his two sons were still working in the tin plate works as picklers. Their mother Sarah died aged 63 in 1916.
James went to Abertillery to enlist in the 2nd Battalion Lancashire Fusiliers, serving as Private 307499.
Stationed at Dover as part of the 12th Brigade of the 4th Division, the 2nd Battalion was, on August 20th 1914, mobilised for war and landed at Boulogne. The Division engaged in various actions on the Western Front during the year including The Battle of Le Cateau, The Battle of the Marne, The Battle of the Aisne and The Battle of Messines. The Battalion took part in the Christmas Truce of 1914.
During 1915 and 1916 they were involved in the Second Battle of Ypres, The Battle of Albert and The Battle of Le Transloy.
In 1917 the Battalion were engaged in the First and Third Battles of the Scarpe, The Battle of Polygon Wood, The Battle of Broodseinde, The Battle of Poelcapelle and The First Battle of Passchendaele.
1918 saw them returning to France for The First Battle of Arras. Later they were involved heavily in the Battles of Hazebrouck and Bethune, The Advance in Flanders, the Battles of the Scarpe, Drocourt-Queant, Canal du Nord, Selle and

lastly, The Battle of Valenciennes.
The Battalion ended the war in Artres, South of Valenciennes, France.
James was killed on September 2nd 1918 and is remembered on the Vis-en-Artois Memorial in France.

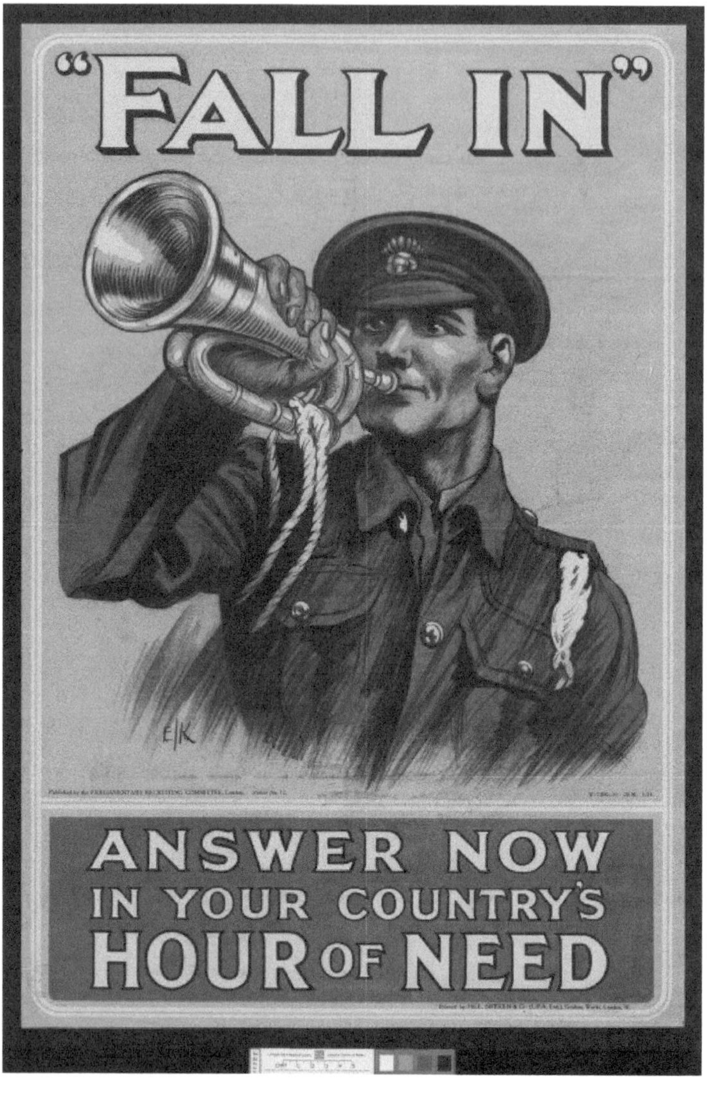
"FALL IN"
E/K
ANSWER NOW
IN YOUR COUNTRY'S
HOUR OF NEED

L

LEONARD FREDERICK WELLINGTON
Gunner, 6th Brigade
Canadian Field Artillery
Service No. 84157
Died 26 April 1917, age 25
Buried Ecoivres Military Cemetery, France

Frederick, born in Coedpenmaen on June 24th 1891, was the son of John and Eleanor Leonard.
John was previously in the South Wales Borderers and fought at Rourkes' Drift during the Zulu Wars.
Living in 28 Tredegar Street, Cross Keys in 1901, John was recorded as being employed as a coal miner. In 1911 Frederick was living as a boarder in 12 St Mary Street, Risca, following his fathers' occupation as a miner for the previous six years.
He was also a member of the Royal Field Artillery, Territorial Force.
Frederick travelled to Canada on March 28th 1914, sailing from Liverpool, England to Halifax, Nova Scotia, Canada aboard the Steamship Tunisian. The records show that he proposed to work as a miner in Canada, but did not intend to live there permanently.
On November 10th 1914, he appeared at London, Ontario to join the Canadian Expeditionary Force in the 6th Brigade, Canadian Field Artillery.
He was recorded as 5ft 7ins tall, medium complexion, brown eyes and light brown hair. He had a vaccination mark on his left arm and his religious denomination was shown as Church of England.
He was killed in action on April 26th 1917. The official report, showed that the brigade was stationed north east of Vimy. It gave the circumstances of his death as *"While asleep in a telephone dugout at about four a.m. on April 26th 1917, he was instantly killed by the explosion of an enemy shell"*
Frederick is buried in Ecoivres Military Cemetery, Mont-St. Eloi, France.
He is commemorated on the memorial in St Mary Church, Risca and the family grave headstone at Risca Old Cemetery, Cromwell Road, Risca.

LEWIS ABNER JOHN
Gunner, Y34th Trench Mortar Battery
Royal Field Artillery
Service No. W/2718
Died 22 May 1918, age 25
Buried Boulogne Eastern Cemetery, France

Born May 10th 1893 in Cross Keys, Abner was one of ten children born to Frank Mark and Laura Lewis, unfortunately only 4 survived, 3 boys and a girl.

In 1901 they lived near the Philanthropic Hotel and Abner attended the Junior Mixed School in Park Street, Cross Keys. He left school on September 18th 1907 and worked as a miner, as did his father and younger brother.

In 1911 the family lived at 1 Oak Terrace, Cross Keys.

Abner married Alice Maud Morgan in 1913, the marriage producing one child. They lived then at 65 High Street, Cross Keys.

He enlisted at Newport into the Royal Field Artillery, serving as a Gunner with the Y34th Trench Mortar Battery, Service Number 2718.

Abner was killed in action and is buried in Boulogne Eastern Cemetery, France. He is remembered on the Pontywaun Wesleyan Church and School Memorial.

LEWIS DAVID
PIONEER, 312TH RAILWAY CONSTRUCTION COMPANY
ROYAL ENGINEERS
SERVICE NO. 226431
DIED 1 NOVEMBER 1917, AGE 49
BURIED IN LIJSSENTHOEK MILITARY CEMETERY, BELGIUM.

Born in Ebbw Vale in 1868, David was the son of Evan and May Lewis.

David has proved elusive in his early years but in 1891 he was living at 1 Club Row, Ebbw Vale and working as a labourer in steel works.

He next appears aged 49, when he joined the 312th Railway Construction Company (RCC), on January 26th 1917 at Abertillery. He lived at the Lodging House, St Mary Street, Risca.

He passed his medical examination three days later at Cardiff. His occupation was given as labourer, but he had stated he had no next of kin.

David was at home until February 17th when he embarked to go to France with the British Expeditionary Force, serving with the 312th RCC.

David died in the 17th Casualty Clearing Station, at Remy (Sidings) Lijssenthoek, from wounds received in action.

As no next of kin was recorded a message was sent to the Police Superintendent at Risca Station to locate any relatives. Although the police searched, no trace of any relatives at Risca or Ebbw Vale were found.

At a later time, his sister Rose and brother Thomas were located and Rose received his personal items, pipe, purse, razor and knife, ring, 2 keys, souvenir and 1 Franc note. His British War and Victory medals were sent to Thomas.

David is buried in Lijssenthoek Military Cemetery, Belgium.

LEWIS SIDNEY RALPH
LANCE CORPORAL, 6TH BATTALION
SOUTH WALES BORDERERS
SERVICE NO. 21966
DIED 2 NOVEMBER 1918, AGE 31
BURIED PONT-DE-NIEPPE COMMUNAL CEMETERY, FRANCE

Sidney, born in Walford, Ross on Wye on August 20th 1887, was the son of William and Annie Lewis.
He lived with his family in Ross attending Bishopswood School, where he started on July 11th 1891 until 1896.
Sidney later moved to Risca, and married Ada E Williams in 1917, living in 5 Grove Road, Risca.
Sometime after 1915 he enlisted at Newport in the 6th Battalion South Wales Borderers.
The 6th Battalion went to France as the Pioneer Battalion of the 25th Division.
They were at Vimy and Neuville St. Vaast in the spring of 1916 consolidating the craters of mines blown under the German lines.
They were continuously employed during the Battle of the Somme in the summer of 1916, on one occasion digging a 700 yard communication trench from one captured trench to another under heavy shell fire.
Their next major action was at Messines in July 1917. They were moved further north in August for the Third Battle of Ypres. The winter of 1917 was spent digging reserve lines and in March 1918 the 5th and 6th Battalions fought against the German drive on Amiens.
Moved up north after this trying experience the 6th along with 2nd and 5th Battalions met the full force of the new German offensive on the Lys. On April 10th the Battalion lost 80 killed and wounded in a gallant attack on Ploegsteert village. With the 6th Battalion, the 5th shared the Battle Honour of 'Aisne, 1918'. Here the weary Battalions had to undergo the pressure of another attack and suffered 250 casualties.
In the subsequent advance to victory in the summer and autumn of 1918 the battalion was fully employed in repairing the communications, often in most difficult conditions and under heavy fire.
Sidney died at the 8th Casualty Clearing Station, Rouen, on November 2nd 1918 and is buried in Pont-de-Nieppe Communal Cemetery, France.

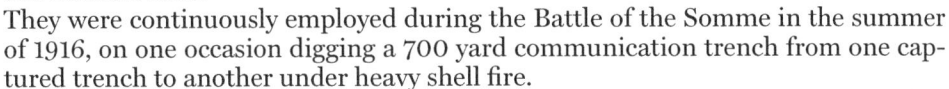

LEWIS WILLIAM
PRIVATE, 5TH BATTALION
SOUTH WALES BORDERERS
SERVICE NO. 14614
DIED 30 JULY 1916
REMEMBERED THIEPVAL MEMORIAL, FRANCE

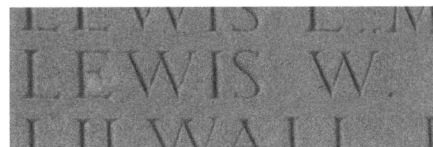

Early details of William are unknown, except that he was born in Cross Keys and lived at Ynysddu at the time of his enlistment into the South Wales Borderers at Newport.
William served as Private 14614 in the 5th Battalion, South Wales Borderers arriving in France on July 17th 1915.
The 5th (Service Battalion) formed at Brecon in September 1914, landed in France on July 16th 1915 as part of the 38th Brigade of the 19th Division.

The 5th was the Divisional Pioneer Battalion, and were used for the duties of trench digging and mining along with bombing and fighting.
The Battalion fought at Loos in September 1915, and remained in the area during winter repairing the infrastructure close to the enemy.
On March 14th 1916, the Germans exploded a mine under the British line known as the "Duck's Bill". The explosion caused devastation to the line and the garrison, killing and wounding a number of a battalion working party.
The Battalion were praised for their work in digging and wiring of a new front line 750 yards in length and 150 yards out in No Man's land in a single night, and so noiselessly as to escape entirely the notice of the enemy.
During the Battle of the Somme in 1916, the 5th Battalion were heavily involved in the fighting alongside its normal duties, the last ten days of July saw the Battalion lose 220 men.
William died on July 30th 1916 and is remembered on the Thiepval Memorial.
He was awarded the 1915 Star and the Victory and British War medals.

LIGHT ALBERT THOMAS
PRIVATE, 10TH BATTALION
SOUTH WALES BORDERERS
SERVICE NO. 14620107
DIED 5 APRIL 1917, AGE 24
REMEMBERED THIEPVAL MEMORIAL, FRANCE

One of eight children of George and Alice Light, (nee Woodward), Albert was born in Newchurch East and baptised on February 28th 1893 in Devauden.
George was shown as being employed as a postman in 1901, when they lived at 17 Nelson Street, Chepstow.
By 1911 they had moved to 2 Hafod Tudor Terrace, Wattsville and both George, Albert and his older brother George are working in the local coal mine.
In 1913 Albert married Edith May Hayes, they lived at 39 Islwyn Road, Wattsville.
He enlisted at Newport into the 10th Battalion South Wales Borderers, serving as a Private.
They fought in the Battle of the Somme where they lost 180 men in the attack on Mametz Wood
Albert was killed on April 5th 1917 and is buried in Essex Farm Cemetery, Belgium.

LLEWELLYN SAMUEL
LANCE BOMBARDIER, 'D' BATTERY 38TH BRIGADE
ROYAL FIELD ARTILLERY
SERVICE NO. 741112
DIED 13 APRIL 1918, AGE 23
REMEMBERED TYNE COT MEMORIAL, BELGIUM

Born in Rogerstone on November 1st 1894, Samuel was one of the 10 children of

Togarmah and Eliza Llewelyn.
The family lived at Brynteg in Rogerstone. His father Togarmah, a tailor, died in 1905.
Samuel attended Tydu Infants School in Rogerstone, before moving onto the Boys School on September 2nd 1901. He left on September 14th 1908, starting at Pontywaun County School on October 1st 1908 and leaving in July 1912.
He enlisted in Newport into the Royal Field Artillery, and served as a Lance Bombardier in D Battery, 38th Brigade, fighting around the Ypres area.
Samuel was killed on April 13th 1918 and as his body was never recovered he is commemorated on the Tyne Cot Memorial, Belgium.
He is commemorated on the Pontywaun County School Memorial, Risca.

LOTT WILLIAM REES
PRIVATE, MOTOR TRANSPORT
ARMY SERVICE CORPS
SERVICE NO. M/348530
DIED 14 OCTOBER 1918, AGE 20
BURIED RISCA OLD CEMETERY, RISCA, WALES

William, born October 10th 1898 was the son of Joseph J. and Annie Lott, of 23 Mount Pleasant Terrace, Pontywain.
He attended Park Street Infants School, Cross Keys, starting on October 14th 1901 until August 12th 1905 when he transferred to the Mixed Department.
William stayed here until August 2nd 1912 when he left to start work.
He was living in Abertillery when he enlisted into the Motor Transport section of the Army Service Corps, where he served as Private, M/348530.
He died at the Fargo Military Hospital, Salisbury.
William is buried in Risca Old Cemetery, Cromwell Road, Risca. He is remembered on the Hope Baptist Church, Cross Keys and the Cwmcarn War Memorials.

G. R.

Recruiting in Carnarvonshire
FOR
LORD KITCHENER'S ARMY.

THE AGE ON ENLISTMENT IS **19—38** YEARS.
For Ex-Soldiers, Ex-Militiamen, Ex-Special Reservists, Ex-Yeomen, Ex-Territorials and Ex-Volunteers, **19—45**.

Standard of Height for Royal Welsh Fusiliers now reduced to 5 ft. 1 in.

CARNARVONSHIRE WELSHMEN

Should now join the 17th Battalion R.W.F., which is at present being formed, as part of GENERAL OWEN THOMAS' Brigade, at Llandudno.

This Battalion is under the command of
COLONEL THE HON. H. LLOYD MOSTYN,
with MAJOR EVAN JONES, of Ynysfor, as second in command, and with 25 Welsh Speaking Officers.

THE BATTALION IS ALREADY HALF FULL! DON'T STOP TO THINK!

For further information apply at the following Recruiting Stations:—

District.	Recruiter.	Address.
1. Aber, Llanfairfechan & Penmaenmawr	Mr. W. Timmins	School House, Llanfairfechan.
2. Bangor and Bethesda District.	Mr. Hugh Griffith	Town Hall, Bangor.
3. Carnarvon, Port Dinorwic & District	Mr. T. S. Ingham	130, High St., Carnarvon
4. Conway and Deganwy	Mr. F. A. Delamotte	Municipal Offices, Conway
5. Criccieth	Mr. T. Burnell	Council School, Criccieth
6. Llanberis and District	Cr. Sergt. H. Pritchard	12, Victoria Terrace, Llanberis.
7. Llandudno	Mr. Arthur Hewitt	Lloyd Street, Llandudno
8. Portmadoc and District	Mr. Llew. Davies	Garth Cottage, Portmadoc
9. Pwllheli and Lleyn District	Mr. W. Cradoc Davies	Town Hall, Pwllheli.
10. Talysarn and Nantlle Vale	Mr. Richard Jones, J.P.	Snowdon View, Talysarn.
11. Trefriw, Bettws y Coed, Penmachno and District	Mr. R. E. Thomas,	13, Church Street, Llanrwst.

H. R. DAVIES,
Supervising Recruiting Officer for Carnarvonshire.

Treborth, Bangor.
March, 1915.

M

MANTLE DAVID JOHN
GUNNER, 185™ SIEGE BATTERY
ROYAL GARRISON ARTILLERY
SERVICE NO. 204658
DIED 13 JUNE 1918, AGE 30
BURIED AIRE COMMUNAL CEMETERY, FRANCE

David, son of John and Ann Mantle, (nee Owens), was born in Dowlais, Merthyr in 1887.
They lived at Penyard, Penydarren where John worked as an ostler in the pit, as did his brother Richard.
David's mother died in 1886 and by 1901 they were living at 4 Charlotte Street, Merthyr with John's father David.
John was employed as a timberman below ground and his son David was a miner. They moved again to Darren View in Merthyr lodging with a Christopher Davies and his family.
John was living at 53 Newport Road, Cwmcarn when he enlisted on September 7th 1914 at Newport. He joined the 5th Service Battalion, South Wales Borderers initially, but was discharged as medically unfit the following month.
He was called up on February 19th 1918 joining the Royal Garrison Artillery going to France. His records of service in France have not survived, but on June 13th 1918 a telegram was sent to his father John informing him that David had been injured.
   "Casualty Clearing Station 51. Dangerously ill with gunshot wounds to abdomen, head, hands and chest. Regret permission to visit him cannot be granted".
A further telegram was sent on June 18th informing John of the death of his son. David is buried in Aire Communal Cemetery, France. He is remembered on the Risca Workingmen's Club Memorial.

MAYBERRY COURTNEY
PRIVATE, 8™ BATTALION
WELSH REGIMENT
SERVICE NO. 11847
DIED 26 SEPTEMBER 1915, AGE 20
REMEMBERED HELLES MEMORIAL, TURKEY

Courtney was born 1895 in Risca, to William and Elizabeth Mayberry. William, originally from Abersychan, was a fitter and turner in the local steel works.
The family lived in Shaftesbury Terrace, Risca in 1901 and in 107 Commercial Street, Risca in 1911.

William was a sewage pipe layer and Courtney was a labourer in the steel works. The census return shows that William and Elizabeth had 14 children, 12 of whom were still alive.

Courtney enlisted into the 8th Battalion, Welsh Regiment at Newport.

The 8th (Service) Battalion (Pioneers) were formed at Cardiff in August 1914 as part of Kitchener's New Army and came under orders of 40th Brigade in 13th (Western) Division. They moved to Salisbury Plain and was at Chiseldon in October 1914 before going into billets in Bournemouth in December.

In January 1915 they converted into a Pioneer Battalion to the same Division. They embarked at Avonmouth on June 15th 1915 landing at Alexandria then moving to Mudros, by July 4th to prepare for a landing at Gallipoli.

The infantry landed at Cape Helles between July 6th and 16th of to relieve the 29th Division.

They returned to Mudros at the end of the month, and the entire Division landed at ANZAC Cove between August 3rd and 5th. They were in action in The Battle of Sari Bair, The Battle of Russell's Top and The Battle of Hill 60, at ANZAC. Soon afterwards they transferred from ANZAC to Suvla Bay.

Courtney landed at Gallipoli on August 4th 1915 and was wounded in one of the battles and transferred to the HM Hospital Ship "Valdivia".

He died of dysentery on board the ship on September 26th 1915, off Suvla Bay and was buried at sea.

Courtney is commemorated on the Helles Memorial and is remembered on the family headstone at Risca Old Cemetery and Bethany Church Memorial.

McGREGOR CHARLES MM
BOMBARDIER, 'D' BATTERY 180TH BRIGADE
ROYAL FIELD ARTILLERY
SERVICE No. 13598
DIED 3 AUGUST 1917, AGE 19
BURIED VLAMERTINGHE NEW MILITARY CEMETERY, BELGIUM

Born in Hopkinstown, Glamorgan in 1897, Charles was the son of Maria McGregor.

In 1900, Maria married Nicholas Cantwell in the Pontypridd district, going to live in 26 Adare Street, Gilfach, Bridgend. In 1911 they were living in 24 New Century Street, Trealaw, Rhondda, Charles and Nicholas were both employed as coal miners.

Charles enlisted in Newport into the Royal Field Artillery, serving as a Bombardier in 'D' Battery, 180th Brigade.

He was awarded the Military Medal which was recorded in the London Gazette on September 17th 1917. Sadly Charles was killed in action just a few weeks previously on August 3rd.

He is buried in Vlamertinghe New Military Cemetery, Belgium and remembered on the Hope Church Memorial in Cross Keys.

MELLISH ALBERT
Private, 2ND / 5TH Battalion
Loyal North Lancashire Regiment
Service No. 245088
Died 26 October 1917, age 22
Buried Cement House Cemetery, Belgium

Albert, son of Albert and Elizabeth Mellish, (nee Williams) was born in Risca on May 24th 1895.
He had five brothers and three sisters and lived at the Sugarloaf Inn, Danygraig, Risca. Albert attended Pontywaun County School before leaving to work as a clerk in the local brewery.
His attestation into The Loyal North Lancashire Regiment took place at Abertillery on December 11th 1915, when he was placed on the Army Reserve.
Albert's records show he lived at 12 Danygraig Rd at that time and he gave his occupation as a colliery clerk.
His height was 5ft 7ins, he weighed 124 lbs and he had a 34ins chest.
Albert was mobilized on October 25th 1916, staying in the UK until February 8th 1917, going to France the following day.
On June 4th 1917 he was admitted to hospital suffering a 'trivial' injury to his foot caused by a nail.
He returned to the Front on June 20th only to be injured again at Etaples on June 29th. On July 7th he reported back for duty with his regiment.
From the Battalion's War Diary:

"Throughout October 25th, the Battalion held the line under the very worst possible weather conditions, the enemy keeping up heavy shelling, which caused fifty-three casualties. About 5 o' clock in the morning of the 26th the companies formed up to attack an objective which was about 1000 yards from the original line. At 5.40 the Battalion moved off in attack formation, three companies being in the front line and one being held in readiness as a counter-attack company, each platoon having a frontage of about 160 yards. The "going" was almost impossible, but the men pushed on steadily if slowly. Owing to the state of their weapons it was practically impossible to use ether rifle or Lewis gun, and the men had to trust to the bayonet, and it is estimated that the NCOs and men accounted for five hundred of the enemy and captured eight machine guns. One sergeant attacked and killed the detachments of two German machine guns single-handed, and was still advancing when he himself became a casualty. 101 men of 2/5th Bn. were killed that day".

Albert's records show that his death was assumed on October 26th 1917. His body was recovered later and identified by his dog tag.
Albert was buried in Cement House Cemetery, Langemarck, Belgium and he is remembered on St Mary's Church, Risca and Pontywaun County School memorials.

MOGFORD GEORGE
PRIVATE, 1ST BATTALION
SOUTH WALES BORDERERS
SERVICE NO. 13242
DIED 19 FEBRUARY 1916, AGE 25
REMEMBERED ARRAS MEMORIAL, FRANCE

George was born in Pontywain on December 5th 1890, the son of William and Harriet Mogford, (nee Purnell). In 1891 William was a miner and the family were living at Main Rd, Cross Keys.
George was a pupil at Risca School, starting on April 17th 1893 until 1896 when he transferred to the Mixed Department.
In 1901 they were living at the Green Meadow Inn where William was a publican as well as working in the pit.
By 1911 George and the family are living at 92 Risca Rd, Cross Keys and he was employed as a collier.
George enlisted at Newport into the 1st Battalion South Wales Borderers, Service Number 13242.
The 1st Battalion, South Wales Borderers were in Bordon serving with 3rd Brigade, 1st Division when war was declared in August 1914. They proceeded to France, landing at Le Havre on August 13th 1914 and fought on the Western Front throughout the war, taking part in most of the major actions.
In 1915 they were in action during The Battle of Aubers and then The Battle of Loos, which George would have been involved in after he landed in France on July 19th 1915.
In 1916 they were in action in the Battles of the Somme.
In February, they were involved in heavy fighting to capture craters south of Loos. The war diary for February 19th 1916 says:

> "Dull day with some rain. Great vigilance was necessary throughout the night of 18th / 19th owing to continued activities of enemy about the craters and reports of probable mining towards our centre Company's trenches. At 4.0 AM our patrols found a party of about 20 men in HARRISON'S CRATER.
> At night we attempted to take HART and HARRISON'S CRATERS and were only partially successful. We captured the NE edge of HARRISON'S CRATER. The attack on HARTS CRATER was foiled by an enfilading machine gun and heavy trench mortar fire. Lt. VCM MAYNE was killed and Lt. GWB WILEMAN and Lt. DORRINGTON were wounded in the attack. Previous to the attack Lt. BUCKLEY was wounded by our own artillery firing short".

It is believed George died during this attack. His body was not found and he is remembered on the Arras Memorial.

MOORE EDWARD
PRIVATE, 2ND BATTALION
GRENADIER GUARDS
SERVICE NO. 14339
DIED 24 DECEMBER 1914, AGE 28
REMEMBERED LE TOURET MEMORIAL,
FRANCE

Edward, the son of John and Louisa Moore was born in Taibach, Glamorgan in 1886.
Living in Inkerman Row East, Margam, Edward followed his father and brothers being employed in the pit as a coal miner.
He moved to Risca and lodged with his Aunt and Uncle, John and Maria Smith at Exchange Road, again employed as a miner.
Edward originally enlisted in the Grenadier Guards on April 19th 1909 and appears to have gone on the Army Reserve as he again took up his old occupation of miner.
He married Jessie McPhee in 1912, the marriage producing a daughter Maria, born in 1914.
When war broke out Edward re-enlisted in Cardiff in the 2nd Battalion Grenadier Guards, serving as Guardsman 14339, arriving in France on November 23rd 1914.
The 2nd Grenadier Guards, an infantry battalion assigned to the British Expeditionary Force, went to France in early August. They fought in the Battles of Mons, the Marne and the First Battle of Aisne. After suffering heavy losses in the First Battle of Ypres, they had been withdrawn from the line to refit and re-organize.
The Battalion spent the first three weeks of December 1914 training replacements in the French town of Mitteren. On December 21st, the 2nd Grenadier Guards went back to the front near Bethune taking over trenches near the Rue de Cailloux. The Battalion diary recorded, the conditions here were terrible.
"Trenches, most improvised from dykes, were full of water. The mud was very bad".
In addition to the awful field conditions, the 2nd Grenadier Guards were also guarding a vulnerable area of the front line. Lt. Col. Ponsonby wrote, *"The enemy had the advantage of the ground, for not only did his trenches drain into ours, but he was able to overlook our whole line".*
The Guards relieved the Royal Sussex Regiment, and moved most of their troops up to the front line. As expected, on the morning of December 24th, they were targeted by snipers and trench mortar fire.
German soldiers had dug to within 10 yards of the British trenches in two places. Without warning, at 11 o'clock, the Germans detonated explosives which blew up one end of Number 2 Company's trench. At the same time the Germans launched an infantry attack against the 2nd Grenadier Guards.
The Grenadier Guards were forced to abandon their first line of trenches, whilst

the survivors of the attack fell back to an improvised second line.
They again made a stand with the remainder of the Battalion and were able to repulse the attacking Germans.
December 24th saw the 2nd Grenadier Guards losing 17 killed, 29 wounded and 9 missing.
Edward, in France for just 1 month, was killed on Christmas Eve; and as he has no known grave, is commemorated on Le Touret Memorial, France.

MOORE WILLIAM JOHN
LANCE CORPORAL, 16TH BATTALION
WELSH REGIMENT
SERVICE NO. 23213
DIED 7 JULY 1916, AGE 26
COMMEMORATED THIEPVAL MEMORIAL, FRANCE

William was born in Risca in 1889 to William and Margaret Moore.
In 1901 they lived at 4 Tredegar Terrace, Risca and in 1911 William and Margaret were living at 13 Mount Pleasant Rd, Risca.
William married Florence May Lighfield in 1909 and they lived off Mill Street, Pontymister in 1911. Later moving to Cardiff they had three children, Frances, William and Hilda.
He enlisted in Newport into the 16th (Cardiff City) Battalion, Welsh Regiment.
The Battalion left Southampton Docks on the SS Margarette, a Paddle Steamer arriving in Le Havre on December 5th. On December 19th the Battalion took over a section of the trenches near Neuve Chapelle. From then until the following June the Battalion held in its turn various sections of the line from Givenchy to Laventie gaining considerable experience of raiding and trench warfare.
In June 1916, the Battalion moved south to the Somme ready for the forthcoming offensive.
The City Battalion experienced very heavy losses at Mametz Wood especially on July 7th when they were involved on the attack on the Hammerhead.
They came under murderous fire from machine gun emplacements in Flatiron Copse and Sabot Copse.
During the Battle of Mametz Wood, it suffered over 450 casualties, with 5 officers and 131 soldiers killed.
William is commemorated on the Thiepval Memorial.

MORGAN ALFRED
LANCE CORPORAL, 3RD BATTALION
ROYAL WELSH FUSILIERS
SERVICE NO. 31166
DIED 1 JANUARY 1916, AGE 31
BURIED RISCA OLD CEMETERY, RISCA, WALES

Alfred, the eldest son of James and Sarah Jane Morgan, was born in Risca about

1885-6.

The family lived at The Laurels, Risca before moving to 12 Wesley Place, Pontymister. Alfred's father James died September 9th 1903 aged 45 and was buried in Risca Old Cemetery, Cromwell Rd.

According to the census returns, Alfred was a brick maker in his teens before becoming a railway foreman by 1911.

Alfred gave his occupation as a labourer when he enlisted on August 29th 1914 at Caerphilly. He joined the Royal Garrison Artillery as a Gunner, Service Number 43841 and was posted on November 6th 1914. He transferred to the 3rd Battalion Royal Welsh Fusiliers, as Gunner 31166 on June 5th 1915 and was promoted to L/Corporal on August 4th later that year.

His service records show he was 5ft 6ins tall, weighed 11 stone 6lbs, and had a fair complexion, blue eyes and light brown hair. It was also noted that he had scars on his chest caused by scalding.

He served in England throughout the war, firstly in Dover as a Gunner and then after his promotion as a Garrison Artillery Instructor in Liverpool.

Whilst in Dover he wrote home to his mother describing not only his determination to defeat the enemy but also his realisation that he may not return.

"Dear Mother - Just a few lines in answer to your most welcome letter and parcel, which I received alright. I am splendid in health, so do not worry mother, for I am glad that I am able to fight for my country in this terrible affair. We will crush them this time, never to dare rise again. I have had to run and leave the letter, as there has been seen some German submarines making for Dover. So we have had to double to our guns to give them a bit more lead if they try to pass us. If they do we are all eager of having a bang at them. Dear mother, do not worry for I shall face anything that will help our country and die with a brave heart for your sake and all the country's sake. So cheer up and keep a good heart, for I hope we will not be long before we shall wipe them out of our country. But we shall want more men before we do that".

Whilst with the Royal Garrison Artillery he was twice confined to barracks for 7 days, firstly for *"neglecting to obey an order"* and later *"being drunk in the battery".*

During his time with the Royal Welsh Fusiliers he was also reprimanded twice for *"improper conduct"* and being *"absent off parade"* and admonished with 2 days loss of pay for being *"absent from tattoo".*

It was while in Liverpool that he contracted pneumonia and was treated at Windy Knowe Military Hospital, Blundellsands, Liverpool. His mother Sarah received news from the hospital that he was seriously ill and later a telegram asking her to come and visit him. She was allowed to see him but when she called at the hospital the following day, New Year's Day, she was told that he had died in the early morning. Arrangements were made for his body to be returned to Risca and his mother travelled on the same train arriving in Risca at 09.30 on the following day.

The funeral took place on Thursday January 6th 1916. The bearers were Army men from the Western Cavalry Depot at Newport and the coffin was of polished elm,

with heavy brass fittings.
Alfred was buried at Risca Old Cemetery in the same plot as his father James.

MORGAN ARTHUR AUGUSTUS
LANCE SARJEANT, 5TH BATTALION
DORSETSHIRE REGIMENT
SERVICE No. 19453
DIED 3 JANUARY 1917, AGE 31
COMMEMORATED THIEPVAL MEMORIAL, FRANCE

Arthur, more commonly known as Gus, was born in Abertillery in 1885, the son of William and Elizabeth Morgan.
Originally living in Bridge Street, Aberystruth, Bedwellty, they moved to the Pontymister Inn by 1901. His father William had died in 1898 and Elizabeth is shown as an Inn Keeper, whilst Gus is employed at a local brewery. Elizabeth later went to Brithdir and took over as the proprietor of the George Inn Hotel.
He enlisted at Cardiff joining the 6th Battalion, B Company, Somerset Light Infantry, as Private 9939.
Gus arrived in France on May 21st 1915 with the Somersets, taking part in the action at Hooge, where the 14th Light Division became the first to be attacked by flame throwers.
Later he transferred to the 5th Battalion, Dorset Regiment serving as Private 19453.
Although the Somme offensive had begun on July 1st, the 5th Battalion first went into the line in the quieter sector south of Arras.
In September, the Battalion moved south, to just below Thiepval at Mouquet Farm. The farm was partly held by the Germans, huge numbers of whom occupied a vast dugout below it. In this and in the attack that followed, two thirds of the 5th were killed or wounded. In the freezing winter of 1916/17 they lost heavily again in an attack near Beaucourt.
Gus was killed on January 3rd 1917 and as he has no known grave, is remembered on the Thiepval Memorial, France.
His brother Charles Ernest Morgan also died in WW1 on April 24th 1915. Their younger brother Albert Austin Morgan was a POW and although repatriated in November 1918, died on March 3rd 1921.
They are all commemorated on the family grave at Tirzah Baptist Church, Michaelston-y-Fedw. Gus and Charles are commemorated on the Brithdir War Memorial.
Elizabeth having lost two sons in the war, died on April 17th 1918 aged 66.

MORGAN CHARLES ERNEST
Rifleman, 1st Battalion
Monmouthshire Regiment
Service No. 123
Died 24 April 1915, age 31
Commemorated Ypres Menin Gate
Memorial, Belgium

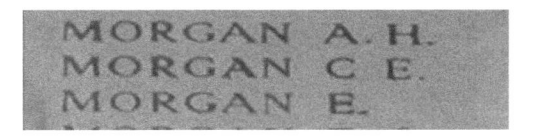

Charles was born in Ebbw Vale in 1884, the son of William and Elizabeth Morgan. They lived in 1 Bridge Street, Aberystruth, Bedwellty, before moving to the Pontymister Inn by 1901. Charles' father William had died in 1898 and Elizabeth is shown as an Inn Keeper. The 1911 census shows Elizabeth as the proprietor of the George Inn Hotel, Brithdir and Charles working as an insurance agent.
He married Susan May Wallis in the Merthyr District in 1914.
Charles enlisted at Rogerstone into the 1st Battalion, Monmouthshire Regiment serving as Private 123.
The 1st (Rifle) Battalion was raised on August 4th 1914 as a Territorial Force with its headquarters at Stow Hill, Newport. They were part of the South Wales Brigade, Welsh Division which landed in France as part of 84th Brigade, 28th Division on February 13th 1915.
The Battalion were in the thick of the fighting round Ypres, where the first German 'gas attack' on April 22nd 1915, had brought a new dimension of horror to war. The 1st Monmouths fought alongside their other two Battalions, the 2nd and 3rd Monmouthshires.
All three Battalions came in for very severe fighting; the 1st had a company involved in supporting the right of the Canadians by counter-attacks as early as April 24th 1915, though most of the Battalion and all the 3rd were holding the 28th Division's front line until the withdrawal to a shorter line nearer Ypres on the night of May 3rd-4th.
Charles was wounded and died whilst being treated by the 85th (3rd London) Field Ambulance. He is commemorated on the Ypres (Menin Gate) Memorial.
As noted elsewhere, Charles' brothers Gus died on January 3rd 1917 in France and Albert, a POW died on March 3rd 1921.
They are all commemorated on the family grave at Tirzah Baptist Church, Michaelston-y-Fedw. Charles and Gus are commemorated on the Brithdir War Memorial.

MORGAN JAMES ARTHUR
Gunner, 'B' Battery 266th Brigade
Royal Field Artillery
Service No. 740184
Died 30 December 1917, age 34
Buried Ramleh War Cemetery, Israel

James, born in Pontymister in 1883, was the son of Mathias and Elizabeth Morgan. In 1901 they lived at the 'Tap Room' Risca along with 2 other children, Emily and

Frederick. Mathias was a tin plater assorter and James was a blacksmith's striker. By 1911 they had moved to 20 Trafalgar Street, Pontymister and James was occupied as a galvanizer in the Galvanized Sheet Mill Works.

He enlisted at Risca presumably into the 4th Welsh Brigade, RFA (Territorial Force). This was redesignated as 266th Brigade, RFA (T.F.) and went to France on November 27th 1915. On December 21st it took over a reserve position near Albert. In early February 1916 it entrained for La Valentine and on the 11th it embarked for Alexandria, joining the 53rd Welsh Division on the edge of the Libyan Desert.

In May 1916 the Brigade became a part of the Suez Canal defences at Ferry Post. During November 1916 the Brigade marched across the desert to Palestine. It was here that it took part in the First and Second Battles of Gaza, the Capture of Beersheba, the Battle of Khuweileh, and the action at Tel 'Asur, ending the war just beyond Akrabeh.

James was killed on December 30th 1917 and is buried in Ramleh Cemetery, now Israel.

MORGAN JOHN GEORGE
RIFLEMAN, 22ND BATTALION
RIFLE BRIGADE
SERVICE NO. 204978
DIED 25 OCTOBER 1918, AGE 30
BURIED STRUMA MILITARY CEMETERY, GREECE

John was born in Cwmcarn in 1888, one of seven children to James and Bessie Morgan.

He lived in Feeder Row, Cwmcarn until he married Mary Jane Jones in 1910, their marriage producing a child Charles Granville born December 23rd 1910.

In 1911 they lived in 5 Tymelin Terrace, Rogerstone and he was working as a labourer in the steel works although he later worked as a miner.

They moved from Rogerstone to 'The Bunch', Ochrwyth by the time he enlisted.

He had previously been in the 1st Monmouthshire Regiment (Territorial Force) as Private 263.

John enlisted at Newport in the Rifle Brigade serving in the 22nd (Wessex & Welsh) Battalion (Territorial) as a rifleman.

The 22nd Battalion was formed on November 29th 1915 from supernumerary Territorial Force Companies, formed from National Reservists that were used for guarding vulnerable points in Great Britain.

The 22nd went to Salonika via Egypt on Garrison duties, being attached to the 228th Brigade in 28th Division.

John died in Salonika of malaria fever and is buried in Struma Military Cemetery, Greece.

The inscription on his headstone is *'Until The Day Break and The Shadows Flee Away Thy Will Be Done'*.

MORGAN WILLIAM RICH MC
Second Lieutenant, 9th Battalion
attached 1st Battalion
South Wales Borderers
Died 2 April 1916, age 33
Buried St. Patrick's Cemetery, Loos, France

William, son of John and Rose Morgan, was born in Abercarn on July 28th 1882.
The family lived at 23 Islwyn St, Abercarn and William was a pupil at Pontywaun County School, Risca.
William employed as a clerk at the Celynen Colliery, was well known locally as an athlete and played football for Abercarn Football Club under the captaincy of his brother, Thomas William Morgan.
With the outbreak of war he attested for service in the Royal Army Medical Corp on September 5th 1914, aged 22 years 4 months. After attaining the rank of Sergeant, in May 1915 he was discharged to a commission in the 9th Battalion South Wales Borderers.
Attached to the 1st Battalion, he entered France on November 26th 1915, joining the Battalion at the front on the Loos Salient on the 29th. William, the Battalion bombing officer, won his Military Cross rescuing a wounded man under heavy fire during the assault on Hart's Crater, February 19th 1916.
He was notified of the award on March 7th and presented with the ribbon by the General Officer Commanding (GOC) on the 9th.
William was killed in action on April 2nd 1916. The 1st Battalion was subject to heavy artillery fire, especially heavy howitzers firing high explosive shells with delayed action fuses which had a burrowing effect. One heavy shell caught 'D' Company's Headquarters in a dug-out at the side of the quarry near Hart's Crater and killed most of the occupants, one of those was William.
The war diary stating that he *"was killed by being buried in a dug-out"*.
William is buried in St. Patrick's Cemetery, Loos.

MORRIS EDGAR
Private, 2nd Battalion
Welsh Regiment
Service No. 44840
Died 8 September 1916, age 29
Buried London Cemetery and Extension, France

According to some army records Edgar was born in St Peter's, Monmouth but other records indicate that he was born in Risca, son of John and Mary Morris.
In 1901 they lived near the Foundry where John is employed as a Labourer in the Iron Foundry.
They lived at No 2 Brooklyn House, Pontymister in 1911. His father John was a labourer in the Tin Works whilst Edgar was working as a labourer in the Steel Works.

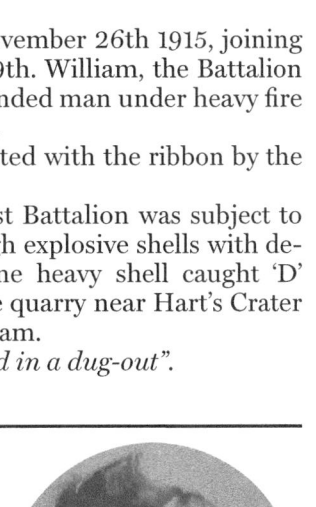

He enlisted sometime after 1915, into the 2nd Battalion Welsh Regiment serving as Private 44840.

The war diary for September states –

"On September 1st 1916, the Battalion was in reserve at Albert and on the second moved up to Lozenge Wood, where it remained until the 5th until it moved up to the North Eastern corner of Mametz Wood. The immediate area was quite free from hostile shelling but the Battalion was very cramped for room and had little shelter. On September 8th the Battalion relieved the South Wales Borderers in High Wood and delivered an attack upon the enemy front line in the wood in conjunction with the 1st Gloucesters who attacked on the left.

The preliminary bombardment commenced at noon, and just before zero (6 pm) the Special Brigade RE used flammenwerfer and a special type of oil drum projectile which burst into flames in the enemy trenches. B and C companies led the assault with D company in close support and A company as reserve carrying company. Our entry into the hostile trench was effected on the right and three platoons of B company and a part of D company occupied about 120 yards of the enemy front line. C company and the left of B and D companies were held up by hostile machine gun fire on the left. They made two unsuccessful attempts to get across and suffered heavy casualties.

On each flank of the portion occupied on the right of the attack, a vigorous bomb fight proceeded with varying success until about 3 am, when, before a violent counter attack our bombers, now very fatigued, were forced to retire. They fought tenaciously but only managed to retain a part of the communication trench which they had dug out to the trench they had taken. The 1st Gloucesters on the left were held up by hostile machine gun fire excepting about 30 men led by their Commanding Officer and these were forced to retire almost immediately after gaining their objective".

Edgar was killed in action on September 8th 1916 and is buried in London Cemetery and Extension, Longueval, France. He is remembered on the Bethany Church Memorial.

MORRIS JAMES
Private, 7ᵀᴴ Battalion
South Wales Borderers
Service No. 7/19046
Died 22 June 1918, age 28
Buried Salonika Military Cemetery, Greece

Born in Cross Keys on August 9th 1889, James was one of seven children to James and Amelia Morris. Their address in 1901 was Canal Side, Risca and later Canal Row.

On February 4th 1902 he started at Waunfawr Junior School, leaving on October 6th 1902.

He was living with his parents at Halls Road Terrace,

Cross Keys in 1911 working as a coal hewer, marrying Alice Maude Evans the following year. Reuben James born in 1913 and Muriel, born in 1916 were their children.
He enlisted at Newport in 7th Battalion, South Wales Borderers as Private 7/19046. The Battalion arrived in Boulogne, France on September 5th 1915 before leaving Marseilles for Salonika, arriving there on November 12th 1915.
When the 7th and 8th Battalions SWB arrived, the Allies were already dropping back and a defensive position covering Salonika was set up.
After a harsh winter the Allies advanced northwards, and took up a line where the British held the right sector for a distance of about 15 miles from Lake Doiran to the River Vardar.
The line remained here until September 1918, and although the Battalions did not see any heavy fighting in this period they took parts in many raids and diversions.
James was injured during this time and died of his wounds on June 22nd 1918.
He is buried in Salonika (Lembet Road) Military Cemetery, Greece.
His brother Serjeant Richard Morris died on August 1st 1917 whilst serving with the 11th Battalion SWB.

MORRIS RICHARD
Serjeant, 11th Battalion
South Wales Borderers
Service No. 22276
Died 1 August 1917, age 33
Buried Dozinghem Military Cemetery, Belgium

Richard was born in Cross Keys in 1884, one of seven children to James and Amelia Morris. Their address in 1901 was Canal Side, Risca and later Canal Row.
He married Elizabeth Jane Murray in 1907, the marriage producing six children.
In 1911 he was living with Elizabeth and three children at 6 Hill Street, Pontymister and was employed as a Labourer in the Steel Works.
He enlisted at Newport in South Wales Borderers as Private 22276 and was later promoted to Serjeant serving with the 11th Battalion.
His wife Elizabeth passed away on 18 May 1918.
As part of the 115th Brigade 38th (Welsh) Division the Battalion was involved in the Third Battle of Ypres, known as the Battle of Passchendaele.
Richard died of his wounds on the second day of this action and is buried in Dozinghem Military Cemetery, Belgium.
His brother James was killed on June 22nd 1918 and is buried in Salonika (Lembet Road) Military Cemetery.
James and Richard are both remembered on the Pontywaun Wesleyan Church and School Memorial.

MURRAY PHILLIP HENRY
Private, 4th Battalion
South Wales Borderers
Service No. 4/13117
Died 10 April 1916, age 28
Buried Amara War Cemetery, Iraq

Philip, one of 13 children, was born in 1887 to John and Elizabeth Murray of Penyrhiw Cottages, Risca.
They later lived near the New Inn and then 9 Hill Street, Pontymister, where Philip was recorded as being employed as a sheet doubler in the Tin Works.
He enlisted at Newport in the South Wales Borderers serving as Private 13117 in the 4th Battalion.
The 4th Battalion was formed at Brecon in August 1914 and became part of 40th Brigade, 13th Division. On June 29th 1915 they embarked from Avonmouth for Mudros arriving on July 12th.
On July 15th they were sent to Gallipoli in an effort to capture the Peninsula. The Battalion served with distinction throughout the campaign and was chosen as the rear guard in the evacuation of Suvla Bay in December 1915, an honour it had fully earned.
The 13th Division were despatched from Egypt to Mesopotamia in February 1916. It was here they took part in the bloody battles of the spring of 1916 fought by the Mesopotamian Expeditionary Force in the vain efforts to relieve General Townshend in Kut. These actions consisted for the most part of desperate attacks on strongly entrenched lines carried out in cold, mud and rain and in circumstances of the greatest hardships to the troops.
On April 4th 1916 the British attacked the Hanna position. The Battalion pushed on under heavy machine gun fire over ground devoid of cover and despite several losses reached a line about 800 yards from the Turkish trenches. During the advance an officer fell and one of his men, going to his help, was hit and disabled. Captain Buchanan therefore dashed out from behind cover and not only carried the officer in despite a heavy fire, but going out again, brought the private in also, for which gallantry he was awarded the Victoria Cross.
A few days later on April 8th came the night assault on the Turkish position at Sannaiyat, with the 4th Battalion in the front line. The attack failed with heavy loss, but the Regiment gained another Victoria Cross. Private Fynn, of C Company, crept out in broad daylight to two men who were lying within 300 yards of the Turkish line, bandaged them and brought them in.
Philip died of wounds on April 10th and is buried in Amara War Cemetery, Iraq.

N

NICHOLAS TREVOR
PRIVATE
ROYAL ARMY MEDICAL CORPS
SERVICE NO. 9962
DIED 30 JUNE 1916, AGE 23
BURIED RISCA OLD CEMETERY, RISCA, WALES

There is a strong possibility that Trevor, born in 1893 at Abercarn, was the son of John and Mary Elizabeth Nicholas of Jamesville, Cwmcarn.
Trevor worked as a coal miner in 1911 but may have later worked for Refuge Assurance as there is a Trevor Nicholas recorded on the firm's war memorial in Cheshire.
When he enlisted at Taunton, Somerset into the Royal Army Medical Corps he gave his birthplace as Newport, and served as Private 9962 in the RAMC.
Trevor married Florence West in 1915 but there is no record of any children, it is believed they lived at 1 Twyncarn Terrace, Cwmcarn.
He died at Cambridge Hospital, Aldershot on June 29th and was buried on July 4th 1916 at Risca Old Cemetery, Cromwell Road.
Trevor is commemorated on the Trinity Church Memorial, Pontywain.

HEROES OF ST. JULIEN AND FESTUBERT

Here's to the Soldier who bled
To the Sailor that bravely did fa':
Their fame is alive, though their spirits have fled
On the wings of the Year that's awa'.

SHALL WE FOLLOW THEIR EXAMPLE?
APPLY AT RECRUITING STATION

O

OGBORNE WILLIAM CHARLES
GUNNER, 838TH AREA EMPLOYMENT COMPANY
LABOUR CORPS
SERVICE NO. 42300
DIED 4 DECEMBER 1918
BURIED RISCA OLD CEMETERY, RISCA, WALES

William was born in Cross Keys in 1884, son of Thomas and Sarah Ogborne, (nee Brown).
Thomas was a stationary engine driver, possibly in the local pit.
On the 1891 census they are recorded as living in Upper Mount Pleasant, Pontywain before showing up in The Grove, Lower Patchway, Bristol in 1901.
The following year they were back in Cross Keys, where their son Trevor was born.
They then moved to 65 Islwyn Road, Wattsville by 1911 where William and Trevor are both shown as coal miners. William enlisted in the Royal Field Artillery, serving as Gunner 13250, going to France on November 9th 1915. He later transferred to the Labour Corps, serving with 838th Area Employment Company.
He died of pneumonia at Seaforth Military Hospital, Liverpool on December 4th 1918.
William is buried in Risca Old Cemetery, Cromwell Road, Risca.

ONIONS WILFRED
SECOND LIEUTENANT, 3RD BATTALION
MONMOUTHSHIRE REGIMENT
DIED 25 APRIL 1915, AGE 26
REMEMBERED YPRES (MENIN GATE) MEMORIAL, BELGIUM

Wilfred was born on May 23rd 1888 in Cross Keys, the son of Alfred and Sarah Ann Onions, (nee Dix).
Alfred worked as a check weighman in the local colliery while living at Back Lane, Risca. They later moved to Abertillery and then onto Tredegar.
By this time Alfred was a miner's agent and Wilfred was a schoolboy at Earl Street Boy's School. Later he attended Tredegar County School playing cricket for the school team. Living at Park Row and then Melrose Villa, Tredegar Alfred was moving up the ranks of the Labour party whilst Wilfred became an Assistant Schoolmaster.
Wilfred went to Cheltenham Training College and it was there that he progressed

into a very good rugby player turning out for the local Tredegar team before having a trial for Newport Rugby Club in 1910.
He was successful and went on to make 43 appearances scoring 6 tries over the next two seasons.
He was described as a useful centre, but unfortunately his career ended when he broke a collar bone at Northampton in November 1911. He joined the 3rd Battalion Monmouthshire Regiment as a Private at the outbreak of war, gaining his commission on October 3rd 1914. His brother Douglas had joined the 2nd Monmouthshires at the same time.
Wilfred was taking part in a movement after news of a German breakthrough. He and his men were crossing an open path with him six yards in advance when he was shot in the head and died without regaining consciousness.
Lieutenant LD Whitehead of the 3rd Mons wrote, *"When the time came Onions stepped out of the trench without the slightest hesitation and showed all the qualities which men expect of their officers"*.
Wilfred's body was lost in the fighting and he is commemorated on the Menin Gate Memorial in Ypres.
He is remembered on the Tredegar War Memorial, the Tredegar Roll of Honour, now housed in Bedwellty House, Tredegar and on a plaque from Wesleyan Methodist Church, Tredegar, unfortunately now lost. He is also named on his father's grave at Risca Old Cemetery. After Wilfred's death his father went onto become the MP for Caerphilly from 1918 until his death in 1921.

ORMAN REUBEN
SERJEANT, 1ST BATTALION
SOUTH WALES BORDERERS
SERVICE NO. 9311
DIED 31 OCTOBER 1914, AGE 26
REMEMBERED YPRES (MENIN GATE) MEMORIAL, BELGIUM

Reuben, the son of Simon and Esther Orman was born in Abertillery in 1888.
The 1901 census shows Reuben and the family living in Cambrian House, High Street, Cross Keys.
He enlisted into the 1st Battalion, South Wales Borderers for 12 years on December 9th 1904 giving his age as 18, when he was in fact only 16. His attestation record shows he was 5ft 4½ins, weighed 8 stone 6 pounds and had a chest size of 36ins. He had a fresh complexion with grey eyes and brown hair.
He was discharged on January 19th 1905 for *'Having been irregularly enlisted'* (Presumably for lying about his age). His service records haven't survived but sometime later he re-enlisted into the same Battalion and entered France on August 14th 1914. A newspaper report told the story of Reuben and his brother Zeph, also killed in France.

> *"Sergeant Reuben Orman lived at Swansea where he was a member of the United Services Brigade and very popular with all classes. Information of his death from shrapnel wounds at Gheluvelt was received by his parents on Christmas Eve. The sergeant had taken part in the battle of the Aisne and other engagements and some of his letters home had been published in the Argus. He was in every sense a soldier and his promotion had been rapid. He is said to have expressed a wish that he might die fighting for his beloved country".*

South Wales Argus 01.01.1915

He died age 26 at Gheluvelt, Belgium along with hundreds of other men from the 1st Battalion South Wales Borderers.

Reuben is commemorated on the Menin Gate Memorial, Ypres, the Swansea Hebrew Congregation Memorial and a Roll of Honour from the Risca Road Synagogue Newport, now held in Gwent Archives, Ebbw Vale.

ORMAN ZEPHANIAH
PRIVATE, 4TH BATTALION
DUKE OF CAMBRIDGE'S OWN (MIDDLESEX REGIMENT)
SERVICE NO. L/13502
DIED 14 OCTOBER 1914, AGE 23
BURIED VIEILLE-CHAPELLE NEW MIL. CEMETERY, FRANCE

Zephaniah, the son of Simon and Esther was born in Abertillery on August 23rd 1891. He used various names throughout his life; the registration of his birth shows Jasapo Chvi Orman, in the 1901 census he was Jepha Orman and he enlisted as Harry Normand.

Simon and his wife were Russian Jews who came to Britain and setup in business as a drapers and outfitters. The couple arrived about 1880 and lived in Blaenavon and Abercarn before settling in Cross Keys.

Zephaniah attended Park Street Junior School in Cross Keys from June 29th 1899 until April 22nd 1904 when he moved to Pontywaun County School.

The 1901 and 1911 censuses show the family living in Cambrian House, High Street, Cross Keys. Zephaniah (Harry Normand) had enlisted in the 3rd Battalion Middlesex Regiment in 1910 and was stationed in India in 1911. Sometime later he transferred to the 4th Battalion and entered France on August 14th 1914.

Zephaniah was an early casualty of the war in France. After surviving the battle and retreat from Mons he was made a despatch messenger; in doing his duty between the regiments he was killed between October 12th and 14th of 1914.

A newspaper report told the story of Zeph and his brother Reuben, also killed in France.

> *"Sympathy of the neighbourhood will be extended to Mr and Mrs S Orman of High St, Cross Keys in the double bereavement which has befallen them and their family. They have given two sons to the cause of freedom, Private Zeph Orman of the 4th Middlesex Regiment and Sergt. Reuben Orman of*

the 1st Battalion South Wales Borderers, having been killed in action. The deceased were among the large number of Jews who have responded to the call of their King and country". Private Zeph Orman was a signaller and he had shown conspicuous bravery at the front. Of him a writer in the "Jewish Chronicle" said "Conversing with a number of wounded men who had recently returned from the front, I chanced to meet a Christian soldier of the 4th Middlesex Regiment who, in glowing language, endorsed the opinions I had already received upon the bravery of our Jewish soldiers in France. Private Orman was reported to me as being the principal signaller of his unit and most popular with all ranks. This Jewish soldier, I was told, had been in many positions of danger and bore a charmed life. My informant observed him moving fearlessly amid 'showers of bullets and shrapnel".
South Wales Argus 01.01.1915
He is buried in Vieille-Chapelle New Military Cemetery, Lacouture, France and commemorated on the Pontywaun County School Memorial and a Roll of Honour from the Risca Road Synagogue Newport, now held in Gwent Archives, Ebbw Vale.

OWEN ALEXANDER PROSSER
Lance Corporal, 10th Battalion
South Wales Borderers
Service No. 20854
Died 10 October 1916, age 34
Buried Essex Farm Cemetery, Belgium

Alexander Prosser Palmer, born in 1882, was the son of Edward George and Margaret Amy Palmer.
He was baptised on December 27th 1882 at St George's Church, Tredegar.
Edward died and Margaret married Evan Owen and moved to Water Lane, Risca with her 4 children. They moved then to 3 Glenbran Terrace, Cwmbran by 1901 and Alexander, who had taken the surname Owen, was working as an Iron Cutter in the Bolt Works. Later they moved again to St Anthony Road, Risca, and Alexander was now working as a packer of tin sheets.
He enlisted in Newport into the 10th Battalion South Wales Borderers as Private 20854, later becoming Lance Corporal.
The 10th Battalion embarked the Empress Queen at Southampton on December 3rd 1915, arriving at Havre at 7 A.M. on the 5th. After spells in the Line at Givenchy in the spring of 1916 the Division moved to the River Ancre on July 3rd at the opening of the Battle of the Somme, and both Battalions had their first real action in the attack on Mametz Wood. Here they had five days' hard fighting in a thick wood flanked by machine guns. It required skill and determination on the part of all ranks to turn the Germans out, and fine work was done with bomb and bayonet by the courage and initiative of junior leaders. The 10th Battalion lost 180 men and the 11th Battalion 220.

They did not return to major action until over a year later although they were engaged in minor actions. Throughout October 1916 they were in the Yser and St Julien areas, near Ypres, Belgium.
The war diary for October 10th shows they were at Irish Farm frontline in the St Julien Sector.
> "Battalion in front line. Enemy Artillery pretty active. Our casualties 3 Other Ranks killed and 5 wounded".

Alexander was killed in action on this day and is buried in Essex Farm Cemetery, Diksmuidseweg, Belgium.

OWEN JONATHAN
PRIVATE, 1ST BATTALION
GRENADIER GUARDS
SERVICE NO. 10329
DIED 25 MARCH 1915, AGE 37
BURIED RISCA OLD CEMETERY, RISCA, WALES

Jonathan, son of John and Eliza Owen was born in Pontypool on December 26th 1875. They lived at 85 Tranch in Pontypool and he attended George St Infants School in Pontypool.
Later the family moved to 35 Wattsville, where father, son and elder brother James were all employed as coal miners. On August 3rd 1898 at Bassaleg, he enlisted into the South Wales Borderers, signing on for 6 years. He is described as being 5ft 5ins tall, 9 stone 6 lbs and a chest measurement of 33 - 35ins. He had a fresh complexion, blue eyes and brown hair and was a Church of England worshipper.
After 49 days of drill instruction he purchased his discharge on May 2nd 1899 and returned to Wattsville and carried on working in the pit.
In 1908 he married Sophia Camp in Brentford, London, returning to Wattsville, living at 46 Old Row (Islwyn St.) They had two sons William Henry and Thomas and a daughter Catherine who sadly died shortly after.
Jonathan enlisted at Pontypridd into the Grenadier Guards serving with the 1st Battalion.
On March 10th 1915, the Battle of Neuve Chapelle, in the Artois region of France, commenced. It was one of the first trench warfare battles and during the conflict Jonathan was severely wounded in the leg by shrapnel.
On Monday March 22nd he arrived by ambulance train in Harrogate and was taken to the Grand Duchess George's Hospital. Shortly after his arrival gangrene set in and he died on Thursday March 25th.
The following day his body was conveyed from Harrogate to his home in South Wales, at Arthur Street, Cwmfelinfach. The procession from the hospital to the railway station was headed by the band of the Yorkshire Hussars playing the "Dead March" from "Saul". Among those following were members of the Russian Royalty, including the Grand Duchess George, Baroness Stoeckl and the Baron Stoeckl

wearing the uniform of a Russian officer. The Mayor, wearing his chain of office was also present. It was announced that the funeral with military honours would take place at 3 o'clock on the following Monday at Risca Cemetery.

There were many impressive scenes and demonstrations of public sympathy as the cortege passed by. The cemetery was thronged with people, while along the route from his home for over two miles the roadside was lined with sympathetic spectators.

The procession, included detachments of the South Wales Borders, the 4th Welsh R.F.A., from Newport, and members of various other regiments, the Shropshires, Somersets and Grenadiers. They passed slowly along, headed by the Cross Keys Band, with drums muffled, playing the *"Dead March"*. On route a halt was made at the Mission Church in Cross Keys for a service conducted by Captain Willet of the Church Army. At the cemetery the coffin, which was draped in the Union Jack, was borne to the grave by six men of the R.F.A. After the reading of the service by Captain Willet the *"Last Post"* was sounded.

As well as floral tributes from members of the family, there were wreaths from the Working Men's Clubs of Wattsville and Risca, together with others from Harrogate, including Comrades, Invalid Comrades, Matron and Nurses of the Hospital. Wreaths were also sent from members of the Russian Royal Family, including the Grand Duke and Duchess George, the Princesses Nina and Xenia, Baron and Baroness Stoeckl.

Jonathan is buried in the Church Section of Risca Old Cemetery.

The following is part of an article written by Bernard Osment for the Risca Directory.

Risca Old Cemetery Revisited

Some months after the burial the "Singapore Free Press and Mercantile Advertiser" published an article headed "Buried Guardsman".

"A remarkable story was telegraphed recently by a Cardiff correspondent. The story originates from the mining village of Risca in Monmouthshire. Spiritualists and psychical research students from all parts of the country are said to be engaged in the investigation of the extraordinary circumstances associated with the death and burial of Guardsman Jonathan Owen who came home wounded from France and died in hospital at Harrogate. He was buried in the cemetery of his native village of Risca in the same grave as his little daughter who had just predeceased him".

"A photograph taken by the family after the funeral, to the astonishment of everybody revealed the faces of Jonathan and his little girl looking out from the foliage. Both are clearly visible, and their resemblance convincing. The astounding incident is expected to arouse much controversy throughout the country".

FACES FROM THE GRAVE.

P

PARKINS WALTER LEWIS
Private, 2ND Battalion
Grenadier Guards
Service No. 30531
Killed 27 August 1918
Buried Mory Abbey Military Cemetery, Mory, France

Walter Lewis was the son of Herbert and Frances Sarah Parkins, (nee Smith). Herbert and Frances married January 26th 1890 at Oxhey Parish Church, Hertfordshire, the marriage producing at least four children.
Charlotte born about 1888 in Hertfordshire, Herbert John, baptised August 12th 1891 in Watford Parish, who died 1894. Walter Lewis baptised May 18th 1894 in Watford Parish and Edith Selina born 1896 in Penygraig, Pontypridd area.
Herbert, a general labourer, Frances and Charlotte were living in Watford in 1891. Frances died in 1900 and the children were adopted by her sister Annie and husband William Grant. They lived in Westbury, Wiltshire. By 1911 Walter had started working for Great Western Railway as a greaser.
The National Union of Railwaymen records show that he joined the union on August 30th 1914, when he was recorded as working as an examiner and employed at Risca. It appears he left the union in December 1915.
Walter joined the Household Battalion possibly in September 1916 with the rank of Trooper. The Household Battalion was an infantry battalion formed from reserve units of the Household Cavalry.
He later joined the 2nd Battalion, Grenadier Guards who fought on the Western Front for the duration of the war.
During 1916 and 1917 they were involved in numerous actions including the Battles of Flers-Courcelette, Morval, Pilkem, Poelkapelle, The First Battle of Passchendaele and The Battle of Cambrai 1917.
1918 saw more action in the Battles of St Quentin, First Battle of Arras 1918, Havrincourt, Cambrai 1918, Selle and the Battle of the Sambre.
Walter was killed in action on August 27th 1918, and buried in a marked grave. His body was later exhumed and moved to Mory Abbey Military Cemetery, Mory, France. He is remembered on the Bethany Chapel Memorial, Risca.

PARSONS GEORGE
Serjeant, 3RD Battalion
South Wales Borderers
Service No. 20727
Died 19 February 1919, age 25
Buried Risca Old Cemetery, Risca, Wales

George, son of George and Sarah Jane Parsons, (nee Davies), was born in Risca on September 25th 1893. He attended Park Street Infant's School in Cross Keys from April 25th 1898 until August 19th 1901 when he transferred to the Boy's School. He left school on April 25th 1908.

At this time they lived in Pontywain, close to the Philanthropic Inn and father George was employed as a coal miner below ground. By 1911 they were living in 8 Western Terrace, Cross Keys and George junior was an apprentice ironmonger.

He enlisted at Abercarn into the 3rd Battalion, South Wales Borderers, Service Number 20727, later transferring to the 10th Battalion, SWB.

After initial training close to home, they moved to Colwyn Bay and joined 130th Brigade, 43rd Division, which was renamed 115th Brigade, 38th (Welsh) Division on April 29th 1915. They moved to Hursley Park near Winchester in July 1915 but then to Hazeley Down for final training.

The Battalion arrived in Le Havre on December 4th 1915 after a voyage from Southampton aboard the Empress Queen.

In July 1916 they were in action at Mametz Wood on The Somme, suffering severe casualties. The Division did not return to major action for more than 12 months. In 1917 they were in action in the Third Battles of Ypres, in 1918 they were at The Somme, in the Battles of the Hindenburg Line and the Final Advance in Picardy. Demobilisation began in December 1918 and was complete by June 1919.

George died of pneumonia at Seaforth Hospital, Liverpol on February 19th 1919.

He is buried in Risca Old Cemetery, Cromwell Rd and is remembered on the memorial at Trinity Church, Pontywain.

PEARCE EDWARD
PRIVATE, 2ND BATTALION
SOUTH WALES BORDERERS
SERVICE No 25077
DIED 13 AUGUST 1915, AGE 46
REMEMBERED HELLES MEMORIAL, TURKEY

Edward was born in Frome, Somerset around 1867. In 1891 he was living as a boarder in 28 The Huts, Trelewis working as a coal miner. By 1901 he had married Sarah Jayne, had a child Mary Ann and moved to Temperance Hill, Risca, later moving to 24 Penyrhiw, Risca.

He enlisted in the 2nd Battalion, South Wales Borderers serving as Private, 25077. The 2nd Battalion served throughout the Gallipoli campaign.

On July 28th 1915, HMT Royal Edward headed for Alexandria with reinforcements of 1,367 officers and men, destined for Gallipoli. Arriving at Alexandria on August 10th, Royal Edward then sailed for Moudros on the island of Lemnos, a staging point for the Dardanelles.

On the morning of August 13th, heading towards Gallipoli, Royal Edward passed the British hospital ship Soudan, heading in the opposite direction.

A German submarine UB-14, was off the island of Kandeloussa and spotted both ships. The Soudan was allowed to pass unharmed, but the unescorted Royal Edward was attacked by one of UB-14's two torpedoes from about a mile away. Hit in the stern, she sank within six minutes.

Royal Edward was able to send an SOS before losing power, and the Soudan made a 180° turn and rescued 440 men in six hours. Another 221 were rescued by other ships.

It was reported that Royal Edward had just completed a boat drill and the majority of the men were below decks re-stowing their equipment. This accounted for the high level of casualties, variously reported as between 132 and 1,865.

The Times in September 1915, published an Admiralty casualty list which named 13 officers and 851 troops as missing believed drowned, a total of 864 lost.

Records show that Edward died by drowning at sea on this day.

He is remembered on the Helles Memorial, Turkey.

PEARSON SYDNEY
PRIVATE, 6TH BATTALION
SOUTH WALES BORDERERS
SERVICE NO. 17183
DIED 9 APRIL 1918
REMEMBERED PLOEGSTEERT MEMORIAL, BELGIUM

Sydney the son of David and Kate Pearson, was born in Brockmoor, Staffordshire in 1879.

His father was an engine driver when the family lived in Sun Street, Kingswinford, Staffordshire in 1881.

They later moved to Brierley Hill, Dudley where Sydney started work in the Tin Mill as a furnace man.

On July 13th 1898 he joined the Worcestershire Regiment, but was discharged on November 2nd 1899 when it was found he had lied about his age on enlistment. He'd stated that he was 19 years 2 months old when he was only 18.

His service records show his details as, height, 5ft 5¼ ins, weight 117 lbs, fresh complexion, brown eyes and hair and a heart tattooed on his left arm. He also stated his occupation was a cycle maker.

He moved to South Wales where he met and married Agnes Eveline Meredith in 1903, sadly she died in 1909 aged just 24.

In 1911, Sydney was living with his in-laws James and Ann Meredith at 23 Raglan Street, Risca. His occupation was shown as a tinplate doubler.

Sydney joined at Newport into the 6th Battalion South Wales Borderers serving as a Private.

The 6th Battalion, raised in South Wales in September 1914, went to France as the Pioneer Battalion of the 25th Division a year later, spending the winter in the Armentieres sector working in flooded trenches.

They were at Vimy and Neuville St. Vaast in the spring of 1916 consolidating the craters of mines blown under the German lines.

They were continuously employed during the Battle of the Somme in the summer of 1916, on one occasion digging a 700 yard communication trench from one captured trench to another under heavy shell fire.

Their next major engagement was at Messines in July 1917, before being moved further north in August for the Third Battle of Ypres. The winter of 1917 was spent digging reserve lines and in March 1918 the 5th and 6th Battalions fought against the German drive on Amiens.

Moved up north after this trying experience, the 6th along with 2nd and 5th Battalions met the full force of the new German offensive on the Lys, where they sought to exploit the limited success gained in the drive on Amiens.

On April 10th, the Battalion lost 80 killed and wounded in a gallant attack on Ploegsteert village.

Sydney's body was never found and he is remembered on the Ploegsteert Memorial.

PERROW WILLIAM
PRIVATE, 15TH BATTALION
ROYAL WARWICKSHIRE REGIMENT
SERVICE NO. 32734
DIED 28 OCTOBER 1917, AGE 21
BURIED LIJSSENTHOEK MILITARY CEMETERY, BELGIUM

William, born in Cross Keys on April 12th 1896, was the son of William and Euphemia Agnes Perrow, (nee Bevan). He started at Waunfawr Infants School on June 13th 1899 whilst living at 25 Salisbury Street, Cross Keys, leaving soon on September 8th as he had *'left the district'*.

They moved to 23 Woodland Terrace, Godreaman, Aberdare, where in 1911 William was working *'Watching belts at the coal washery'*.

William was living in Aberavon when he enlisted at Aberdare in the 3rd Battalion, Dragoon Guards as Private 9617 arriving in France on May 18th 1915. He later joined the 15th Battalion Royal Warwickshire Regiment serving as Private 32734.

The 15th (2nd Birmingham Pals) Battalion, Royal Warwickshire Regiment part of 95th Brigade, 32nd Division arrived in Boulogne, France on November 21st 1915 transferring firstly to the 14th Brigade then the 13th Brigade, 5th Division.

They took over a section of the front between St Laurent Blangy and the southern edge of Vimy Ridge, close to Arras.

In July the Division moved south to the Somme and were in action at High Wood and the Battles of Guillemont, Flers-Courcelette, Moval and Le Transloy.

In October they moved to Festubert and stayed there until they moved in preparation for the Battles of Arras.

In September 1917 the 5th Division moved out of the line for rest before being in action during the Battle of Passchendaele.

It was during this battle that William died of wounds on October 28th 1917.

He is buried in Lijssenthoek Military Cemetery, Belgium.

PETERSON CHARLES
Private, 11ᵀᴴ Battalion
South Wales Borderers
Service No. 20037
Died 23 August 1917, age 27
Remembered Tyne Cot Memorial, Belgium

Charles born in Newport about 1890, he was the brother of Mrs Hannah Goodwin of 21 Coronation Place, Pontywain.
Living in Pontywain when he enrolled at Newport into the South Wales Borders, he served as Private 20037, in the 11th Battalion.
The 10th Battalion (1st Gwent) and 11th Battalion (2nd Gwent) were both raised in October 1914, as part of the 115th Brigade of the 38th (Welsh) Division. In December 1915, they went to France, where their Division was to remain until the end of the War, winning much glory for Wales.
After spells in the line at Givenchy in the spring of 1916 the Division moved to the River Ancre on 3rd July at the opening of the Battle of the Somme, and both Battalions had their first real action in the attack on Mametz Wood.
After an uneventful winter in the trenches the Welsh Division found itself attacking the Pilckem Ridge on July 31st 1917, the opening day of the Third Battle of Ypres. On the next day the Germans opened a terrific artillery barrage along the Steenbeeke and on Iron Cross Ridge, which seemed to herald a counter attack.
The following day, after playing a part second to none in a most successful action, both Battalions were relieved. Their Division had gone straight through to its final objective, had consolidated the ground won, and had smashed up the famous German 3rd Guards Division.
The war diary shows that during the early part of August 1917, the 11th Battalion were resting and training at 'Staines Camp' before moving up into the line at 'Canal Bank' in Elverdinge, Belgium.
They arrived at Canal Bank on August 18th and immediately went into the front line relieving the 14th Welch Battalion. D Company was sent out to take position in shell holes whilst the enemy shelled Canal Bank throughout the night.
"19 August At Chien Farm a carrying party of 100 suffered 20 casualties. The enemy artillery was quiet, whilst the Allies artillery were busy all night. The following day was taken up with Lewis Gun training.
21 August The artillery opened up an intense bombardment on enemy positions on the right and kept up an intermittent shelling throughout the day. The enemy put about 15 4.2 shells in the Canal and dug outs but no damage was incurred.
22 August Saw the enemy drop 4.2s and gas shells in and around the Canal. Our artillery opened heavy bombardment which lasted for 5 hours. 8 enemy planes passed over and dropped bombs on E and W side of Canal. Orders received to relieve 13th Welch in the line.
23 August Battalion started to move from Canal Bank in parties of 20 at 100 yards interval.
Battalion HQs with Major Monteith in command are at Alouette Farm. The 17th

RWF and 6th Border regiment are on our right and left respectively. When the Battalion was on its way up a SOS was being sent from Alouette Farm by lamp. Shortly after our artillery opened a very intense bombardment and the signal Stop was read. The enemy barrage just escaped us. Our casualty coming up was 1 officer wounded. Artillery of both sides active".

After taking part in the battle of Langemarck, in which the 10th Battalion lost another 100 men and the 11th only slightly less, the Welsh Division was relieved and sent down to Armentieres.

Charles died age 27, on August 23rd 1917 and is remembered on the Tyne Cot Memorial, Belgium.

He is remembered on the Cwmcarn War and Cwmcarn Institute memorials.

PHILLIPS GODFREY REES
PRIVATE, 9TH BATTALION
CHESHIRE REGIMENT
SERVICE NO. 53224
DIED 12 APRIL 1918, AGE 19
REMEMBERED PLOEGSTEERT MEMORIAL, BELGIUM

Godfrey was born in 1889, one of five children to John and Elizabeth Phillips.
The family lived in 2 Station Road, Risca, and his father was shown as being employed as a railway carman.
Godfrey was a crane driver when he signed his attestation papers to the Army Reserve on September 1st 1916 at Abertillery.
He was mobilized on October 13th 1917 and posted to the 3rd Battalion Royal Welsh Fusiliers on October 15th. After training he was sent to France on March 26th 1918 and transferred to the 9th Battalion Cheshire Regiment on March 31st. Just 12 days later he was reported missing.
In 1918 the Cheshire Regiment fought on The Somme during The Battle of St Quentin and The Battle of Bapaume and in the Battles of the Lys at Messines and Bailleul.
Godfrey was initially reported missing and then killed in action on April 12th 1918. As his body was never recovered he is remembered on the Ploegsteert Memorial, Belgium.

PHILLIPS GRIFF
PRIVATE, 8TH BATTALION
BORDER REGIMENT
SERVICE NO. 29494
DIED 27 MAY 1918, AGE 18
REMEMBERED SOISSONS MEMORIAL, FRANCE

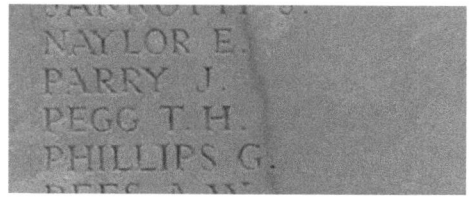

Griff, the son of David and Mary Anne Phillips, was born in Risca in 1900. The family lived in Tredegar Cottages, Risca before moving to 5 Mount Pleasant Road, Risca.

David initially worked as a smelter in the steel works before becoming a ladle man.
Griff enlisted at Abertillery in the Cheshire Regiment as Private 3700, before transferring firstly to the Manchester Regiment as Private 74622 and finally the 8th Battalion of the Border Regiment as Private 29494.
He must have enlisted sometime after 1915 as he was only entitled to the British War and Victory medals, not a 1915 Star.
The 8th Battalion Border Regiment arrived in France on September 27th 1915, but it is not known when Griff joined them.
They fought in the Battles of the Somme, Messines, Lys and Aisne.
On May 27th 1918 they were fighting at Ventelay, Roucy and La Paite Farm in NE France. The enemy were moving toward Ventelay and the 8th had to put up a spirited resistance whilst dropping back as they were being encircled. They eventually managed to break through the German line and join up with the French 21st Infantry Regiment as the British troops could not be located.
It was on this day that Griff, age just 18 was killed. He has no known grave and is remembered on the Soissons Memorial, France.

POOLE WILLIAM FRANK TREWAVAS
Driver, 147th Brigade, Ammunition Column
Royal Field Artillery
Service No. 19723
Died 8 August 1915, age 19
Buried Lancashire Landing Cemetery, Turkey

Known as Frank, he was the eldest son of Frank and Mary Hannah Poole, and was born November 4th 1895 in Cross Keys.
He attended Park Street School (Infants), Cross Keys, starting on November 1st 1898 until September 1st 1902 when he transferred to the Mixed School. He left school on November 8th 1908.
In 1901, living near the Hope Church, Frank senior was a coal miner. In 1911 they had moved to 12 High Street, Cross Keys and Frank junior was also now employed as a coal miner.
Frank enlisted in the 147th Brigade, Ammunition Column, Royal Field Artillery serving as a Driver.
After his initial training, he arrived overseas on April 1st 1915.
Frank was killed during the fighting in Gallipoli and is buried in Lancashire Landing Cemetery, Turkey.
He is remembered on the family grave at Risca Old Cemetery, Cromwell Road, Risca.

POTTER ALBERT HENRY
Lance Corporal, Military Foot Police
Military Police Corps
Service No. P/13536
Died 28 October 1918, age 21
Buried St. Cattwg Churchyard, Gelligaer, Wales

Albert was born in Risca on September 30th 1897 to Joseph Ernest and Lily Elizabeth Potter, (nee Hambleton).

In October 1900 they were living in Rhiwderin as Albert attended Rhiwderin Infants School. He only stayed there a few weeks leaving on November 16th to go to Bargoed.

The family then lived at 10 Francis Street, Gelligaer in 1901.

In 1911 Albert was living with his parents, brother Melvin and sister Doris at 15 Hanbury Street, Pengam, he was working as a Blacksmith's Striker.

He enlisted in Mumbles in the Military Foot Police, serving as A/Lance Corporal P/13536.

Albert died of illness at the Military Hospital, Aldershot on October 28th 1918 and is buried in St. Cattwg Gelligaer Churchyard.

He is remembered on the Mumbles War Memorial, Swansea.

POWELL CHARLES
Gunner, 'D' Battery 317th Brigade
Royal Field Artillery
Service No. 740158
Died 23 July 1918, age 23
Buried Bagneux British Cemetery, France

Charles was born in Ewyas Harold in Herefordshire, son of James and Nellie Powell.

James was a miner and the family had moved to Risca by 1911, living in 9 Wyndham Terrace, where Charles is also shown as a miner.

He enlisted into the Royal Field Artillery serving as a Gunner with D Battery 317th Brigade.

Charles died of wounds on July 23rd 1918.

He is buried in Bagneux British Cemetery, Gezaincourt, France and remembered on the memorial at Moriah Church, Risca.

POWELL JOSEPH HENRY
Private, 1st Battalion
South Wales Borderers
Service No. 13412
Died 22 December 1916, age 21
Buried AIF Burial Ground, France

Joseph, born in Newport on January 16th 1894, was the son of Joseph and Mary Powell, (nee Hill).

Living at 11 Bolt Street, Newport, he attended Bolt Street

Boy's School from August 19th 1901 until January 17th 1908 when he left to start work. His mother had died earlier in the year.

In 1911 they were living at 28 South Market Street, Newport where Joseph was shown as being a coke hauler.

He later worked at Risca as a packer in the Engineering Depart for the Great Western Railway Company.

Joseph enlisted at Newport into the 1st Battalion South Wales Borderers and went to France on August 23rd 1915.

The SWB were involved in many arenas of conflict during the war. In 1915 they were at Festubert, Givenchy and Loos before moving to the Somme in the middle of 1916. Although not directly involved in the main battles of the Somme they were in action at Contalmaison in mid July, near High Wood in the second half of August and near Flers at the end of September.

In December the Battalion had moved to the Mametz Wood area, the scene of terrific fighting earlier in the year.

The war diary records what the Battalion were doing at this time.

> *18th December 1916*
> *MAMETZ WOOD (Front Line): Commanding Officer's Orderly Room 10.00 am. During the morning Companies carried their packs and blankets to the Quartermaster's stores. At 1.30 pm the Battalion marched off for the trenches. They relieved the 1/GLOUCESTERS in the centre sector. On the way up a halt was made at HIGH WOOD for tea.*
> *19th December 1916*
> *IN THE FRONT LINE: Very hard frost owing to which movement was easier. At night, while going up to the front line, No 6043 CQMS WH Rickards and No 39123 Pte G Breach were killed instantaneously. The loss of Sergeant Rickards is a great blow to the battalion and is keenly felt by all ranks.*
> *20th December 1916*
> *Heavy shelling by enemy throughout the day in retaliation for our bombardment of the maze. TURK DUMP was shelled. Here we lost several casualties while water was being drawn.*
> *21st December 1916*
> *Fairly quiet day nothing to report.*
> *22nd December 1916*
> *2Lt TPM Robertson rejoined from leave. In the evening the Battalion were relieved by the 2/WELCH and moved back to Site 3 BAZENTIN-LE-PETIT. All were in Camp by 11.00 pm except Capt AAC Garnons-Williams with half D Company who did not arrive till 2.00 am owing to the relief being stuck in the mud. Total Casualties were: Killed - 6, Died of Wounds - 2, Wounded 15.*

(This is the day that Joseph Powell was killed and I believe he was one of the 6 who died that day)

Joseph is buried in the A.I.F. Cemetery, Flers, France.

POWELL PERCY
SERJEANT, 17TH BATTALION
WELSH REGIMENT
SERVICE NO. 26255
DIED 25 NOVEMBER 1917, AGE 21
REMEMBERED CAMBRAI MEMORIAL, FRANCE

Percy, born on September 4th 1896, was the second eldest son of William and Sarah Powell.
On May 6th 1901 he attended Waunfawr Infants School, where he stayed until August 15th 1904 when he moved up to the Junior School; at this time they were living at 26 Wattsville.
In 1911 they lived at 52 Islwyn Road, Wattsville where Percy was recorded as being an errand boy.
He was a miner when he enlisted at Newport in the 17th Battalion Welsh Regiment. The 17th (1st Glamorgan) Battalion Welsh Regiment was raised as a Bantam Battalion in Cardiff in December 1914. After initial training close to home they moved to Rhyl, Rhos, Prees Heath and then onto Aldershot for their final training.
They landed in France in June 1916 and went to the front line near Loos. Later they saw action at the Somme during the Battle of Ancre.
In 1917 they were involved in the German retreat to the Hindenburg Line, the capture of Fifteen Ravine, Villers Plouich, Beaucamp and La Vacquerie.
In November they were part of the Cambrai Operations including the capture of Bourlon Wood.
Percy died in action on November 25th 1917 in the attack on Bourlon Wood and is commemorated on the Cambrai Memorial, Louverval, France.

PRITCHARD CLARENCE HENRY
PRIVATE, 9TH BATTALION
WELSH REGIMENT
SERVICE NO. 60315
DIED 23 MARCH 1918, AGE 19
REMEMBERED ARRAS MEMORIAL, FRANCE

'Clarrie' as he was called, was born in Pontymister on April 9th 1898 and baptised on May 8th at St Mary's Parish Church, Risca. One of seven children, his parents were Henry and Rose Pritchard, (nee Laskey).
In 1901 they lived near the Drill Hall, Risca before moving to 10 Commercial Street, Risca.
By 1916, he was working as a shop assistant in a grocery store, whilst living at 62 Park Place, Risca.
On June 1st he travelled to Abertillery, joining the Army Reserve, later joining the Welsh Regiment on May 23rd 1917. The service records show that until December 28th 1917 he was in the UK before travelling to France on the following day.

He served with 'C' Company 3rd Battalion Welsh Regiment before being posted to the 19th Battalion on December 31st 1917 and then 15 days later to the 9th Battalion. He was killed on March 23rd 1918 during the Battle of St Quentin, and as he has no known grave he is commemorated on the Arras Memorial, France.
Clarrie is remembered on the memorial in St Mary's Church Risca.

PROTHERO WILLIAM JAMES
PRIVATE, 11TH BATTALION
LANCASHIRE FUSILIERS
SERVICE NO. 48617
DIED 28 MAY 1918, AGE 18
REMEMBERED SOISSONS MEMORIAL, FRANCE

William, born in 1900, was the son of William Richard and Ada Ann Prothero, (nee Matthews). Originally living in the Tap Room, Pontymister, they later moved to 10 Wellspring Terrace, Pontymister.
William enlisted in Cardiff as Private 41867 in the 11th Battalion Lancashire Fusiliers.
The 11th (Service) Battalion was formed in 1914 at Codford as part of the Third New Army.
They moved to Boscombe to join the 74th Brigade of the 25th Division and then again moved to Hursley and then on to Malplaquet Barracks.
On September 29th 1915 they were mobilised for war and landed at Boulogne. The Division were engaged in various actions on the Western Front including the German attack on Vimy Ridge, The Battle of Albert, The Battle of Bazentin, The Battle of Pozieres and The Battle of the Ancre Heights.
In 1917 they saw action at The Battle of Messines and The Battle of Pilckem. The following year they were in action at the Somme during the Battle of the Lys.
William died on May 28th 1918 age 18.
He is commemorated on Soissons Memorial, France and remembered on Bethany Baptist Church Memorial, Risca.
His father William Richard who served in 4th Welsh Brigade, Royal Field Artillery, survived the war.

PROUT CHARLES GEORGE
SERJEANT, 11TH BATTALION
SOUTH WALES BORDERERS
SERVICE NO. 12489
DIED 31 JULY 1917
BURIED BARD COTTAGE CEMETERY, BELGIUM

Charles was born in Clifton Wood, Bristol, Gloucestershire in 1887 to George Washington and Amy Elizabeth Prout, (nee Calver). Amy died in 1892 and George married Emma Ada Calver in 1894, possibly Amy's sister.
His father George was a Police Constable and the family lived in Clifton and then Bristol where he served in the police force.

Charles had moved by 1911 and was staying with Henry Watkins and his family in Star Cottage, Risca, being employed as a delivery clerk for a Brewery Company. One of Henry's children was Fanny Watkins who Charles married in 1912. They had two children, Barbara born December 5th 1913 and Eric born April 15th 1915.

Charles enlisted at Newport into the South Wales Borderers, going abroad to Gallipoli on July 19th 1915, possibly with the 4th Battalion South Wales Borderers.

Whilst in Gallipoli he wrote home to his mother in law Elizabeth Watkins, explaining her son Herbert had been killed. He also wrote that he himself had been wounded in the back.

At some stage he was evacuated from Turkey and went to France where he transferred to the 11th Battalion South Wales Borderers serving as a Serjeant.

Battle of Passchendaele.

The 11th Battalion, as part of the 115th Brigade 38th (Welsh) Division attacked Pilckem Ridge on July 31st 1917, the opening day of the Third Battle of Ypres.

The attack started at 3.50 a.m.

Their first two objectives were taken but there was hard fighting at Iron Cross, and when the 11th Battalion reached that area about 9 a.m. to pass through, they came under machine gun fire from some still untaken pillboxes.

The 11th completed the capture of the Iron Cross Ridge and swept down to the Steenbeeke, dealing with the pillboxes on their way.

The leading companies of the 11th Battalion crossed the Steenbeeke and started to establish their bridgeheads.

This work completed so well, that when the Germans advanced to counter attack at 3 p.m., the 11th were in position to attack with their rifles and Lewis guns.

Unfortunately, the Battalion on their left was driven back, and with their left thus exposed to enfilade machine gun fire the 11th was forced to withdraw across the Steenbeeke.

Rain, mud and shells were making conditions very difficult later in the afternoon and the 11th lost heavily, the enemy was only 100 yards from the Steenbeeke, and his machine guns and snipers made movement very dangerous.

Charles was killed during this action and is buried in Bard Cottage Cemetery, Belgium.

He is remembered on the memorial in St Mary's Church, Risca.

PUGH DAVID JOHN
Private, 8th Battalion
Welsh Regiment
Service No. 11805
Died 8 August 1915
Remembered Helles Memorial, Turkey

David was born in Atherton, Lancashire to David and Sarah Pugh. His early life was in Lancashire before moving to Cwmmer, Llantrisant, Wales between 1881 and 91. David's father was employed as a coal miner as was his son when he left school.

In 1911 he was a boarder, living with the England family in Ty Isha Road, Gelli, Rhondda. He later moved to Risca before enlisting into the 8th Battalion, Welsh Regiment, where he served as a Private, 11805.

The 8th Welsh Regiment were sent to Gallipoli and were involved in the attack called the Battle of Chunuk Bair.

Allied units that reached the summit of Chunuk Bair early on August 8th 1915 to engage the Turks were the Wellington Battalion of the New Zealand and Australian Division, 7th Battalion, Gloucestershire Regiment and 8th Battalion, Welch Regiment of the 13th (Western) Division.

The troops were reinforced in the afternoon by two squads of the Auckland Mounted Rifles Regiment, New Zealand and Australian Division. The first troops on the summit were severely depleted by Ottoman return fire and were relieved at 10:30 pm on August 8th by the Otago Battalion (NZ), and the Wellington Mounted Rifles Regiment New Zealand and Australian Division.

The New Zealand troops were relieved by 8:00 pm on August 9th by the 6th Battalion, Loyal North Lancashire Regiment and 5th Battalion, Wiltshire Regiment, who were massacred and driven off the summit in the early morning of August 10th, by an Ottoman counter-attack led by Mustafa Kemal.

The capture of Chunuk Bair, (Turkish: Çanak Bayır Basin Slope, now Conk Bayırı), the secondary peak of the Sari Bair range, was one of the two objectives of the Battle of Sari Bair, the British August Offensive at Anzac Cove and Suvla, to try to break the stalemate that the campaign had become.

The capture of Chunuk Bair was the only success for the Allies of the campaign but it was fleeting as the position proved untenable. The Ottomans recaptured the peak for good a few days later.

David was killed during the attack on August 8th and is remembered on the Helles Memorial, Gallipoli, Turkey.

"FALL IN"

ANSWER NOW
IN YOUR COUNTRY'S
HOUR OF NEED

R

RAFFERTY THOMAS ALFRED
Private, 1st Battalion
Royal Welsh Fusiliers
Service No. 27982
Died 27 August 1916, age 20
Remembered Thiepval Memorial, France

Thomas, son of Thomas and Caroline Rafferty was born August 9th 1896 in Abergavenny. His father was a tinman and his mother a hawker, in 1901 the family lived in 4 Wells Street, Brynmawr. Thomas was one of six children, having two brothers and three sisters.

He attended Abergavenny School before moving to Merthyr and starting at St Mary's Roman Catholic School, Merthyr Tydfil on March 22nd 1909, he lived at 4 Riverside, Merthyr.

Thomas was living at 3 Chapel Row, Pontywain when he enlisted into the Royal Welsh Fusiliers at Kingsway, London on August 2nd 1915.

Luckily his service records have survived and show that he was 5ft 2¼ins tall, weighing 7st 11 lbs with a 32 ½ins chest.

He gave his age as 19 years and 1 month on enlistment and his occupation was a cook's assistant.

Thomas was vaccinated on August 10th and 22nd.

On October 28th 1915 he was admitted to hospital in Bangor with tonsillitis for 13 days. His tonsils were removed and he was recommended for a period of leave to recover. He had further inoculations at Kinmel Park on February 23rd 1916.

He had a medical examination on June 28th 1916 and 2 days later embarked at Folkestone and landed the next day in France as part of the Expeditionary Force. At Etaples he was transferred to 14th Battalion RWF and then on July 12th 1916 he was posted to 1st Battalion RWF.

As part of the 22nd Brigade 7th Division the 1st Battalion Royal Welsh Fusiliers were involved in the 1st Battle of the Somme. The war diaries show they were involved in the following actions.

1st July	Attack between Mametz and Fricourt.
3rd July	South of Mametz Wood.
5th July	Capture of a part of Quadrangle Trench.
14th July	Capture of Bazentin-le-Petit.
16th July	Mametz Wood.
19th July	Bazentin-le-Petit.
20th July	Attack on right of High Wood.
26th August	Bernafay Wood.
28th August	Attack of Brewery Trenches (East of Delville Wood).

Thomas was killed on August 27th, and as he has no known grave is commemorat-

ed on the Thiepval Memorial.
His British and Victory medals were sent to his mother Caroline after the war.

RALLISON BERNARD
Corporal, 'D' Battery 76th Brigade
Royal Field Artillery
Service No. 4724
Died 23 June 1916, age 20
Buried Ferme-Olivier Cemetery, Belgium

Born in Risca and baptised on 6 October 1895, Bernard was the son of a soldier, Edward and wife Emily Rallison, (nee Battin).
Edward was a career soldier, enlisting on March 25th 1873 until September 4th 1905, serving in 59th Regiment, East Lancashire and South Wales Borderers Regiments. He saw service at home, India and Afghanistan and signed up again when the war started in 1914. He later became Sergeant Instructor to Volunteers at the Drill Hall, Risca.
Bernard, a colliery worker, was one of nine children and in 1911 the family lived at 78 St Mary Street, before moving later to Commercial Street, Risca.
He enlisted in 'D' Battery, 76th Brigade, Royal Field Artillery serving as a Corporal, Service Number 4724 arriving in France on August 22nd 1915.
He was killed in action on June 23rd 1916 and is buried in Ferme-Olivier Cemetery, Belgium.
He is remembered on the Moriah Church Memorial and the family grave at Risca Old Cemetery, Cromwell Road, Risca.
His brother Victor Edward Rallison, Manchester Regiment, was killed on April 7th 1917.
Frederick Charles, 1st Battalion South Wales Borderers and Ivor, 2nd Battalion South Wales Borderers, Bernard's other brothers, survived the war.

RALLISON VICTOR EDWARD
Second Lieutenant, 17th Battalion
Manchester Regiment
Service No. 7662
Died 7 April 1917, age 29
Buried London Cemetery, France

Victor, son of Edward and Emily Rallison, (nee Battin), was born in Newry, Northern Ireland on June 20th 1887.
Edward was a career soldier who enlisted into the 59th Regiment on 4 April 1873. He also served with the East Lancashire Regiment and South Wales Borderers, fighting in Afghanistan and later re-joining for service in World War 1.

In 1891 the family lived in Ivy House, Risca later moving to near the Drill Hall and then in 1914 they were at 78 St Marys Street, Risca.

Victor, along with his brother Frederick, attended Risca School both being admitted on April 7th 1891.

In 1901 Victor was employed as a moulder in the steel works. He then joined the army enlisting in the East Lancashire Regiment and was home on leave in 1911 staying at the family home.

He married Evelyn Mary Sheffield in 1916 at Rugby, Warwickshire.

On October 24th 1916 he was promoted from Sergeant to 2nd Lieutenant and transferred to the Manchester Regiment.

The Manchesters had taken part in the attack on Flers in the Somme, and although they fought tremendously it was a disaster.

The Battalions lost 12 Officers and 213 Other Ranks killed, wounded or missing for very little ground gained.

The Manchesters were in reserve at Bailleulval until November 6th before taking over the line at Bellacourt which was known as a 'quiet sector'.

They were here until the January 6th 1917 before marching to Sus St Leger for various types of training.

Work was carried out on the construction of a railway ready for the Battle of Arras. On March 20th, the Battalion went into the line in front of Agny and South of Mercatel, relieving the 2nd Bedford's.

The Germans had been gradually falling back from the Somme to Arras and each night the men would attempt to keep in touch with the enemy. It was during one of these patrols that Victor, along with Officer Hobbs and four men, were killed when they encountered the enemy in a ruined mill and were thrown off guard when they were challenged in English.

His brother Bernard Rallison, Royal Field Artillery, was killed on June 23rd 1916. Some of this information was taken from www.themanchesters.org/17th_20batt.htm

Victor is buried in London Cemetery, Neuville-Vitasse, France and he is commemorated on the family grave at Risca Old Cemetery, Cromwell Road, Risca.

RAWLINGS ARTHUR JOHN
Private, 1st Battalion
King's (Liverpool Regiment)
Service No. 7662
Died 16 April 1918, age 28
Remembered Arras Memorial, France

Born in Cross Keys in 1890, Arthur was the son of Joseph and Mary Ann Rawlings. They lived in 1 Foresters Row, Risca and later in 57 High Street, Cross Keys, both father and son worked as coal miners in the local pit.

In 1914 he married Winifred Clara Bishop and they had two children Arthur J, born 1914 and Kathleen E born 1918.

Arthur enlisted in Cross Keys into the 1st Battalion, Liverpool Regiment, serving as a Private.
The King's Liverpool Regiment fought at The Battle of Cambrai in November 1917 and followed this up with defensive activities until the New Year.
On March 21st 1918, a five-hour artillery and gas shell barrage across a 50 mile front heralded the beginning of the Battle of St. Quentin and the Spring Offensive in the Somme.
The 1st King's, occupying positions near Vélu Wood during the Battle of Bapaume, came under attack on the 24th but held out until a retreat was ordered. The Battalion commander, Lieutenant-Colonel Murray-Lyon, had just 60 men at his command when they arrived at Beaulencourt later in the day.
On March 28th, the German offensive reached Arras, but was soon repulsed by the Allies.
Having suffered about 250,000 casualties, comparable to Allied losses, Germany abandoned the operation on April 5th. Despite the losses, on April 9th, the German Army launched Operation Georgette in Flanders.
The German forces made significant gains, capturing Armentieres and on April 11th, British Commander-in-Chief, General Haig, issued his *"backs to the walls"* order of the day.
Arthur was killed on April 16th 1918 and is remembered on the Arras Memorial, Pas de Calais, France.
He is remembered on the family grave at Risca Old Cemetery, Cromwell Road, Risca.

RICHARDS GEORGE
DRIVER
ROYAL FIELD ARTILLERY
SERVICE NO. 19999
DIED 27 MAY 1918
BURIED HAGLE DUMP CEMETERY, BELGIUM

George, born in Landore, Glamorgan was one of eight children to George and Annie Richards.
George senior was a pitman in the steelworks. In 1901 their address was Water Lane, Risca, later to become Mill Street where they lived at number 13 in 1911.
George junior enlisted at Newport in the Royal Field Artillery, serving as Driver 1999.
There are few details about his military service apart from he went to France on December 5th 1915 with the RFA and was killed on May 27th 1918, leaving a wife Gertrude.
George is buried in Hagle Dump Cemetery, Belgium.

RICHARDS JOHN READ
Able Seaman
Royal Naval Volunteer Reserve
Service No. Wales Z/103
Died 26 January 1917, age 18
Remembered Thiepval Memorial, France

John was born September 26th 1898 to parents John Reed and Ellen Augusta Richards, (nee Simpson).
(There are various spellings of the middle name Read)
In 1901 John and his eleven siblings lived at Lower Golynos Farm, Rogerstone where father John was employed as a farm bailiff.
In 1911 the family had moved to 1 Clifton St, and father John was now employed as a stoker in the local gas works.
John enlisted January 22nd 1915 and his records describe him as 5ft 5 ½ins tall, fresh complexion with light brown hair and green eyes. He had a scar on his left knee and his occupation was a tin worker.
He gave his date of birth as September 26th 1896 which was two years earlier than when he was actually born.
After initial training he was posted to firstly the Anson Battalion and then the Hood Battalion as part of the British Expeditionary Force. He landed with them in Boulogne on September 25th 1916.
Anson and Hood Battalions were part of the Royal Naval Division which was a unique formation in World War 1, raised by the Admiralty to serve in their then traditional role as Infantrymen fighting *"shoulder to shoulder"* alongside their Army comrades in an emergency.
The RND, including Anson and Hood were involved in the Battle of the Ancre (November 13-18 1916), which was the final large British attack of the Battle of the Somme.
After the Battle of the Ancre, British attacks on the Somme front were stopped during inclement weather. For the rest of the year and early January 1917, military operations by both sides were mostly restricted to surviving the rain, snow, fog, mud fields, waterlogged trenches and shell-holes. As preparations for the offensive at Arras continued, the British attempted to keep German attention on the Somme front.
An ambitious plan for the spring was an attack into the salient that had formed north of Bapaume, during the Battle of the Somme in 1916. The attack was to be directed northwards from the Ancre valley and southwards from the original front line near Arras to meet at St Léger, as soon as the ground dried and was intended to combine with the effect of the offensive planned at Arras. British operations on the Ancre from January 10th - February 22nd 1917, forced the Germans back 5 miles on a 4 mile front, and eventually took 5,284 prisoners.
It was during this time that John was reported missing on 26 January 1917.
His body was never recovered and he is commemorated on the Thiepval Memorial in France.

RICHARDS LEWIS GARFIELD
PRIVATE, 12TH BATTALION
SOUTH WALES BORDERERS
SERVICE NO. 23359
DIED 21 SEPTEMBER 1916, AGE 21
BURIED BARLIN COMM. CEMETERY EXT., FRANCE

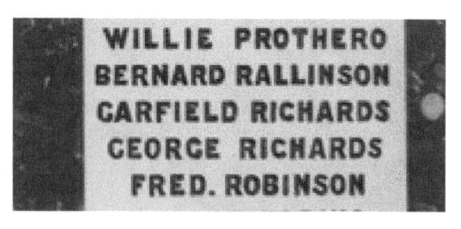

Garfield, was born in Pontymister in 1895, son of William and Matilda Richards, (nee Thomas).
William and Matilda were married in 1888 and had three sons Thomas, Idwal and Garfield, sadly Matilda died in 1897 aged 32.
In 1901 Garfield was living with his brothers, father and grandfather Thomas Thomas at Shaftsbury Terrace, Pontymister. By 1911 they had moved to 9 Wellspring Terrace where they were living with John Richards, Garfield's' grandfather.
He was employed as a tin worker, but later went to work in the colliery.
Garfield enlisted at Newport into the South Wales Borderers serving as Private 23359 in the 12th Battalion.
The 12th (Service) Battalion was raised in Monmouthshire in March 1915, and became part of the Welsh Bantam Brigade. Recruits were confined to the height of 5ft to 5ft 3ins. Progress in forming the battalion was slow, as many Monmouthshire men had already enlisted in the 17th and 18th (Bantam) Battalions, The Welsh Regiment. After training at Prees Heath, Shropshire and Aldershot the Battalion eventually went to France, landing at Le Havre on June 2nd 1916, in the 119th Brigade of the 40th Division.
They went into the front line near Loos and were later in action in the Battle of the Ancre on the Somme.
Garfield, age 21, died of wounds on September 21st 1916 and is buried in Barlin Communal Cemetery Extension, France.
He is remembered on the Bethany Church Memorial, Risca.

RIDEOUT FRANCIS BENJAMIN
PRIVATE, 1ST BATTALION
SOUTH WALES BORDERERS
SERVICE NO. 7979
DIED 13 NOVEMBER 1914, AGE 28
BURIED POPERINGE OLD MILITARY CEMETERY, BELGIUM

Frank was born in St James, Bristol in 1886 to William Charles and Charlotte Rideout, (nee Hallett).
He was baptised on September 21st 1887 in Bristol. The family lived in Bristol before Frank moved to the Risca area, where he worked in the United Colliery.

Frank married Ada Mary Blackwell in 1907, having three daughters, Edith Emily, Harriett Maud and Doreen, they also had a son William.
In 1911 Frank, Ada and two daughters were living in 4 Rogerstone Terrace Rogerstone.
He enlisted in the 1st Battalion, South Wales Borderers and landed at Le Havre, France with them on August 13th 1914 as part of the British Expeditionary Force.
The 1st Battalion took part in earlier battles of the war including Mons, Aisne and at Gheluvelt on October 31st 1914. It was here, where its defence of Gheluvelt Chateau stands out as its greatest achievement.
For another fortnight the remnant of the Battalion continued fighting, repulsing several more attacks and when it was taken out of the line it had lost all but four of its officers and over 800 NCOs and men.
Frank was wounded and moved to 4 Clearing Hospital at Poperinge, where he died on November 13th 1914.
He was buried in the Poperinghe Old Military Cemetery, Belgium.

ROBATHAN DOUGLAS PARKER
CAPTAIN, 5TH BATTALION
WELSH REGIMENT
DIED 10 AUGUST 1915, AGE 27
REMEMBERED HELLES MEMORIAL, TURKEY

Douglas, born in Risca on January 28th 1888, was the fifth son of George Beckett and Frances Elizabeth Robathan, of The Grove, Risca; he was baptised at St Mary's Church, Risca on March 25th.
Educated at Llandaff Cathedral School and Cranbrook School, Kent he became a mining engineer at Insoles Colliery Porth, he was also a member of the Homfray Lodge of Freemasons at Risca.
Douglas joined the Monmouth Volunteers as a 2nd Lieutenant in January 1908 and transferred to the 5th Welsh Territorials in April 1908, passed the School of Instruction and obtained his certificate as a Musketry Instructor in 1909.
He became a Lieutenant on April 7th 1909 and Captain on July 1st 1914. He volunteered for foreign service after the outbreak of war and left England with the 53rd Welsh Division on July 18th 1915 for the Dardanelles.
The war diary shows that the 1/5th Welsh were on the HMT Huntsgreen which arrived at Suvla Bay at 6.30 pm on August 8th preparing to disembark onto 'C' Beach.
Disembarking the following morning at 12:30 a.m. they prepared to attack and advanced on Turkish positions at 8:30 a.m..
They reached Anafarta Ova and bivouacked there that night. At 05:30 a.m. on August 10th they continued their advance and were pushed forward into Turkish trenches
They suffered the following casualties.
Killed:One officer and 17 Other ranks.

Wounded: 5 Officers and 107 Other ranks.
Wounded and Missing: Two Officers
Missing: One Officer
His Colonel wrote of him as
> "devoted to his duty and always to be relied on" and a brother officer said that when wounded "lying on the ground he still cheered his men on - 'Stick it Welsh' he shouted, and kept shouting until another bullet came along and got him in the lung.
> He died the best death any man could die and as game as possible. His lot did wonderfully well and fought like 'good uns' and it was a hot shop they were in".

A private also wrote
> "He led his men into one of the fiercest fights that has ever been fought on Gallipoli Peninsula. He was loved by his men and admired by all. He fought as gallantly as any as long as he was able to lead and I am expressing the thoughts of all the Battalion when I say it has lost one of its best soldiers".

Labour Voice newspaper December 4th 1915:
> "From Corporal J. Thomas, 1-5th Welsh Regiment, who has just returned to his home at Berry Square, Dowlais, after being wounded in the Dardanelles, we now learn how Captain Robathan, late surveyor at Tarreni Collieries, and commanding A Company, Pontypridd, met his fate on the Gallipoli Peninsula.
> After landing at Suvla Bay in the dead of night the British troops were subjected to a hail of shrapnel and Maxim gun fire, and subsequently in an attack on the Turkish lines, Captain Robathan was shot by a sniper. The fire, however, was so intense that he could not be rescued, and he was burned to death. Lieut. Phillips of Cardiff was the only officer then left in charge of the company, and he rallied his men with words of encouragement and praise".

He is commemorated on the Helles Memorial, Turkey as well as Llandaff School Memorial at Llandaff Green, Cardiff, Ystalyfera War Memorial and the Scout's Memorial in St David's Ystalyfera.

ROBBINS HERBERT GEORGE
GUNNER, 'C' BATTERY 62ND BRIGADE
ROYAL FIELD ARTILLERY
SERVICE NO. 19571
DIED 27 OCTOBER 1918, AGE 27
BURIED BOIS GUILLAME COMM., CEMETERY EXT., FRANCE

Born about 1893, Herbert was the son of George and Annie Robbins, (nee Yeoman). Some records give his birth place as Cross Keys but it appears he was born in the Fishponds area of Bristol.
Living in Bristol, George was a core maker in the iron works, whilst Herbert worked

as a pawn brokers assistant.
He may well have moved to Cross Keys after 1911 as he enlisted at Newport in the 62nd Brigade, Royal Field Artillery.
He arrived in France on September 2nd 1915 with the Royal Field Artillery.
They were in action at the Battle of Loos, repelling a German attack on October 8th going on to take part in an action of the Hohenzollern Redoubt, a defensive strongpoint of the German 6th Army on the Western Front.
During their time at Loos, 117 officers and 3237 men were killed or wounded.
Frequently in and out of the front line during the winter, they moved to Baizieux in June the following year. In August they fought in the Battle of Pozieres before moving north. 1917 saw them at Arras and the Battles of the Scarpe and Arleux before suffering heavy losses during the Cambrai offensive. In 1918 they went to Albert seeing action in the Battle of Bapaume and later the Battle of Amiens. October 1918 saw them fight in the Final Advance in Artois reaching the Scheldt Canal by the 27th.
Herbert died of disease at 8 General Hospital, Rouen, France and is buried in Bois Guillaume Communal Cemetery Extension, France.
He is commemorated on the Pontwaun Wesleyan Church and School Memorial, Cross Keys.

ROBBINS WILLIAM GEORGE
PRIVATE, 2ND BATTALION
WELSH REGIMENT
SERVICE NO. 9389
DIED 20 SEPTEMBER 1914, AGE 29
REMEMBERED LA FERTE-SOUS-JOUARRE MEMORIAL, FRANCE

Known more usually as George, he was born in Glamorgan in 1885, the son of William and Esther Robbins, (nee Jones).
The family moved to Bristol as father William worked as a labourer in the chemical works. Returning to Ystradyfodwg, Pontypridd, William worked as a coal hewer and George an assistant coal hewer in the mines.
William and Esther later moved to 2 Coronation Row, Pontymister where she was heavily involved with the Salvation Army.
George enlisted in the 1st Battalion Welsh Regiment early in 1907 serving as a Private, in 1911 they were in Abbassia, Cairo, Egypt.
Sometime prior to the outbreak of war, he transferred to the 2nd Battalion Welsh Regiment. They were stationed at Bordon training camp in Hampshire, as part of 3rd Brigade in 1st Division. As part of the British Expeditionary Force they landed at Le Havre on August 13th 1914.
They were involved in the Battle of Mons and the subsequent retreat, the Battle of the Marne from September 6-10 and the Battle of the Aisne, September 10-13.
George was killed in action on September 20th 1914 and is remembered on La Ferte-Sous-Jouarre Memorial, France.
A South Wales Gazette report of October 16th 1914 recorded his death.

ROBERTS ALBERT
No further information found
Commemorated on St John's Church Memorial, Risca, Wales

There are 54 casualties named Albert Roberts in WW1, none of which seem to have a link with Risca.

ROBERTS WILLIAM HENRY
Sapper, 257th Tunnelling Company
Royal Engineers
Service No. 79502
Died 21 March 1918, age 28
Buried Faubourg D'Amiens Cemetery, France

On the memorial in Moriah Baptist Church, WH Roberts is listed as a Private in the Royal Engineers.
The only man who fits this criteria is written about here, although no link to Risca has yet been found.
William was the son of Charles Benjamin and Clara Roberts, (nee Hawkes).
Born in Staffordshire, he was baptised on February 19th 1890 at St Michael's Church, Tividale, West Midlands.
Living in Tipton, Dudley, Charles worked as a nail caster, later becoming a moulder, the same occupation that William took up.
William married Ann Griffiths in 1913, having two children William and Elizabeth.
He enlisted at Dudley into the Worcester Regiment arriving in France on March 26th 1915. While in France, William transferred to the 257th Tunnelling Company of the Royal Engineers. The 257th Tunnelling Company was one of the tunnelling companies of the Royal Engineers created by the British Army during World War I. They were involved in the placing and maintaining of mines under enemy lines, as well as other underground work such as the construction of deep dugouts for troop accommodation, the digging of subways, saps (a narrow trench dug to approach enemy trenches), cable trenches and underground chambers for signals and medical services. In 1916 they were at Chipgny Sector, north of Neuve Chapelle, Rouen and Bethune. The following year saw them tunnelling at Vimy and Nieuport. Attached to VI Corps they fought at the Battle of St Quentin March 21-23 1918.
March 21st was the first day of the German Spring Offensive where the German army hoped to push through the Allied lines and advance in a north-westerly direction to seize the Channel Ports, which supplied the British Expeditionary Force (BEF) and to drive the BEF into the sea.
The offensive ended at Villers-Bretonneux, to the east of the Allied communications centre at Amiens, where the Allies managed to halt the German advance; the German Armies had suffered many casualties and were unable to maintain supplies to the advancing troops.
William died of his wounds on March 21st and is buried in Faubourg D'Amiens Cemetery, France.

ROBINSON FRED
Rifleman, 1st Battalion
Monmouthshire Regiment
Service No. 2142
Died 11 May 1915, age 29
Buried Tyne Cot Cemetery, Belgium

Fred, son of George Harry and Rhoda Robinson, (nee Stephens), was born on November 27th 1885 and baptised on April 6th 1886 at St Mary's Church, Brynmawr. The family moved to Rogerstone and George worked as a school attendance officer for the local education board.
Fred started on August 31st 1892 at Tydu Infants School, Rogerstone before moving to Tydu Boy's School on October 7th 1892. He left school on July 5th 1899.
In 1911 he was working as a butchers assistant while living at 163 Corporation Road, Newport, the home of Sidney Hockey and his family.
Fred enlisted at Newport in the 1st Battalion Monmouthshire Regiment, landing in France with them on February 13th 1915.
He was severely injured on May 8th during the Battle of Ypres and taken prisoner by the German army. He died of wounds at a German Field Hospital in Staden, Belgium on May 11th.
Fred was initially buried in the German Military Cemetery at Staden before being exhumed and reburied at Tyne Cot Cemetery, Belgium at a later date.
His headstone inscription reads *"He maketh the storm to cease so that the waves thereof are still"*.
Fred is remembered on a number of local memorials in Risca and surrounding areas including Bethany Baptist Church, Bethesda Church, St. Basil's Church Gates and St. Woolos Cathedral Memorial, Newport.

ROSE JOHN
Stoker, 1st Class
Royal Navy, HMS Vivid
Service No. 9389
Died 2 April 1918, age 24
Buried Risca Old Cemetery, Risca

Born June 17th 1895, in Gloucester, John was the son of James and Elizabeth Rose.
It appears that James died early 1901 as in the 1901 census, Elizabeth was a widower in 38 St Mary's Square, Gloucester with John, Emily aged 3 and Lily V aged 2 months. Elizabeth gave birth to another son, William Rose in 1902.
Elizabeth moved to south Wales and married Edward Kirkpatrick in 1905, and went to live firstly at 23 Full Moon Cottages, then 1 Full Moon Road, Cross Keys,

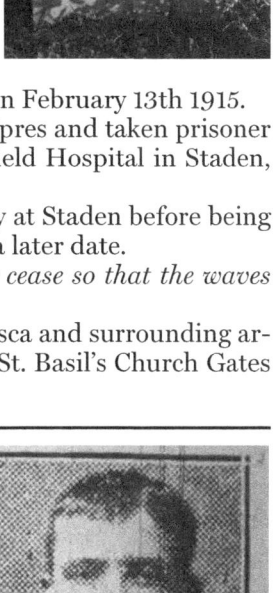

later living at 36 Bright Street, Cross Keys.
John joined the Royal Navy on October 7th 1913 and was stationed at HMS Vivid, the RN Barracks at Devonport. John served as a stoker on HMS Marlborough, Sandhurst and Rowena, being at the Battle of Jutland aboard the Marlborough.
His service record shows he was 5ft 3ins tall with a 36ins chest. He had brown hair, hazel eyes and a fresh complexion, with a number of tattoos on both arms.
Whilst serving on HMS Rowena he contracted pneumonia and died from pulmonary embolism on April 2nd 1918.
John is buried in Risca Old Cemetery, Cromwell Road, Risca.

ROWLANDS DAVID FRANCIS
GUNNER, 124TH BRIGADE
ROYAL FIELD ARTILLERY
SERVICE NO. 740919
DIED 16 OCTOBER 1917, AGE 20
BURIED LOCRE HOSPICE CEMETERY, BELGIUM

David, the son of John and Rose Ann Rowlands, (nee Brewster), was born in France on January 1st 1897.
He attended Pontywaun County School being admitted on November 13th 1909 and leaving in the summer of 1913, prior to this he attended Cwmcarn Council School.
In 1911 he lived in 2 Jamesville, Cwmcarn with his three brothers and sister. After leaving school he became a Pupil Teacher in Cwmcarn School.
David enlisted in Newport as a Signaller in the Royal Field Artillery.
During the Battle of Arras, he, with an officer, laid a telephone wire back to the observing station, and for this was recommended for the Military Medal.
Age 20, he died of wounds in a French Field Hospital on October 16th 1917 and is buried in Locre Hospice Cemetery, Belgium.
David is remembered on the Pontywaun County School, Cwmcarn Institute and Cwmcarn War memorials.
His younger brother Tudor Stephen Rowlands was killed in WW2.

SAGE WILLIAM JAMES
PRIVATE, 2ND BATTALION
MONMOUTHSHIRE REGIMENT
SERVICE NO. 265269
DIED 30 NOVEMBER 1917, AGE 23
REMEMBERED CAMBRAI MEMORIAL, FRANCE

William, son of Isaac and Elizabeth Sage, (nee Hewlett), was born in Risca in 1895.
They lived in Pontywain in 1901 and Isaac's occupation was shown as a coal miner below ground.
Their address in 1911 was given as Cross Keys; Isaac was still employed as a miner, as was his son Charles, William was shown as a baker. The census also shows that Isaac and Elizabeth had eleven children but only five were still living.
In May 1913, William enlisted in the Territorial Army serving as Private 1707 with the Monmouthshire Regiment; he was living at 52 Twyncarn Road, Pontywain at this time.
He went to France with the 2nd Monmouthshire Battalion, part of the British Expeditionary Force, on November 5th 1914 sailing from Southampton.
They spent the winter taking part in trench warfare near Armentieres.
William was admitted to No 2 Clearing Hospital on 4 January 1915 with frostbite.
They subsequently took part in the Second Battle of Ypres in April and May 1915, fighting alongside the 1/1st and 1/3rd Monmouths in the 28th Division. Such were the losses that the three battalions were temporarily amalgamated. By July 1915 the 1/2nd had been brought up to strength and resumed its own existence.
On January 30th 1916 they left the 4th Division moving to the Lines of Communication, becoming a Pioneer Battalion on May 1st 1916.
In July they went into action at the Battle of the Somme. William was wounded and on July 4th 1916 he returned to England suffering from a gunshot wound to his arm sustained three days earlier. He was released from hospital on July 15th 1916.
He remained in England until May 23rd 1917 when he returned to France once again.
The Battalion was involved in the Battle of Langemarck near Ypres, from August 16th-18th 1917 and the Battle of Passchendaele before moving south to contest the Battle of Cambrai.
William was reported missing on November 30th 1917 and is remembered on the Cambrai Memorial, Louverval, France.
He is commemorated on the Trinity Church, Pontywain, Roll of Honour.

SALATHIEL EWART GLADSTONE
2ⁿᵈ Lieutenant, 4ᵗʰ Battalion
South Wales Borderers
Died 17 July 1916, age 27
Buried Rogerstone (Bethesda) Chapel Yard, Wales

Ewart was born at Newport in 1889, the son of Philip and Justina Salathiel, (nee Protheroe).
In 1891 the family lived at 3 Wilson's Row, Lower Machen, where Philip was recorded as a labourer in the tinworks. In 1901 their address was Ochrwyth and in 1911 they lived at Cwmynant, Pontymister. At this time though, Ewart was a student and boarding with a Richard Lewis in Towyn, Montgomeryshire.
He later studied at Aberystwyth University where he was a keen sportsman, playing tennis and football. He also played cricket for Pontymister Cricket Club 2nd X1.
After the outbreak of war, on October 9th 1914, Ewart was commissioned into the 4th Battalion, South Wales Borderers, which was attached to 40 Brigade, 13th (Western) Division.
The Division had fought at Gallipoli in 1915, before being evacuated to Egypt. On February 12th 1916 the Division began to move to Mesopotamia, to strengthen the force being assembled for the relief of the besieged garrison at Kut al Amara.
Ewarts medal card shows he arrived in Egypt on April 22nd 1916.
He then appears to have been sent to France and was attached to the 1th Battalion, South Wales Borderers which was attached to 115 Brigade, (38th Welsh) Division. Ewart was wounded by a sniper during the attack of 115 Brigade at Mametz Wood on July 7th 1916. He returned home for treatment, dying in hospital at London before his parents, Phillip and Justina could get there.
He died on July 17th 1916 aged 27 years and is buried in Rogerstone (Bethesda) Baptist Chapel yard.
Ewart is remembered on the Aberystwyth University and Pontywaun County School memorials.
Some of the above information was kindly supplied by the late Mrs Bernice Williams of Risca and Steve John, West Wales War Memorial Project.

SHEEHAN DANIEL
Corporal, 'A' Battery 86ᵗʰ Brigade
Royal Field Artillery
Service No. 74622
Died 13 November 1918, age 23
Buried Premont British Cemetery, France

In the 1881 census, Daniel Sheehan, born in Ynysddu, was shown as a driver in the Royal Artillery at Sheffield Barracks.
He married Emily Moore in Sheffield, Yorkshire, early 1884. In 1891 the family

including 3 children are living in The Castle on Holy Island, Northumberland, where Daniel is now shown as a Gunner with the Royal Artillery.

A son, Daniel was born in Scarborough in 1895. By 1901 the family had moved from Yorkshire and were living in Bright Street, Cross Keys where Daniel senior was working in a local colliery as a coal labourer below ground.

In 1911, still living in Bright St, Daniel Jnr was employed as a coal miner hewer's boy. On October 8th 1913, he followed his father's footsteps and joined the Royal Field Artillery.

His service records appear not to have survived but his Medal Index Card shows that he was in the 42nd Brigade RFA.

He was stationed at Preston and Salisbury Plain and in his letters home, he told how he enjoyed his army life apart from a period on Salisbury Plain where he complained about the food and the lack of coal *"for months at a time"*.

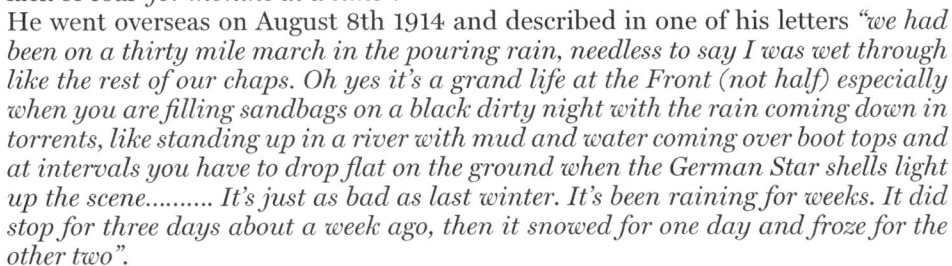

He went overseas on August 8th 1914 and described in one of his letters *"we had been on a thirty mile march in the pouring rain, needless to say I was wet through like the rest of our chaps. Oh yes it's a grand life at the Front (not half) especially when you are filling sandbags on a black dirty night with the rain coming down in torrents, like standing up in a river with mud and water coming over boot tops and at intervals you have to drop flat on the ground when the German Star shells light up the scene........... It's just as bad as last winter. It's been raining for weeks. It did stop for three days about a week ago, then it snowed for one day and froze for the other two"*.

At some stage he transferred to 'A' Battery 86th Brigade.

On October 31st 1918 he was admitted to the 50th Casualty Clearing Station where he died of broncho pneumonia (after effects of influenza) on November 13th, two days after the Armistice.

He was buried on November 14th at the British Soldier's Cemetery at Premont near Bohain, France.

SHORE JOSEPH
PRIVATE, 1ST BATTALION
WELSH REGIMENT
SERVICE NO 22573
DIED 25 MAY 1915, AGE 24
REMEMBERED YPRES (MENIN GATE)MEMORIAL, BELGIUM

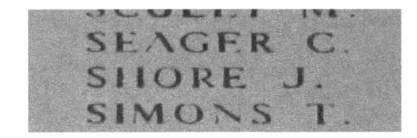

Joseph, born in Risca in 1890, was the son of Thomas and Jane Shore.
They lived near the New Inn Public House in the 1891 and 1900 censuses; by 1911 they had moved to 7 Coronation Street, Pontymister.
Joseph worked at the Tin Works as a tin sheet doubler as did his younger brother William.

He married Ellen Turner in 1913, the marriage producing a son, Joseph a year later. Joseph enlisted at Newport into the 1st Battalion Welsh Guards going to France on January 18th 1915. He was killed whilst fighting around Ypres just a few months later on May 25th 1915.

As he has no known grave, Joseph is commemorated on the Menin Gate Memorial, Ypres, Belgium.

SIBLEY JOHN DAVID
Driver, Guards Division, Ammunition Column
Royal Field Artillery
Service No. 20008
Died 1 August 1917, age 37
Buried Dozinghem Military Cemetery, Belgium

John was born in 1880 in Ynysddu, son of John and Gwen Sibley.

Employed as a miner, he married Sarah Ann Ashman in 1900, living in Bright Street, Cross Keys before moving to 23 Railway Street, Risca by 1911.

According to the census they had five children, two who died in infancy. The children living with them were Annie, David and Oliver.

John enlisted at Newport into the Royal Field Artillery, serving as a Driver, Service Number 2008, with the Guards Division, Ammunition Column.

His medal card shows that he went abroad on July 27th 1915 to Gallipoli. He later went to France where he was wounded and died in No 61 Casualty Clearing Station on August 1st 1917.

John is buried in Dozinghem Military Cemetery, Belgium.

This cemetery was one of many that was used for casualties of the Battle of Passchendaele.

SKINNER FREDERICK
Private, 1st Battalion
South Wales Borderers
Service No. 8690
Died 31 October 1914
Remembered Ypres (Menin Gate) Memorial, Belgium

Fred, born in the Cwmbran area, was baptised on December 30th 1881 at Llanfrechfa Upper, the son of William and Mary Skinner, (nee Quilford).

Brought up with his family in Cwmbran, he moved to the Risca area to work in the local pit as a miner.

He enlisted in Cwmbran in the 1st Battalion, South Wales Borderers as Private 8690, going to France on August 13th 1914.

The 1st Battalion South Wales Borderers were at the forefront of the action at Gheluvelt where Fred along with hundreds of others, was killed just a few weeks after arriving in France.

Fred is remembered on the Menin Gate Memorial, Ypres, Belgium.

SMITH ERNEST WILLIAM
PRIVATE, 16TH BATTALION
CHESHIRE REGIMENT
SERVICE NO. 200768
DIED 22 OCTOBER 1917
REMEMBERED TYNE COT MEMORIAL, BELGIUM

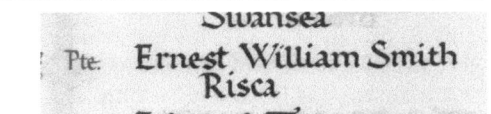

Swansea
Pte. Ernest William Smith
Risca

Very little is known about Ernest apart from he was born around 1895, supposedly in Risca. His grandmother was Mary Smith, his mother was called Elizabeth and he had an Aunt Agnes.
He enlisted in the 16th Battalion Cheshire Regiment at Birkenhead, Liverpool presumably after 1915 as he wasn't awarded the 1914 or 1915 Star.
The 16th (Service) Battalion (2nd Birkenhead) landed at Le Havre as part of the 105th Brigade in the 35th Division in January 1916.
They fought at the Battles of the Somme where they suffered severe losses. New recruits were received but many were found not to be of the same physical standard as earlier recruits and were transferred to the Labour Corps.
The following year they saw action in the push to the Hindenburg Line and at the Second Battle of Passchendaele.
Ernest was killed in action on October 22nd 1917 and is commemorated on the Tyne Cot Memorial.
He is commemorated in the Welsh National Book of Remembrance.

SMITH WILLIAM HENRY
PRIVATE, 130TH (ST JOHN) FIELD AMBULANCE
ROYAL ARMY MEDICAL CORPS
SERVICE NO. 48190
DIED 1 MAY 1918, AGE 31
BURIED RISCA OLD CEMETERY, RISCA, WALES

William, the son of Henry John and Margaretta Smith, (nee Roberts), was born in St John's, Cardiff in December 1886.
His father Henry, who worked as a plasterer, moved with his family to 24 Jamesville, Cwmcarn. By 1901 they moved again to Back Lane, Cross Keys and afterwards to 2 North Road, Pontywain.
William, along with his brother George also worked as a plasterer and slater.
Trained in first aid and ambulance duties and a member of the St John Ambulance Association at Abercarn Colliery, he underwent a medical examination at Abercarn on December 7th 1914 and was passed fit. He duly enlisted in the army on December 12th 1914 at Cardiff, serving as a Private in the 130th (St John) Field Ambulance, Royal Army Medical Corps.
His records described him as 5ft 11ins tall, weighed 154 lbs with a sallow complexion, brown eyes and light brown hair.
After undergoing initial training in Wales until August 1915, the 130th travelled to Winchester to finalise their instruction. On December 3rd 1915 they marched to

Southampton and boarded the SS Kamak which left for Le Havre at 5.00 pm.
William, and the 130th were attached to the 38th Welsh Division which saw action at the first battles of Ypres and La Bassee. Later in 1916 they were at Mametz Wood during the Battle of the Somme and the following year at Passchendaele.
On October 13th 1917, he reported sick in France with shortage of breath and low blood pressure.
William was admitted to East Leeds War Hospital, Yorkshire where he was diagnosed with Morbus Addisonii – Addison's Disease. This is a long-term endocrine disorder in which the adrenal glands do not produce enough steroid hormones.
In 3 months he had lost nearly two and a half stone in weight.
It was recorded that although the condition was not caused by his military service it was aggravated by it along with exposure and strain.
His discharge papers were signed at Woking on January 10th 1918 as he was deemed no longer fit for war service.
William returned home to North Road, Pontywain where he died on May 1st 1918 and is buried in Risca Old Cemetery, Cromwell Road, Risca.
He is remembered on the Cwmcarn War Memorial.

STACEY EXTON JAMES
PRIVATE, 6TH BATTALION
SOUTH WALES BORDERERS
SERVICE NO. 19648
DIED 2 MAY 1916, AGE 33
BURIED ECOIVRES MILITARY CEMETERY, FRANCE

Born in Abercarn in 1882, Exton was the son of John and Sarah Ann Stacey, (nee Jones).
John was a tinplate worker living in Pantyresk, Mynyddislwyn. He married Sarah in 1881 and they had three children from the marriage.
John died in 1889 and Sarah then married a Richard Fletcher.
Exton lived in The Spiteful, Cwmcarn before moving with the family to Provident Place, Risca, later moving to Thornes House, Wattsville.
He was a miner when he enlisted as a Private in the 6th Battalion South Wales Borderers, Service Number 19648.
Exton arrived in France on September 24th 1915. The 6th Battalion went to France as the Pioneer Battalion of the 25th Division spending the winter in the Armentieres sector working in flooded trenches.
They were at Vimy and Neuville St. Vaast in the spring of 1916 consolidating the craters of mines blown under the German lines.
Exton was injured and died of his wounds on May 2nd 1916 and is buried in Ecoivres Military Cemetery, Mont-St. Eloi, France.

STEPHENS RICHARD EVAN
Gunner, 112ᵀᴴ Battery, 24ᵀᴴ Brigade
Royal Field Artillery
Service No. 97035
Died 7 March 1916, age 20
Buried Etaples Military Cemetery, France

Richard, born in Treorchy in 1895 was the son of George and Mary Stephens.
The family lived in the Rhondda area before moving to Cross Keys. In 1911 Richard was living with his Grandmother, Rachel Jones in 7 Medart Place, Cross Keys.
Richard enlisted in Newport into the Royal Field Artillery, serving with the 112th Battery, 24th Brigade. He went overseas with them on March 11th 1915. Richard was admitted to No 18 General Hospital on February 12th 1916 and diagnosed with a fractured spine caused by gunshot. An operation was carried out on February 29th when it was found he had two fractured vertebrae.
Richard died of his wounds on March 7th 1916 and is buried in Etaples Military Cemetery, France.

STEVENS JOHN MM
Private, 4ᵀᴴ Battalion
South Wales Borderers
Service No. 13221
Died 15 February 1917, age 29
Remembered Basra Memorial, Iraq

John, born in Risca on November 20th 1887, was the son of Albert and Annie Stevens, (nee Rogers). In 1891 the family lived in Providence Place, Risca and Albert was employed as a coal miner.
John attended Risca Town School starting on September 28th 1891.
By 1901 they were still living in the same house and John had joined his father as a coal miner in the local colliery.
In 1908, John married Annie Maria Court in Cheltenham. They had a son John Alfred, born in Cheltenham in 1909. By 1911 they had moved to the Rhondda, living at 55 Madeline Street, Pontygwaith.
He went to Newport to enlist into the army joining the 4th Battalion, South Wales Borderers.
On June 29th 1915, the 4th Battalion embarked from Avonmouth for Mudros (a small Greek port on the Mediterranean island of Lemnos) arriving on July 12th 1915. On July 15th they landed in Gallipoli and fought through the campaign with distinction until being evacuated to Mudros and then on to Egypt. On February 15th 1916 they left Suez arriving in Basra on March 4th 1916.
As part of the 13th Division the 4th SWB took part in the battles of the spring of 1916 fought by the Mesopotamian Expeditionary Force to relieve Kut. These ac-

tions consisted mainly of desperate attacks on strongly entrenched lines carried out in cold, mud and rain with great hardships to the troops.

After the failure to relieve Kut, operations ceased until December 1916 until the next attempt to complete the advance through the Turkish defences. This was achieved and the troops advanced to Baghdad, the Battalion being the first British troops to enter the main city on April 11th 1917.

It was during this campaign that John Stevens won a Military Medal, the award being announced in the London Gazette on October 21st 1916.

John was killed on February 15th 1917 and is remembered on the Basra Memorial.

STEVENS TOM ALBAN
PRIVATE, 2ND BATTALION
SOUTH WALES BORDERERS
SERVICE NO. 30312
DIED 5 OCTOBER 1917, AGE 20
BURIED BLEUET FARM CEMETERY, FRANCE

The son of Arthur John and Emily Stevens, Tom was born in Risca on August 10th 1897. The family were living at that time in 10 Temperance Hill, Risca; Arthur was employed as a coal miner.

Tom attended Risca School starting on May 7th 1901 before transferring to the Mixed Department on August 14th 1905.

In 1911, Tom was employed as a tinplate worker, still living at Temperance Hill. The family later moved to 38 Grove Road, Risca.

It is not known when he enlisted into the 2nd Battalion South Wales Borderers at Abertillery, serving as Private 30312 but appears to be after 1915.

The 2nd Battalion saw action at Tsingtao in China in 1914 and Gallipoli in 1915 before arriving in France in March 1916. Here they fought at the Battle of the Somme. In 1917 they fought through the Third Battle of Ypres (Passchendaele) and then at Cambrai in November and December.

Tom was killed on October 5th 1917 and is buried at Bleuet Farm Cemetery, Belgium.

Originally his grave was marked with a cross, albeit with the wrong initial, H.

STROUD CHARLES HENRY
PRIVATE, 2ND BATTALION
ROYAL WELSH FUSILIERS
SERVICE NO. 6238
DIED 25 SEPTEMBER 1915, AGE 33
BURIED CAMBRIN CHURCHYARD EXTENSION, FRANCE

Charles, born in Monmouth in 1882, was the son of Charles and Adelaide Stroud, (nee Williams).

He was baptised on December 4th 1882, although his name is incorrectly recorded as that of his brother, James Henry who was born in 1880.

In 1891 they lived at Chippenham Gate Street, Monmouth with elder son James Henry; father Charles was employed as a painter.

On March 30th 1898 Charles, employed as a plasterer's labourer, enlisted into the Royal Monmouthshire Royal Engineers for 6 years. Age 16 years and 2 months, he is described as a *'Growing lad'*. He transferred to the Royal Welsh Fusiliers on December 7th 1899, serving as a Private.

Whilst with the RWF he went abroad and for 6 months served with the Garrison Police and Station Police in China, as well as serving in Agra, India.

He was discharged to the Army Reserve on October 1st 1907.

Charles joined the Monmouthshire Constabulary as a 3rd Class Constable on January 20th 1908.

He was at Head Quarters from January 20th 1908 until March 30th 1908. Charles transferred to Cross Keys on April 1st 1908 until May 10th 1908, when he moved the next day to Risca.

He resigned on July 31st 1908 after being suspended from duty for being under the influence of drink and causing a disturbance at Monmouth.

Charles married Jane Emma Chant in Neath in 1909, the marriage producing three children, Jane Emma (1910), Charles H (1912) and Frances J (1914).

In 1911 Charles, Jane and daughter Jane lived at 7 Ynysarwed Cottage, Neath Rd, Resolven. Charles was now employed as an underground labourer at Ynysarwed Colliery.

When war was declared he was called from the reserve into his old unit of the Royal Welsh Fusiliers, serving as Private 6238 in the 2nd Battalion. It appears he had returned to Monmouth where he enlisted; his wife's address given as Cinderhill Street, Monmouth.

In August 1914 the 2nd Battalion were in Portland before being mobilised and landing on August 11th, moving to Rouen as Lines of Communication troops.

On August 22nd 1914 they came under orders of 19th Infantry Brigade, which was not allocated to a Division but was an independent command at this time.

His medal card shows he was one of the first British troops to go overseas landing in France on September 22nd 1914.

Charles was killed on September 25th 1915, the first day of the Battle of Loos.

He is buried in Cambrin Churchyard Extension, Cambrin, France along with 34 other men of the 2nd Royal Welch Fusiliers who also died on the same day.

He is commemorated on the Monmouth War Memorial.

STROUD WILLIAM
REGIMENTAL SERGEANT MAJOR
130ᵀᴴ (ST JOHN) FIELD AMBULANCE
ROYAL ARMY MEDICAL CORPS
SERVICE NO. 48071
DIED 18 DECEMBER 1918, AGE 51
BURIED RISCA OLD CEMETERY, RISCA, WALES

William, born at Bramley, Hampshire in 1867 was the son of William and Jane Elizabeth Stroud, (nee Wickens). They lived in Pamber Heath, Hampshire where father William was a grocer and baker.
At the age of 14 he worked as a page boy for Thomas Peregrine, a London Physician, at his home in Silchester, Basingstoke.
Age 21, he married Keren Happuch Beale at Wallingford Register Office on March 6th 1888. They moved with their two children, Eleanor Martha and Agnes Sarah to 3 Feeder Row, Cwmcarn, living with her brother Job.
William was employed as a miner and was also a member of St John Ambulance, training in First Aid.
Sadly his daughter Agnes, aged 1 died in 1892; another child also died before 1911. They moved to Provident Terrace, Risca before moving back to Feeder Row living at No. 14.
At the outbreak of war, as he was First Aid trained, he joined the 130th (St John) Field Ambulance on December 12th 1914. For the first half of 1915 he trained with the unit at Prestatyn rising through the ranks to Regimental Sergeant Major.
They sailed to France on December 3rd 1915 and saw service at among other places, Mametz Wood in July 1916 and Pilkem Ridge during the third Battle of Ypres in July - August 1917.
Injured by shrapnel and poisoned by gas in May 1917 he continued until he was no longer fit for service and was discharged on August 15th 1918.
Admitted to hospital suffering from pleurisy and rheumatism, he died on December 18th 1918 in the Royal Mineral Water Hospital, Bath age 52.
He is buried at Risca Old Cemetery, Cromwell Road, Risca and is remembered on the Cwmcarn War Memorial, along with his son William John Stroud.

STROUD WILLIAM JOHN
DRUMMER, 1ˢᵀ/2ᴺᴰ BATTALION
MONMOUTHSHIRE REGIMENT
SERVICE NO. 1312
DIED 19 DECEMBER 1916, AGE 24
BURIED ST. SEVER CEMETERY EXTENSION, FRANCE

William John, one of twelve children to William and Keren Happuch Stroud, (nee Beale) was born in Risca in 1892.

In 1901 the family were living in Provident Terrace, Pontywain before moving to 14 Feeder Row by 1911.
William John, like his father was a miner employed in the local colliery.
The military records show he enlisted at Abercarn and joined the 2nd Battalion Monmouthshire Regiment as a drummer, landing at Le Havre, France on November 7th 1914.
They spent the winter taking part in trench warfare near Armentières, France and subsequently took part in the Second Battle of Ypres in April and May 1915, fighting alongside the 1/1st and 1/3rd Monmouths in the 28th Division. They later fought on the Somme before moving back to Ypres in 1916. In early October the Battalion again returned to the Somme battlefield occupying a camp at Montauban. As they were now a Pioneer Corp, their work was extremely hard, dangerous, and exhausting. Throughout November they battled against the mud and enemy and completed two long communication trenches, known as Flank Avenue and Flers Alley.
This work was heart-breaking as due to the weather the trenches would either collapse or be full of water when the men returned to carry on their duties. The weather in December got even worse and the men were exhausted from their efforts. They were rumoured to be relieved but no-one believed them as there had been rumours before. Sometime in this period William was injured and succumbed to his wounds on December 19th 1916. The Battalion were relieved the next day and moved to Foudrinoy for three weeks rest.
William is buried in St Sever Extension Cemetery, Rouen, France. He is remembered on the family grave at Risca Old Cemetery, and with his father William Stroud on the the Cwmcarn War Memorial.

SULLIVAN WALTER ERNEST
Second Lieutenant
Welsh Regiment
Died 19 April 1918
Buried Doullens Communal Cemetery Extension, France

Walter Ernest, born in Pontymister, Risca in 1891, was the son of John and Kate Sullivan, (nee Powell).
More commonly known by the name of Ernest, he lived in Pontymister until about 1897 when the family moved to 19 Tower Street, Treforest, Pontypridd, later 19 Laura Street.
His father John was a furniture dealer, whilst Ernest worked as an assistant teacher.
On September 17th 1914, he joined the Royal Army Medical Corps (Territorials) serving with the Second (Reserve) Welsh Field Ambulance.
His height was 5ft 8ins, with a chest measurement of 35 1/2ins, he had good vision

and good physical development.
He stayed with the RAMC (T), until November 11th when he enlisted into the Regular Army, serving with the Welsh Regiment.
Ernest was promoted to Temp 2nd Lieutenant on January 25th 1917 and sometime later was awarded the Military Cross. He was with B Company, 13th Battalion Welsh Regiment
His citation read: *"T. / 2nd Lt. Walter Ernest Sullivan, Welsh Regiment For conspicuous gallantry and devotion to duty in leading his platoon. He was the first to enter an enemy strong point, which he captured, afterwards personally searching several dug-outs and collecting a number of prisoners from them. During the whole action he set a splendid example, and was untiring in his efforts to cheer his men in most adverse weather conditions."*
He was attached to 114th Brigade, H.Q. when he died of his wounds on April 19th 1918.
Ernest was buried in Doullens Communal Cemetery, France.

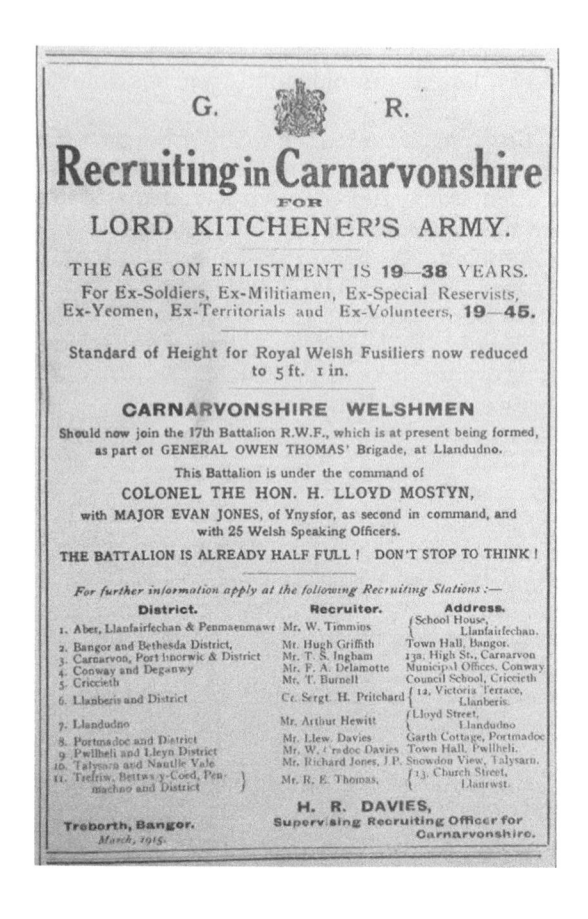

G. R.

Recruiting in Carnarvonshire
FOR
LORD KITCHENER'S ARMY.

THE AGE ON ENLISTMENT IS **19—38** YEARS.
For Ex-Soldiers, Ex-Militiamen, Ex-Special Reservists, Ex-Yeomen, Ex-Territorials and Ex-Volunteers, **19—45**.

Standard of Height for Royal Welsh Fusiliers now reduced to 5 ft. 1 in.

CARNARVONSHIRE WELSHMEN

Should now join the 17th Battalion R.W.F., which is at present being formed, as part of GENERAL OWEN THOMAS' Brigade, at Llandudno.

This Battalion is under the command of
COLONEL THE HON. H. LLOYD MOSTYN,
with MAJOR EVAN JONES, of Ynysfor, as second in command, and with 25 Welsh Speaking Officers.

THE BATTALION IS ALREADY HALF FULL! DON'T STOP TO THINK!

For further information apply at the following Recruiting Stations:—

District.	Recruiter.	Address.
1. Aber, Llanfairfechan & Penmaenmawr	Mr. W. Timmins	School House, Llanfairfechan.
2. Bangor and Bethesda District,	Mr. Hugh Griffith	Town Hall, Bangor.
3. Carnarvon, Port Dinorwic & District	Mr. T. S. Ingham	13a, High St., Carnarvon
4. Conway and Deganwy	Mr. F. A. Delamotte	Municipal Offices, Conway
5. Criccieth	Mr. T. Burnell	Council School, Criccieth
6. Llanberis and District	Cr. Sergt. H. Pritchard	12, Victoria Terrace, Llanberis.
7. Llandudno	Mr. Arthur Hewitt	Lloyd Street, Llandudno
8. Portmadoc and District	Mr. Llew. Davies	Garth Cottage, Portmadoc
9. Pwllheli and Lleyn District	Mr. W. Cradoc Davies	Town Hall, Pwllheli.
10. Talysarn and Nantlle Vale	Mr. Richard Jones, J.P.	Snowdon View, Talysarn.
11. Trefriw, Bettws-y-Coed, Penmachno and District	Mr. R. E. Thomas,	13, Church Street, Llanrwst.

Treborth, Bangor.
March, 1915.

H. R. DAVIES,
Supervising Recruiting Officer for Carnarvonshire.

T

TAYLOR CHARLES
Private, 10ᵗʰ Battalion
Royal Welsh Fusiliers
Service No. 33843
Died 29 September 1917
Buried Dozinghem Military Cemetery, Belgium

Charles was born about 1885 in Risca, but no other details of his early life are known.
In 1915 he lived in Tywn Gwyn Terrace, Cross Keys, working as a collier, and his father John lived in No 3 Villa, near Roger's Shop, Cross Keys.
Charles enlisted at Newport on July 5th 1915 into the South Wales Borderers and was assigned to the 3rd Battalion as Private 35041.
His service record shows he was 5ft 8 ½ins tall, with a 32ins chest and had tattoos on his hand and arm.
The following month he transferred to the 1st Garrison Battalion of the Royal Welsh Fusiliers and went to Gibraltar. Whilst in Gibraltar he was reported for a few misdemeanours.
In July 1916 he was drunk in the barracks, which resulted in a punishment of being confined to barracks for five days. He was also admonished on two further occasions, once for causing a nuisance and damaging bedding and later for being drunk and returning to barracks late in the evening on June 29th 1917.
On September 5th 1916, Charles passed a swimming test of 100 yards in saltwater.
He embarked at Gibraltar on July 22nd 1917 for transfer to the British Expeditionary Force in France, where he joined the 10th Battalion Royal Welsh Fusiliers on August 25th 1917. He would have been in action at the Battle of the Menin Bridge Ridge, between September 20th to 25th 1917.
Charles was wounded and died on September 29th 1917 at No. 47 Casualty Clearing Station.
He is buried in Dozinghem Military Cemetery, Belgium.

TAYLOR JOHN WILLIAM
Lieutenant, 1ˢᵗ / 2ⁿᴰ Battalion
Monmouthshire Regiment
Died 12 March 1915, age 37
Buried Calvaire (Essex) Military Cemetery, Belgium

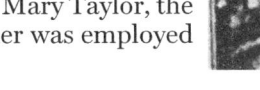

Born in Leicester in 1881, to John and Mary Taylor, the family moved to Wales where his father was employed as a miner.

In 1901, John, still living with his parents, was employed as an Assistant Schoolmaster. A very accomplished rugby player he captained Cwmcarn Rugby team and played at both wing and outside half for them. He was also selected as a reserve wing three quarter for the Welsh team in 1901.

He married Ethel Hester Sweet, in 1909. They had two children, Doreen and Frederick and lived at Fronheulog, Cwmcarn in 1911.

At the time of the outbreak of WW1, John had been on the staff of Pontywaun County School for over eleven years, formerly as a mathematical master and later as Head of the Commercial Department.

In 1912, he received his commission as Second Lieutenant in the 2nd Mons Territorials and was appointed First Lieutenant a couple of months before the outbreak of war. Part of the British Expeditionary Force in 1914, he was killed in action at Ypres on March 12th 1915.

The War Diary states: *"March 12th Lieutenant JW TAYLOR killed, B3 trench, shot in head".*

John is buried in Calvaire (Essex) Military Cemetery, Belgium.

He is commemorated on a number of local memorials, including the Cwmcarn and Pontywaun County School Memorials.

THOMAS EVAN HENRY
PRIVATE, 1ST BATTALION
WELSH GUARDS
SERVICE NO. 713
DIED 10 SEPTEMBER 1916, AGE 27
REMEMBERED THIEPVAL MEMORIAL, FRANCE

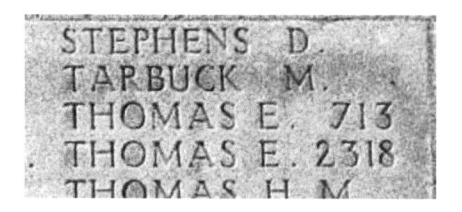

Evan, son of David and Ann Thomas, was born in Risca in 1888.

The family lived in Colliery Row, Risca in 1901 before moving to 20 Well Place, Aberdare by 1911 where children David and Ann were born. The census shows they had been married for 25 years and that they had 9 children but that 3 had died.

Both David and Evan were employed as coal miners.

From his service record, we know that Evan was a 5ft 10¼ins tall with a 39ins chest, weighed 11 st 12 lb and was of good character.

Age 26, Evan enlisted into the 12th Service Battalion Royal Welsh Regiment on January 4th 1915 but just 9 days later was discharged as being medically unfit due to *'flat feet'*.

Undeterred Evan travelled to Mountain Ash and enlisted again, but this time into the Welsh Guards as Private 713.

His service number indicates he joined in early March 1915, whilst his Medal Index Card shows he landed in France on August 17th 1915.

The following is an extract from *'Welsh Guards at War'* by Major LF Ellis.

"The Welsh Guards were formed on February 26th 1915 and in three days had recruited around 600 men, many of these coming from other Guards regiments. The Welsh Guards sailed for France on August 17th 1915 whilst recruiting continued in Britain. They landed at Le Havre on August 18th

and joined the 3rd Guards Brigade, Guards Division.
A month later the Welsh Guards went into action for the first time in the Battle of Loos and their bearing was held to have been "up to the best Brigade of Guards standard." "Loos" is the first Battle Honour borne on the Colours of the Regiment.
During the winter of 1915-16 the Battalion was occupied with the rest of the Guards Division in trench warfare. In the summer of 1916 they fought at the battle of the Somme, taking part in actions at Ginchy, Flers-Courcelette and Morval, all three of which were awarded to the Regiment as further Battle Honours.
Ginchy, 1½ km north east of Guillemont and situated at the crossing of six roads, stood on a high plain that defended Combles and was a forward position in the German defence.
The 7th Division had captured Ginchy on September 3rd but over the next few days heavy fighting saw attack and counter attack before it was finally recaptured on the 9th.
The Germans again counter attacked on the 10th and the Guards Division were forced to fight off a number of attempts to retake the village".

Evan and another Welsh Guardsman, Edwin White were killed during this day. Evan is remembered on the Thiepval Memorial, France and in St Margaret's Church, Risca.

THOMAS FRANK
PRIVATE, 4TH REGIMENT SOUTH AFRICAN INFANTRY
SERVICE NO. 2938
DIED 19 NOVEMBER 1916
BURIED IN ALDERSHOT MILITARY CEMETERY, HAMPSHIRE.

Frank was born in Aberystruth around 1866.
There is not much detail about his life but it appears that he attended Blaina Boy's School being admitted on June 20th 1870.
He lived with his grandmother Ann Thomas in Queen Street, Aberystruth in 1871 before moving to live with his uncle John Hayes and family at Old Cwmcarn Road, Pontywain. The census recorded him as working in the lamp house at the local pit.
The next record shows that he had enlisted in the South African Infantry and was killed on November 19th 1916. It is possible that he joined the army earlier and went to South Africa, fought in the Boer War and stayed there after the war finished.
He is buried in Aldershot Military Cemetery, Hampshire.

THOMAS GEORGE DAVID MM
Private, 14ᵀᴴ Battalion
Welsh Regiment
Service No. 58458
Died 30 October 1918, age 19
Buried Montay-Neuvilly Road Cemy. Montay, France

George, the son of Evan and Mary Thomas, was born in Nantymoel in 1899.
Living at 16, Commercial Street, Nantymoel, Llandyfodog, Bridgend, Evan was an ironmonger and painter.
In 1911, George and his younger brother Emlyn, were living with their uncle Rhys Prothero at 18 Hillside, Risca.
Aged just 17, George enlisted in the South Wales Borderers on November 27th 1916. He went on the army reserve until mobilised on April 19th 1918 joining the British Expeditionary Force in France on September 5th 1918. He then transferred to the 14th Battalion Welsh Regiment, the 'Swansea Pals' a week later.
The 14th, as part of 38th Welsh Division, fought from September 12th to October 12th 1918 in the Battles of the Hindenburg Line. This was a series of very large scale offensive operations to advance to and break through the Hindenburg Line system. Their objectives were achieved in what is now regarded as one of the British Army's greatest military achievements. Capitalising on their success they pushed across the Selle and Sambre rivers recapturing Valenciennes and then liberating Mons.
George was killed in action on October 20th 1918 and is buried in Montay-Neuvilly Road Cemetery, Montay, France. He is commemorated on the Bethany Church Memorial, Risca.
He was awarded the Military Medal and this was reported in the London Gazette Supplement on May 14th 1919.

THOMAS WILLIAM
Private, 6ᵀᴴ Battalion
Welsh Regiment
Service No. 265422
Died 15 November 1917
Buried White House Cemetery, Belgium

William, born in Risca, enlisted at Maesteg as a Private in the 1/6th (Glamorgan) Battalion Welsh Regiment.
The 1/6th (Glamorgan) Battalion Territorial Force was stationed at Swansea as part of the South Wales Brigade.
He landed in Le Havre, France as part of the British Expeditionary Force on October 29th 1914 working in the Lines of Communication.
In July 1915 they transferred to the 84th Brigade of the 28th Division, later being

transferred to the 3rd Brigade of the 1st Division.
They became a Pioneer Battalion of the 1st Division and saw action on the Somme. The following year they were involved in the German retreat to the Hindenburg Line and The Second Battle of Passchendaele.
William died on November 15th and is buried in White House Cemetery, St. Jean-Les-Ypres, Belgium.

THOMAS WILLIAM GEORGE
Private, 11th Battalion
South Wales Borderers
Service No. 21988
Died 2 July 1916
Buried Loos British Cemetery, France

William was born in Maesteg about 1879. He married Elizabeth Ann Francis in 1899 and they lived in 7 Charles Street, Ystradyfodwg, Pontypridd, with their daughter Ethel. They later moved to Cwmbran, living at 23 St Dials Road in 1911, with their six children.
At the time of his enlistment, he gave his place of residence as Risca, although no other record of this can be found.
He joined the 11th Battalion South Wales Borderers as Private 21988, landing in Le Havre, France on December 4th 1915. He was at some stage attached to 220th Field Company Royal Engineers.
In the spring of 1916 the 11th Battalion, as part of the 38th Welsh Division, spent time in the line at Givenchy before being involved in the Battle of the Somme.
William was killed on July 2nd 1916 and is buried in Loos Cemetery, France.

TUDOR DOUGLAS
Rifleman, 1st Battalion
Monmouthshire Regiment
Service No. 3343
Died 15 October 1915, age 23
Buried Sailly-Labourse Communal Cemetery, France

Douglas, son of Lloyd and Eleanor Tudor, (nee Morrell), was born March 16th 1892 in Maesycwmmer. In 1901 they lived at 16 Ffrwd Terrace, Llanbradach and on July 8th 1902 he was admitted to Coed-Y-Brain Elementary and Junior School in Llanbradach.
School records show that he stayed there until June 1904 when he left to start work. They later moved to 2 Glen View, Ynysddu, by 1911 where Lloyd, Douglas and elder brother George are all working as coal miners.

Sometime after 1911 they moved to 36 Garden Suburbs, Pontywain, Cross Keys.
Douglas enlisted at Newport into the 1st Battalion Monmouthshire Regiment, serving as Private 3343.
The 1st Battalion had been in France from February 1915, and was involved in very heavy fighting straight away on the Ypres Salient, including being the target of the first German 'gas attack' on April 22nd 1915. Douglas, along with other reinforcements, didn't arrive in France until August 18th 1915.
On September 3rd 1915 they transferred as a Pioneer Battalion to 46th (North Midland) Division.
The Actions of the Hohenzollern Redoubt took place from 13-19 October 1915, at the Hohenzollern Redoubt (Hohenzollernwerk) near Auchy-les-Mines in France. In the aftermath of the Battle of Loos (September 25th – October 8th 1915), the 9th (Scottish) Division captured the strongpoint and then lost it to a German counter-attack. The 46th Division attack on October 13th failed and resulted in 3,643 casualties, mostly in the first few minutes. In the British Official History, J. E. Edmonds wrote that

"The fighting (from 13-14 October) had not improved the general situation in any way and had brought nothing but useless slaughter of infantry".

Douglas was injured and transferred No 3 Field Ambulance where he died of wounds on October 15th 1915, just 2 months after arriving in France.
He is buried in Sailly-Labourse Communal Cemetery, France.

TUTTON HARRY
Driver
Royal Engineers
Service No. 3343
Died 11 October 1918, age 28
Buried in Bangalore (Hosur Road) Cemetery, India

Harry, born September 1st 1890 in Risca, was the son of Arthur and Mary Ann Tutton, (nee Phillis). His parents were originally from Somerset before moving to Wales. He was baptised the following year in Shepton Mallet, Somerset on August 7th 1891, his address was recorded as Buddings Factory Cottages, Pontymister. The family later moved to The Bunch, Risca and then onto 3 Dixon's Place, Risca.
Harry was a boarder at 5 Tredegar Street, Cross Keys in 1911, working as a coal miner.
He enlisted at Newport as a Driver in the Royal Engineers, being posted to India, where he died of influenza on October 11th 1918.
Harry was buried in Bangalore (Hosur Road) Cemetery, India and also commemorated on the Madras 1914-1918 War Memorial, Chennai, India.
His brothers Alfred George, a Private in the Royal field Artillery and Reginald, a stoker on HMS Caesar, both survived the war.

TYLER GEORGE EDWARD VICTOR
GUNNER, 'D' BATTERY 177TH BRIGADE
ROYAL FIELD ARTILLERY
SERVICE NO. 13200
DIED 13 SEPTEMBER 1916, AGE 22
BURIED IN DELVILLE WOOD CEMETERY, FRANCE

Victor, one of five children to George Henry and Ellen Tyler was born in Newbridge on July 6th 1894. In 1901 the family were living in 23 Greenfield, Newbridge. When Victor attended Pontywaun County School in Risca on January 14th 1907, his address was 11 Twyn Gwyn Terrace, Newbridge. He left school on April 7th 1909 to work as a grocer's assistant, later employed as a coal miner.

He enlisted in Newport into the Royal Field Artillery, serving as Gunner 13200 in 'D' Battery, 177th Brigade, Royal Field Artillery.

CLXXVII Brigade, Royal Field Artillery, joined 16th (Irish) Division on the February 22nd 1916 in France. They were in action on the Somme during the Battle of Guillemont in which the Division captured the village and the Battle of Ginchy. The Brigade War Diary shows on September 13th 1916: Hardecourt

"Very quiet morning. Very misty and slight rain made observation difficult during the day. No infantry action – our artillery very active during the afternoon. The enemy retaliated on Leuze Wood and Ginchy. Special night shooting on enemy communications, tracks and roads.
No 13200 GR Tyler. V.J. D Bty Killed whilst repairing telephone lines".

His brother Ivor Tyler, Royal Welsh Fusiliers, was a Prisoner of War in WW1.

Victor was awarded the British War and Victory medals and is commemorated on the Pontywaun County School Memorial as well as the Celynen Collieries Roll of Honour, Zion Chapel and Newbridge War Memorials.

He is buried in Delville Wood Cemetery, Longueval, France.

HEROES OF ST. JULIEN AND FESTUBERT

Here's to the Soldier who bled
To the Sailor that bravely did fa':
Their fame is alive, though their spirits have fled
On the wings of the Year that's awa'.

SHALL WE FOLLOW THEIR EXAMPLE?
APPLY AT RECRUITING STATION

V

VENN WILLIAM GEORGE MM
Serjeant, 9th Battalion
Welsh Brigade
Service No. 53715
Died 6 February 1920, age 26
Buried in Risca Old Cemetery, Risca, Wales

William George was born in Nantyglo in 1893, his parents were George and Sarah Venn. In 1901 the family, along with a daughter Dorothy, lived at 67 Princess Street, Abertillery.
In 1911 they lived at Alexandra House in Six Bells where both father and son's occupations are listed as coal hewer. On February 22nd 1912 William enlisted for four years into 1/3rd Battalion Monmouthshire Regiment, a Territorial unit based at Abergavenny. His Service Number was 1263. When war was declared in August 1914, they were part of the Welsh Border Brigade, Welsh Division. They were mobilised to Pembroke Dock but had moved to Oswestry by August 10th and went on to Northampton by the end of August.
On October 6th 1914 he married Ethel Bright and they had three children, William George Stephen, Gilbert John and Kenneth.
In December the regiment moved to Bury St Edmunds and then to Cambridge in January 1915. On the February 14th they left the Division and proceeded to France to join 83rd Brigade, 28th Division who were concentrating in the area between Bailleul and Hazebrouck. In 1915 they were in action in The Second Battle of Ypres, suffering heavy casualties. On May 27th they amalgamated with the 1/1st and 1/2nd Battalions, resuming their own identities on August 11th. He suffered a gunshot wound to the knee on May 10th 1915 and was admitted to No 11 General Hospital and then returned to England.
On August 3rd 1915 he returned to France and was promoted to Corporal on August 10th. Just over a year later, on August 24th 1916 William joined 9th Entrenching Battery.
On September 21st 1916 he transferred to the 4th Reserve Battalion Welsh Regiment and then posted to the 9th Battalion Service Number 53715. In May 1918 he was injured in France, promoted to Searjant on August 15th 1918 and was awarded the Military Medal on November 26th 1918.
William returned to England on December 2nd 1918 and was diagnosed with VDH (valvular disease of the heart) attributable to the war.
He was demobilised on January 11th 1919, living at Glenrose, Cromwell Rd, Risca. He was awarded a pension for his wife and two children until August 3rd 1920 but died on February 6th 1920 at Risca.
William is buried in Risca Old Cemetery, Cromwell Road, Risca and remembered on Abertillery War Memorial.

COUNTY OF CARNARVON

MEN ARE URGENTLY REQUIRED

FOR

THE ROYAL WELSH FUSILIERS

KITCHENER'S ARMY.

All information can be obtained and Recruits can be enlisted at any of the following Stations:

District.	Recruiter.	Address.
1. Aber, Llanfairfechan and Penmaenmawr	Mr. W. Timmins	School House, Llanfairfechan
2. Bangor & Bethesda	Mr. L. D. Jones	Town Hall, Bangor
3. Bettwsycoed, Trefriw and Penmachno	Penr.-Sergt.-Major Chesterman	Pont-y-Pair Hotel Bettwsycoed
4. Conway & Deganwy	Penr.-Q.-M.-Sgt. Thos. Ellis	Town Hall, Conway
5. Llandudno	Mr. Arthur Hewitt	Lloyd St., Llandudno

Treborth,
Bangor.
Oct. 26th, 1914.

H. R. DAVIES
Recruiting Officer for Carnarvonshire.

GOD SAVE THE KING.

Jarvis & Foster, Printers, Bangor.

W

WALKER EDWARD JAMES
Company Quartermaster Sergeant
3rd Australian Pioneers
Service No. 1608
Died 4 March 1917, age 27
Buried in Risca Old Cemetery, Risca, Wales

Edward was born in Clifton Hill, Victoria, Australia in 1889, the son of Edward Aquila and Lilly Mary Walker, (nee Harvey).
Edward Aquila, who emigrated to Australia in the early 1880's, had been the organist at the Bethany Baptist Church, Risca. He married Lilly in 1887 in Victoria.
Edward James married Dorothea Francis Ellen Austin in 1916 also in Victoria, living at Jenkin Street, Northcote, Victoria.
His service records show that he was a Hardware salesman, 5ft 8ins tall, weight 10 stone 8 lbs with a chest measurement of 34-36ins. He is described as having a sallow complexion with blue eyes and dark brown hair.
Edward enlisted into the Australian Military forces on January 24th 1916, serving firstly with the 10th Depot Battalion, as a Private, before transferring to the 3rd Pioneer Battalion.
The Battalion sailed for the United Kingdom aboard HMAT Wandilla, on June 6th 1916 arriving at Plymouth on July 26th, before transferring to Larkhill Garrison on Salisbury Plain for training.
Edward was admitted to Fargo Military Hospital on February 16th 1917, being promoted to Acting Company Quartermaster Sergeant on March 1st 1917. He died of pneumonia at 08:15 pm on Sunday March 4th 1917.
Following his death, Sergeant Walker's body was brought to Risca, to the home of his cousin John Walker. On Saturday March 10th 1917 the residents of Risca witnessed a full military funeral. A service was held in the Bethany Baptist Church before the coffin, covered with the Union Jack, was conveyed to his last resting place of Risca Cemetery. A squad of the Royal Defence Corps formed the escort and firing party.
In response to a request from his widow on the circumstances of his death, Assistant Matron EM Bowes, wrote the following:

"He was admitted on Feb 16th. He was very ill from the day of admission but we were in hopes of his recovering. The last 2 or 3 days however he got very much worse and died of pneumonia on March 4th. His body was sent to his uncle, MJ Walker, 4 Tredegar Tce, Risca, Newport, Monmouth. QMS Walker's aunt came down to see him just a few days before he died and I understand she has written to his relatives in Melbourne. Please convey to his wife our sincere sympathy".

WALLACE JOSEPH
Lance Corporal, 5th Battalion
South Wales Borderers
Service No. 17527
Died 10 November 1916, age 42
Buried in Risca Old Cemetery, Risca, Wales

Joseph, born in 1874 in Risca, was the son of John and Mary Wallace, (nee Bacon). The Wallace family led an unorthodox way of life with Mary after having three children with her husband, had a son by her father in law, then John having a bigamous marriage before returning to live with Mary. He also spent time in Pennsylvania, America before returning and buying property including houses in Sarn Place, Mill Street, Church Road and American Villas, Risca.
In 1891 the family lived at Colliery Row, Risca.
Joseph married Eleanor Sarah Beechey on November 2nd 1896 at Newport Register Office.
They also lived in Colliery Row before moving in with Eleanor's (Lena) parents in Mount Pleasant Farm, Ochrwyth, where according to the 1911 census they had five children.
Joseph appeared numerous times in the local papers for his misdemeanours including poaching, trespassing in pursuit of rabbits, assault and riotous behaviour, at one time he was sentenced to three years' penal servitude.
Whilst working as a miner in the colliery, he enlisted in the South Wales Borderers as Private 17527, arriving in France with the 5th Battalion on July 17th 1915.
The South Wales Borderers had their first real taste of action at Loos in September 1915. The Battalion was kept busy in that area throughout the winter repairing roads, constructing tramways, improving trenches, and in mining in close proximity to the enemy. For this type of work the men of South Wales were unequalled.
On March 14th 1916, the Germans exploded a mine under a salient in the British line known as the 'Duck's Bill'. Half the salient was destroyed, and most of the garrison, including a working party of the battalion, were killed or wounded. A party of volunteers of the Battalion rushed across the open under heavy fire, losing two men killed on the way, reached the Duck's Bill, and with the rest of the garrison put up a fight which prevented the enemy from exploiting the success of the mine.
The Battalion showed their efficiency and courage by the digging and wiring of a new front line 750 yards in length and 150 yards out in No Man's Land in a single night, and so noiselessly as to escape entirely the notice of the enemy.
During the great battle of the Somme in 1916 the Battalion lost 220 men in the last ten days of July.
On July 26th 1916 whilst at Mametz Wood, Lance Corporal Joseph Wallace was carrying his friend, Private Mercy, wounded by an exploding shell, back to the trenches when a second shell exploded. A fragment of shrapnel penetrated his back

and lodged in his lung.
Joseph was treated at No 3 Casualty Clearing Station on July 27th before being transferred two days later.
He was evacuated back to England for treatment but on November 10th 1916 in the 1st Eastern General Hospital, Cambridge, he died from his wounds received in France.
Joseph is buried in Risca Old Cemetery, Cromwell Road, Risca.

WALSH THOMAS
PRIVATE, 5TH BATTALION
ROYAL IRISH REGIMENT
SERVICE NO. 10500
DIED 4 NOVEMBER 1918
BURIED CROSS ROADS CEMETERY, FONTAINE-AU-BOIS, FRANCE

Thomas was born in Cork, Ireland around 1880, the only other details are that his mother's name was Hannah.
The information of his time in th UK is also sketchy. It is known that he lived in 3 Clyde Street, Pontymister when he enrolled at Abertillery in the Royal Irish Regiment. He served with the 5th Battalion as Private 10500 probably signing up after 1915.
The 5th Irish fought in Gallipoli before being involved in the Palestine Campaign. On April 1st 1918, they transferred to the 52nd (Lowland Division) and moved soon after to France. Initially concentrated near Abbeville, they moved to the front line close to Vimy on May 6th.
On May 31st they transferred to the Lines of Communication and then to the 50th (Northumbrian) Division as a Pioneer Battalion on July 14th 1918. October 1918, saw them in action at the Battles of the Hindenburg Line, the Pursuit to the Selle and in the Final Advance in Picardy.
Thomas was killed on November 4th 1918 and was buried in Cross Roads Cemetery, Fontaine-Au-Bois, France.

WALTERS THOMAS HENRY
PRIVATE, 6TH BATTALION
SOUTH WALES BORDERERS
SERVICE NO. 17189
DIED 1 SEPTEMBER 1916, AGE 33
BURIED BLIGHTY VALLEY CEMETERY, FRANCE

Thomas Henry Walters was born in Cwmdows, Newbridge, on January 21st 1883, son of Henry and Margaret Walters.
On June 2nd 1890 he was admitted to Newbridge Boy's School, leaving on June 19th 1896 to start work as a collier, at this time he was living at 20 Whitethorne, Newbridge.

Thomas signed up at Cardiff for 6 years to the 3rd Battalion, Welsh Regiment on January 27th 1901, serving as Private 1340.

His service records record his Height as 5ft 4ins, Weight 124 lbs, Chest 32 ½ins, Fresh Complexion, Brown Eyes, Brown Hair and gave his religion as Protestant.

In 1905 he married Edith Harriett Griffiths and in 1911 they lived at 3 Hawthorn Row, Pontywain. Thomas was employed as a coal miner and they had 6 children, William Henry, Edith May, Iris Irene, Thomas, Lilian and John.

Thomas enlisted into the South Wales Borderers at Newport and was assigned to the 6th Battalion serving as Private 17189.

After training, the Battalion left Tourney Barracks, Aldershot to travel to Southampton Docks. They embarked for Le Havre on board the Archimedes arriving in France on September 24th 1915.

As the Pioneer Battalion of the 25th Division they spent the winter in Armentieres sector doing heavy work in flooded trenches. The following spring saw the battalion in Vimy and Neuville St. Vaast consolidating the craters blown under the German line. They were continually shelled and at times had to break off their work to repel attacks, but eventually handed over a thoroughly well organised position to the relieving infantry. This exploit was rewarded with two Military Crosses and five Military Medals. In the Battle of the Somme the battalion was continuously employed. On one occasion they carried out a magnificent piece of pioneer work by digging 700 yards of communication trench from one captured trench to another (the Regina Trench) under heavy shell fire.

Only good discipline and a fine spirit could have accomplished this task and the battalion was deservedly complimented upon it.

(The above information was taken from the 6th Pioneer Battalion South Wales Borderers WW1 factsheet published by the Royal Welsh Museum.)

The war diary for September 1st 1916, although very difficult to read, shows the battalion was at Aveluy, a village north of Albert.

'A' and 'C' Company working in Leipsic Salient, 'B' on a light tram line and 'D' at 4th Avenue in Brimstone.
Killed in action 1106/17189 Pte WALTERS. T

Thomas was buried in Blighty Valley Cemetery, Authuille Wood, France. He is remembered on the Cwmcarn Institute and Cwmcarn War Memorials.

WARD DANIEL
No further information found
Commemorated on Risca Workingmen's Club Memorial, Risca, Wales

The name Daniel Ward is commemorated on the Risca Workingmen's Club memorial in Risca.

There were only 2 men killed in WW1 that fit the name criteria, none of which seem

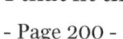

to have any link to Risca.
Daniel Ward : Lance Corporal I/3435 - 1st/1st Bn. Monmouthshire Regiment Age 19. Died 21.08.1916 - Buried Bienvillers Military Cemetery, France - Son of Edward Ernest and Annie Elizabeth Ward, of 3 Gordon St., Newport.

Daniel Charles Ward - Private 49454 - 1st/4th Battalion Welsh Regiment - Age 28. Died 03.11.1917 - Buried Beersheba War Cemetery, Israel - Son of Charles John Thomas and Sarah Ward, of 38, Bishton St., Newport.

WATKINS HERBERT GEORGE
PRIVATE, 4TH BATTALION
SOUTH WALES BORDERERS
SERVICE NO. 12473
DIED 9 AUGUST 1915, AGE 24
BURIED AZMAK CEMETERY, TURKEY

Herbert was born in Risca in 1891, one of eight children to George Henry and Elizabeth Leah Watkins, (nee Chivers).
He was baptised on September 4th 1892 along with his sisters Hilda May and Fanny at St Mary's Parish Church, Risca. In 1893 he was admitted to Risca School.
According to the 1901 census they lived near the Viaduct, their address in 1911 was the Star Cottage, Risca. George was employed as a colliery stoker and Herbert as a collier, also shown on the census was Charles George Prout, a visitor.
He enlisted at Newport into the South Wales Borderers serving with the 4th Battalion as Private, 12473.
The 4th Battalion was formed at Brecon in August 1914 and became part of 40th Brigade, 13th Division. On June 29th 1915 they embarked from Avonmouth for Mudros on the Greek island of Lemnos, arriving on July 12th.
On July 15th they were sent to Gallipoli in an effort to capture the Peninsula. The Battalion served with distinction through the campaign and was chosen as the rearguard in the evacuation of Suvla Bay in December 1915, an honour it had fully earned.
He arrived in Gallipoli on July 19th 1915 and was killed just 20 days later.
The following was published in the South Wales Gazette on Friday September 17th 1915.
"Bore Himself as a Soldier Should"
A letter relating to the circumstances in which Private Hebert Watkins, of Risca, was killed in action has been received by Mrs. Watkins his mother, from Sergeant Charles Prout, son in law, to whom about twenty Turks surrendered some time ago.
The letter says :
"It is with sincere regret that I have to inform you that your son Herbert was killed on the 9th. instant by shrapnel, while carrying a message to headquarters to the officer commanding "A" Company. He always bore himself as a soldier should and died doing his duty for his King and

country. It will give you some comfort to know that he was decently buried and a rough wooden cross marks his grave.
Today, Wednesday, August 11th. is the first intimation I had of it, and I hasten to let you know I am quite alright and have been in the thick of the firing line. I have given and taken some hard knocks.
Several Risca boys out here have been wounded - one named Durban, who was hit by shrapnel in the leg, the others whom I do not know. I believe the general situation is favourable but we get little or no news from the other fronts. The engagement we are now in has been on continuously for five days and nights. We hope to bring the matter shortly to a successful and satisfactory finish."
In a postscript Sergeant Prout says that he has been wounded in the back, but says that the wound is slight.
Charles Prout was later killed in France on July 30th 1917.
Herbert is buried in Azmac Cemetery, Suvla, Turkey and commemorated on St Mary's Church Memorial in Risca.

WATTS HERBERT IVOR
DRIVER, 'D' BATTERY 110TH BRIGADE
ROYAL FIELD ARTILLERY
SERVICE NO. 740695
DIED 27 AUGUST 1918
BURIED DANTZIG ALLEY BRITISH CEMETERY, FRANCE

Born in Risca in 1897, Herbert was the son of Edgar George and Elizabeth Ann Watts, (nee Richards).
In 1901 they lived at 4 Tredegar Place, Pontymister with their three children, Gwladys, Herbert and Archie.
By 1911 their address had been redesignated to 7 Tredegar Terrace, Pontymister and they were now living with seven children.
Edgar was a coal miner whilst Herbert aged 13 was a tin worker.
Herbert enlisted at Newport into the Royal Field Artillery, serving as a Driver in 'D' Battery, 110th Brigade.
The 110th Brigade, Royal Field Artillery was raised to support the 25th Division, and landed in France on September 25th 1915.
The 25th Division was heavily involved in the Battle of the Somme in 1916. The following year in May and June, it took part in the Battle of Messines, and in July and August, in the Third Battle of Ypres, also known as Passchendaele.
During the German offensive of March 1918 near Bapaume on the Somme, the 25th Division lost half of its strength. They were moved close to Ploegsteert and were caught in the renewed German attack in the Battle of the Lys in April. Here they lost two thirds of the strength during five days of heavy fighting whilst withdrawing to Bailleul.
The Third Battle of The Aisne, from May 27th to June 6th 1918 again saw the Division take heavy losses which resulted in the Service Battalions broken up and the Divisional HQ returned to England to rebuild.

The remnants of the Divisional Artillery stayed in France supporting other formations.
They were then attached to the 12th Division, which after a brief rest, attacked again on August 22nd, pushing right across the wilderness of the old Somme battlefield, capturing Meaulte, Mametz, Carnoy, Hardecourt and Faviere Wood, which was reached after a week's continuous fighting.
Herbert was killed during the battle and is buried in Dantzig Alley British Cemetery, Mametz, France.
He is remembered on the Bethany Church Memorial in Risca.

WATTS PERCY EDWIN
PRIVATE, 2ND BATTALION
SOUTH WALES BORDERERS
SERVICE NO. 11827
DIED 25 JULY 1915, AGE 19
BURIED PINK FARM CEMETERY, TURKEY

Percy, eldest son of Edwin and Elizabeth Ann Watts, was born in Risca in 1895.
Living in 1 Tredegar Place in 1901, Edwin's occupation was a florist. The 1911 census shows the family are living in the same house although the address was now 10 Tredegar Terrace and Edwin was a gardener, whilst Percy was employed as a colliery labourer.
He joined the 2nd Battalion South Wales Borderers, in Newport.
On January 12th, 1915, the Battalion on its return from China, landed at Devonport, and joined the 87th Brigade of the 29th Division billeted at Coventry, Rugby and neighbouring towns.
They left England in March for the attack on the Gallipoli Peninsula. They hoped to open a passage for ships through the Straits of Helles into the Sea of Marmora and on through the Bosporus at Constantinople into the Black Sea. This would enable the Russians to export the grain needed by the Allies and to import munitions of war.
On April 25th, 1915, the 29th Division made the historic landing at Helles. Landing in broad daylight on open beaches defended by barbed wire, they were attacked by the enemy with rifles and machine guns at close range. The Battalion landed three Companies at S Beach on the shores of Morto Bay just inside the Straits at the comparatively light cost of 2 officers and 18 men killed and drowned and 2 officers and 40 men wounded. 'A' Company and the King's Own Scottish Borderers and Marines landed at Y Beach on the Mediterranean shore.
Although successful, the attack was unsupported and they had to withdraw. 'A' Company encountered heavy fighting during the retreat, losing the Company Commander and 26 men killed and missing, and an officer and 42 men wounded. The Battalion served throughout the rest of the Gallipoli campaign. In the efforts to advance from Cape Helles in May and June it fought with great determination and stubbornness.
On July 24th and 25th the Battalion were involved in the decking of new trenches

and raising the level of the road and constructing a containing wall.
Percy, age 19, was injured and taken to the 87th Field Ambulance for treatment, but died of his wounds on July 25th 1915.
He is remembered on the Special Memorial at Pink Farm Cemetery, Helles and on the memorial at Moriah Baptist Church, Risca.

WEBB WILLIAM
PRIVATE, 5TH BATTALION
ROYAL BERKSHIRE REGIMENT
SERVICE NO. 39028
DIED 19 SEPTEMBER 1918, AGE 21
REMEMBERED VIS-EN-ARTOIS MEMORIAL, FRANCE

William was the eldest son of William and Annie Webb, (nee Thomas). Born in Llanwonno, Glamorgan in June 1897, he was one of 14 children to the couple; 5 of whom died before 1911.
In 1901 the family with five children, lived at Canal Parade, North Risca with Annie's mother Ellen.
William attended Park Street School, Cross Keys from September 24th 1901 until February 5th 1904 when he moved to the Junior School. He stayed here until January 11th 1913 before leaving to start work.
They also lived at 31 Tredegar St before going on to 27 Islwyn Road, Wattsville.
William was recorded as working at the Nine Mile Point colliery.
William enlisted at Newport into the Army Service Corps as Private T4/035785, later transferring to the 5th Battalion Royal Berkshire Regiment as Private 39028. The 5th (Service) Battalion was part of the First New Army, part of Kitchener's Army, and joined the 35th Brigade attached to the 12th (Eastern) Division. They saw their first action in 1915 at Loos, then in 1916 at the Battle of Albert and Pozières in 1917. In 1918 the 5th Battalion was transferred to the 36th Brigade, still with 12th Division.
William was killed on September 19th 1918 and is commemorated on the Vis-en-Artois Memorial, France.
He is remembered on the Pontywaun Wesleyan Church and School Memorial.

WELCH ERNEST AUGUSTUS
CORPORAL, 1ST BATTALION
MONMOUTHSHIRE REGIMENT
SERVICE NO. 2115
DIED 13 MAY 1915, AGE 25
REMEMBERED YPRES (MENIN GATE) MEMORIAL, BELGIUM

Born in 1890 in Abertillery, Ernest was the son of Frederick and Clara Welch, (nee Edwards).
After being brought up in Abertillery, Ernest moved with his family to Birmingham where his father

worked as a night watchman. By 1911, Ernest had moved to Ammanford working as a miner.
His parents had moved to 4 Clifton Road, Rogerstone, later living at 11 Newport Road, Pontymister.
He was living in Rogerstone when he enlisted at Newport in the 1st Battalion, Monmouthshire Regiment, where he served in 'C' Company as a Corporal.
Ernest landed in France on February 13th 1915, with the 1st Battalion, which had been posted to the 28th Division along with the 3rd Monmouthshire Battalion. Almost immediately they were in action in the Ypres Salient. Joined by the 2nd Monmouthshires, all three Battalions came in for very severe fighting; the 1st had a company involved in supporting the right of the Canadians by counter-attacks as early as 24th April 1915, though most of the Battalion and all the 3rd were holding the 28th Division's front line until the withdrawal to a shorter line nearer Ypres on the night of May 3rd-4th.
The intense fighting of May 8th, saw the 1st and 3rd Battalions severely depleted in the defence of the Frezenberg position.
On May 8th, arguably one of the worst days in the whole struggle, the 3rd Monmouths, near Frezenberg and the 1st, away to their left, north-east of Wieltje were both in hastily constructed defences. Here they felt the full force of a tremendous period of shelling by an attack in great force.
Both Battalions were so badly decimated, that by the end of the day their survivors between them hardly amounted to a war-strength Company.
Ernest was killed in action on May 15th and is remembered on the Menin Gate Memorial in Ypres. He is commemorated on the memorial in Bethany Baptist Church, Risca.

WELCH GILBERT GEORGE
PRIVATE, 13TH BATTALION
DURHAM LIGHT INFANTRY
SERVICE NO. 54240
DIED 13 OCTOBER 1917, AGE 19
BURIED GODEWAERSVELDE BRITISH CEMETERY, BELGIUM

Gilbert was born in Pontywain on November 30th 1897, son of George and Beatrice Welch, (nee Tuck).
He attended Park Street Infant's School, Cross Keys, starting on May 7th 1901 until moving to the Mixed Department on August 15th 1904.
At the time the family were living at 15 Provident Terrace, before moving to 23 Park Street, Cross Keys.
Gilbert left school on October 21st 1910 to start work, although on the 1911 census he is not shown as being employed. He was later employed as a coal miner.
On August 26th 1914, he was living at 1 Park View, Cross Keys when he enlisted at Newport in the South Wales Borderers as Private 13151. He was discharged

on October 12th 1914 for lying about his age on enlistment. He said he was 19 years 9 months old when he was only 16 years 8 months old.
He signed up again on April 22nd 1915 at Newport, this time with the Royal Field Artillery. He was again under age being 17 years and 4 months old.
His service records show him as 5ft 5ins, with a 36ins chest and with no distinctive marks.
Gilbert married Beatrice Caroline Tuck on May 31st 1916 at Portsmouth Registry Office.
Beatrice had a child Mona born in 1915 but the man she was due to marry was killed when his ship, HMS Cressy was torpedoed on September 22nd 1914.
They had a child, Beryl Georgina, born February 6th 1917 and baptised on February 25th at St Mary's Church, Portsea.
There is a possibility of another child Phyllis Beatrice, as her birth was recorded at the same time as Beryl's birth with the same mother's name.
Gilbert spent a period of time in the Training Reserve Battalion before being posted to the Durham Light Infantry on January 11th 1917 and arriving in Boulogne on April 1st 1917.
He contracted Bronchitis in June 1917 and was admitted to No. 16 General Hospital at Le Treport before returning to England for further treatment where he was hospitalised for 26 days.
After treatment he was posted to the 4th Battalion on August 4th 1917.
On August 23rd he was awarded 10 days detention for being absent from parade and a day later given another 14 days for insubordination and making a false accusation against an NCO.
Returning to France he was now with the 13th Battalion, which was in action in September, during the Third Battle of Ypres, fighting on the Menin Road.
Gilbert was admitted to 41 Casualty Clearing Station, where he died on October 13th, from his wounds received in action.
He was buried in Godewaersvelde British Cemetery, Belgium.

WEST WILLIAM JAMES
LANCE CORPORAL, 130th FIELD AMBULANCE
ROYAL ARMY MEDICAL CORPS
SERVICE NO. 48217
DIED 7 JULY 1916, AGE 31
REMEMBERED THIEPVAL MEMORIAL, FRANCE

William, son of David and Emma West was born in Cwmcarn in 1895. They are shown as living in 14 Feeder Row, Cwmcarn in 1891 and 1901 before the family moved to 1 Twyncarn Terrace by 1911.
William married Melinda Jones in 1909. They had 3 children, Melvyn George born in 1910, Trevor in 1912 and William Elvet in 1914. In 1911 they were living at 4 Twyncarn Terrace, Cwmcarn.
He enlisted in Cardiff into the Royal Army Medical Corps and served with the 130th Field Ambulance unit, landing in France on December 4th 1915.
The 130th Field Ambulance unit generally consisted of men who were St John first aiders and stretcher bearers employed in the mines. They were unique in World

War 1 as the only unit allowed to wear the St John insignia as part of their uniform.

The 130th were at the attack on Mametz Wood in July 1916, where William was acting as a stretcher bearer recovering wounded men from the 11th Battalion, South Wales Borderers and the 16th Battalion Welsh Regiment who were both fighting to capture the wood.

The duties of the stretcher bearers were hazardous as they had to leave the comparative safety of the trenches to carry the wounded men over open ground back to the Triangle, a rendezvous point where the injured men were transferred to the field hospitals.

William was making his second trip back over the open ground when he was decapitated by an allied shell which fell short, fragments of which injured two other men.

He was buried the following morning and the site marked with a wooden cross and William's details.

The grave was lost in the ensuing fighting and he is recorded on the Thiepval Memorial as well as a headstone and Roll of Honour at Trinity Church, Pontywain.

WHEELER WILLIAM BERTRAM
PRIVATE, 10TH BATTALION
SOUTH WALES BORDERERS
SERVICE NO. 23134
DIED 3 APRIL 1916, AGE 23
BURIED GUARDS CEMETERY, WINDY CORNER, FRANCE

William Bertram, known as Bert or Bertie, was the son of Richard and Rosina Wheeler, (nee West). Born on March 27th 1893 he attended Risca School being admitted on June 1st 1897 and transferred to the Mixed Department on July 31st 1901.

He had four sisters and they lived at 19 Colliery Row, Risca, where in 1911, he was working as a coal miner.

Bert enlisted in Newport into the South Wales Borderers serving with the 10th Battalion.

The 10th Service Battalion was raised by the Welsh National Executive Committee in October 1914. On April 29th 1915 they became 115th Brigade, 38th (Welsh) Division. They moved onto Hursley Park, Winchester then onto Hazeley Down in Southampton.

They embarked on the Empress Queen at Southampton and travelled to Le Havre, France landing on December 4th 1915.

Throughout December the Battalion were engaged in *'usual training'* at Robecq. After Christmas they were attached to the Guards Division and then instructed in Trench Warfare. On December 27th they went into the forward trenches for the first time at Levantie.

January 1916 was much the same with training at Robecq and in the trenches at Pont du Hem.

On January 30th the men were inspected by Lloyd George at Locon. February and March saw them in billets and trenches at Croix Barbee, Marmeuse, Le Touret and Festubert.

The Battalion moved to Givenchy on March 28th to give their support and relieved the 11th Battalion SWB on April 1st moving into the trenches. On April 3rd the Germans blew up a mine killing seven and wounding twenty men.

It was during this attack that Bert was killed just 6 days after his 23rd birthday.

He is buried in Guards Cemetery, Windy Corner, Cuinchy, France and remembered on the Ebenezer Primitive Methodist Church Memorial, Risca..

WHITE EDWIN
PRIVATE, 1ST BATTALION
WELSH GUARDS
SERVICE NO. 2129
DIED 10 SEPTEMBER 1916
REMEMBERED THIEPVAL MEMORIAL, FRANCE

Edwin, son of Rupert William and Martha Jane White, (nee Nicholls), was born in Smethwick, Shropshire around 1894.

Sometime before 1899 they moved to Ledwell, Sandford St Martin, Woodstock, Oxfordshire where Rupert worked as a farm labourer. They stayed here until at least 1911, when it appears the family moved to south Wales.

Edwin enlisted at Newport in the Welsh Guards, serving as a Private in the 1st Battalion. His Service Number of 2129, indicates he joined up between October and November 1915.

The Welsh Guards were only formed in February 1915 and were mobilised for war on August 18th 1915 and landed at Havre before joining the 3rd (Guards) Brigade of the Guards Division.

The 1st Welsh Guards fought in the Somme Offensive of 1916 and it was here that Edwin died in action.

He is commemorated on the Thiepval Memorial as well as the memorials in Bedwas and Trethomas and St Margaret's Church, Risca.

WIGMORE FRANK HAROLD
PRIVATE, 6TH BATTALION
SOUTH WALES BORDERERS
SERVICE NO. 6/17117
DIED 13 AUGUST 1917, AGE 21
BURIED LIJSSENTHOEK MILITARY CEMETERY, BELGIUM

Born in Risca in 1895, Frank was the son of Daniel and Sarah Ann Wigmore, (nee Flook).

In 1901 they lived at 14 Foundry Row, Pontymister, where Daniel worked in the foundry, before moving to 26 Grove Place, Griffithstown, Pontypool.

Daniel was employed as a cast iron dresser whilst Frank was a tinplate case maker's assistant in the Galvanised

Steel factory.
He enlisted into the South Wales Borderers, serving as Private, 6/17117, in the 6th Battalion.
The 6th Battalion was raised in South Wales in September 1914. They went to France as the Pioneer battalion of the 25th Division on 24 September 1915, spending the winter in the Armentieres sector working in flooded trenches.
They were at Vimy and Neuville St. Vaast in the spring of 1916 consolidating the craters of mines blown under the German lines.
They were continuously employed during the Battle of the Somme in the summer of 1916, on one occasion digging a 700 yard communication trench from one captured trench to another under heavy shell fire.
Their next major engagement was at Messines in July 1917. They were moved further north in August for the Third Battle of Ypres.
It was during this period, also known as the Battle of Passchendaele that Frank died of his wounds on August 13th 1917.
Frank is buried in Lijssenthoek Military Cemetery, Belgium and is remembered on Panteg Memorial.

WILCOX RAYMOND
No further information found
Commemorated on Bethany Church Memorial, Risca

The name of Raymond Wilcox is commemorated on the Bethany Chapel Memorial in Risca.
There were a few men killed in WW1 that fit the name criteria, none of which seem to have any link to Risca.
One possibility is Raymond Nathan Wilcox who died March 26th 1917.
He was born in 1896 in Forden, Montgomeryshire the son of Nathan and Mary Wilcox, (nee Jones).
He joined the 7th Battalion Royal Welsh Fusiliers, which fought in Gallipoli as part of the 158th Brigade, 53rd Division.
He is buried in Gaza War Cemetery, Gaza.
There were a number of Wilcox people living in Risca during WW1, including William Wilcox who was caretaker of Risca Cemetery and his son Edward James who later became Deacon of Bethany Chapel. As yet I cannot find a link between the families.

WILDE BENONI REX
Private, 6th Battalion
South Wales Borderers
Service No. 33173
Died 27 August 1918, age 21
Buried Arneke British Cemetery, France

Rex, born in Bassaleg on June 29th 1897, was the youngest son of Augustus 'Gus' and Margaret Ann Wilde, (nee Mallett).
In 1891, Gus and Margaret along with children, Gus and Jacqueline, were living at

17 Woodland Terrace, Rogerstone. Gus' occupation is shown as a carpenter and joiner. Another daughter Rosa was born in 1892.

His father Gus died in 1897 a few months before Rex was born. This had a massive impact on the family as in 1901 apart from Rex, the other children were living away from home. Gus was in an Orphanage in Bethnal Green, Jacqueline was living with a William and Alice Edwards in Abergavenny as their adopted daughter, and Rosa was living with her Uncle John and Aunt Rosa Jones in Stow Hill, Newport.

Margaret and Rex were living in 10 Nettlefold Terrace, Rogerstone and she was working as a dress maker.

Rex attended Tydu Boy's School in Rogerstone and later Rhiwderin Mixed School until leaving to go to Pontymister.

By 1911 they had moved to 2 Lyne Road, Pontymister and the family are all back together. Gus was a tin worker, Jacqueline 'Lena' was employed on domestic duties whilst Rosa was a shop assistant, whilst Rex had followed his father's occupation and was a joiner's apprentice. Margaret was now working as a certificated midwife.

Records show that she was enrolled on the Midwives Roll on June 30th 1904 after passing the Examination of the Central Midwives Board. She had been in practice since July 1901.

Gus and Rex, living now at 21 Commercial Street, Pontymister, both signed up to the army. Gus initially into the 1st Battalion Monmouthshire Regiment, later transferring to the Military Police.

Rex enrolled in the South Wales Borderers at Risca, serving as Private 33173. He served in the 11th, 7th and then 6th Battalions.

The 6th Battalion, raised in S Wales in September 1914, went to France as the Pioneer Battalion of the 25th Division a year later, spending the winter in the Armentieres sector working in flooded trenches.

They were at Vimy and Neuville St. Vaast in the spring of 1916 consolidating the craters of mines blown under the German lines.

They were continuously employed during the Battle of the Somme in the summer of 1916, on one occasion digging a 700 yard communication trench from one captured trench to another under heavy shell fire.

Their next major engagement was at Messines in July 1917, after which they were moved further north in August for the Third Battle of Ypres. The winter of 1917 was spent digging reserve lines and in March 1918 the 5th and 6th Battalions fought against the German drive on Amiens.

On April 10th the battalion lost 80 killed and wounded in a gallant attack on Ploegsteert village.

With the 5th Battalion, the 6th shared the Battle Honour of 'Aisne, 1918'. Here the weary battalion had to undergo the pressure of another attack, and performed the same heroic acts shown at the Battle of the Lys. It cost the battalion 250 casualties.

This was the last infantry fighting the Battalion encountered. In the subsequent

advance to victory in the summer and autumn of 1918 it was fully employed in repairing the communications, often in most difficult conditions and under heavy fire.
Rex was injured and moved to the 62nd Casualty Clearing Station at Arneke, Northern France where he died of his wounds on August 27th 1918.
He was buried in Arneke British Cemetery, France and remembered on the Bethany Church Memorial, Risca.

WILKIE CHARLES JOSEPH
LIEUTENANT COLONEL, 17TH BATTALION
WELSH REGIMENT
DIED 18 OCTOBER 1916, AGE 47
BURIED MAROC BRITISH CEMETERY, FRANCE

Charles was born in Melbourne, Australia on January 8th 1869, the only son of Joseph and Frances Elizabeth Muirhead Wilkie, (nee Paull). He was baptised at Christ Church, South Yarra on February 10th 1869. Joseph was a Captain in The Victoria Mounted Rifles, of Melbourne. He later became a proprietor of Wilkie, Webster & Allan, who owned a pianoforte and music warehouse in Melbourne.
Charles' father died on December 10th 1875 at Blacklands House, Chelsea.
The 1881 census shows him as a boarder at a school, in 37 and 38 Montpelier Crescent, Brighton aged 12 years. He later went on to be educated at Owen's College, Manchester.
His mother Frances married George Robathan, a surgeon from Risca in 1877. By 1891, they had moved to Grove Cottage, Risca and Charles was recorded as being a Lieutenant in the Militia.
Charles was gazetted as 2nd Lieutenant, The Oxfordshire and Buckinghamshire Light Infantry, from the Militia, on April 9th 1892 and was promoted to Lieutenant on July 18th 1893, becoming Captain on October 23rd 1899.
He married Dora George of Derw-allt, Rogerstone in 1897.
During 1897/98 the 2nd Battalion, Oxfordshire and Buckinghamshire Light Infantry was stationed at Tirah on the North West Frontier of India and Lieutenant Wilkie served with the Tirah Expeditionary Force, for which he received a medal with two clasps.
In 1899 he was invalided with malaria and dysentery and as a consequence he was unable to pass the medical board on the mobilization of the 1st Battalion, and was not allowed to go to South Africa.
Instead he was sent to Ireland and placed in command of mixed troops at Buttevant in 1900 for eight months.
During the period 1899-1902 he personally trained over 5,000 young officers and recruits, despatching them as drafts directly to the front in South Africa. He was Brigade Major in the Cork district for the manoeuvres in 1901. The following year he was appointed Adjutant to the South Middlesex Volunteer Battalion and to the

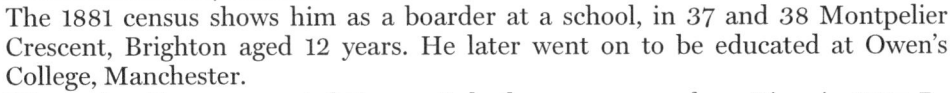

26th Middlesex (Cyclist) Battalion, London.
He retired from the Army on May 8th 1907 and joined the Reserve of Officers. He was appointed Brigade-Major for the South Wales Infantry Brigade in 1908, and in 1909 took over the secretarial duties of the Glamorgan Territorial Force Association. He took part in carrying out the mobilization in August and September 1914, was appointed Major in the 9th Battalion The Welsh Regiment on October 8th 1914 and promoted to Lieut.-Col. Commanding 17th Battalion on November 26th.
Lieutenant Colonel Wilkie was in command of the 17th Battalion The Welsh Regiment when it departed for France on June 2nd 1916 until his death at the age of 47.
He was tragically killed, together with his Second in Command, as recorded in the War Diary for October 18th 1916.

"Col. C. J. Wilkie (Commanding Officer) and Capt C. V. Lyne (acting Second in Command) were killed at about 3:45 p.m. by a High Explosive Shell at the junction of SOUTH STREET and ST JAMES STREET whilst on a tour of the trenches occupied by this unit as Support Battalion".

An officer who served under him wrote;

"Colonel Wilkie was a man amongst men and a soldier amongst soldiers. His attributes as a man were only equalled by his exceptional and far-reaching capabilities as a soldier. In the field his was a leader with a knowledge and personality which created absolute faith and trustfulness, and in the orderly room his administration was just exemplary. I had the honour and privilege of serving under him as an officer from Dec. 1914, until June 1916. During the time I learned his character as a man and his qualities as a soldier. Both were the finest I have known, and during that period I heard no word of complaint or reproach against him from any rank. The officers, non-commissioned officers and men of the Welsh Regiment knew him first as a soldier, and secondly as a gentleman, and as such they loved him as only soldiers know how to love. They would have followed him through anything, and would have rejoiced to have had the chance to do so. They knew that no injustice would be done to them provided Colonel Wilkie had a say in the matter. His loss will be felt amongst all ranks so deeply and so terribly that it is impossible for mere words to describe it".

Charles was buried in Maroc British Cemetery, Grenay, France.
He is commemorated on a stained glass window in St Basil's Church, Bassaleg and a memorial in Lisvane, Cardiff.

WILLIAMS ALBERT STANLEY
GUNNER, 'C' BATTERY, 312TH BRIGADE
ROYAL FIELD ARTILLERY
SERVICE NO. 740752
DIED 22 NOVEMBER 1918, AGE 22
BURIED MOUNT HUON MILITARY CEMETERY, FRANCE

Albert, son of William and Louisa Williams, (nee Whitmarsh), was born in Risca on January 5th 1896.

He started at Risca School on January 9th 1899 before transferring to the Mixed Department on July 31st 1903.

In 1901 William was a grocer living at 15 Church Terrace, Risca, before moving to 1 Sarn Place by 1911 where Albert was shown as working as a grocer's assistant.

Albert enlisted at Newport into the Royal Field Artillery, serving as Gunner 740752 in "C" Battery, 312th Brigade, Royal Field Artillery.

The 312th Brigade were a Territorial Force with the 62nd Division from formation in February 1915 until November 1918.

On August 31st 1914 the War Office issued instructions for all units of the Territorial Force to form a reserve unit. The men who had agreed to serve overseas were separated from the rest. Those left as 'home service only' were formed into 'second line' units, which would be this reserve. They were joined by many new recruits from September 1914 onward.

In March 1915, Divisional HQ moved to Matlock Bath and a number of moves were made in 1915 and 1916 before being inspected by King George V on July 26th 1916. The units made a final move to Northampton in October 1916, where orders were received to embark for France.

The Division crossed to France between December 30th 1916 and January 18th 1917 with concentration between the rivers Canche and Authie.

The Division then remained on the Western Front in France and Flanders for the rest of the war and took part in the many engagements including in 1917, the Operations on the Ancre, the German retreat to the Hindenburg, the Battle of Bullecourt, the Cambrai Operations and the capture of Bourlon Wood.

Further engagements in 1918 saw them in action at the Battle of Bapaume, the First Battle of Arras, and the Battles of the Scarpe, Selle and Sambre.

On November 9th the Division entered the southern outskirts of Maubeuge, crossed the Sambre and reached the Maubeuge-Avesnes road. The Division was selected to form part of the army which would advance across Belgium and occupy the Rhine bridgeheads, the only Territorial formation to receive this honour.

The move began on November 18th, although the Division halted December 1st – 9th between Ciney and Rochefort. The German border was crossed on December 15th and the last units reached the allotted area around Schleiden on Christmas Day.

Albert was wounded around this time and taken to the Le Treport Hospital, Northern France where he died of his injuries on November 22nd 1918.

He was buried in Mont Huon Military Cemetery, Le Treport and commemorated on the Ebenezer Primitive Methodist Church Memorial, now housed in the Chapel at Risca Old Cemetery, Cromwell Road, Risca.

WILLIAMS EDWARD BOURTON
Private, 1/5th Battalion
Welsh Regiment
Service No. 242129
Died 26 April 1917, age 20
Remembered Jerusalem Memorial, Israel

Edward, born in Wattsville in 1896, was the son of John and Isabella Jane Williams, (nee Symonds).
Initially living with Isabella's family at Llanover Terrace, Abercarn, they later lived at 41 Islwyn Street, Wattsville, Edward was working in the local pit alongside his father.
He initially enlisted as Private 28442 with the Liverpool Regiment before transferring as Private 242129 in the 1/5th Battalion, Welsh Regiment.
The 1/5th Battalion were a Territorial Force, part of the South Wales Infantry Brigade. Edward arrived in Gallipoli with the 1/5th on September 27th 1915.
On March 26th 1917, as part of the 53rd (Welsh) Division, they were involved in the First Battle of Gaza. Along with three other brigades, they advanced over open ground, suffering rifle and machine gun fire along with shrapnel to capture the Turkish fortifications in and around the town of Gaza.
Edward was presumed dead a few weeks later and is commemorated on the Jerusalem Memorial.
His brother Isaac, Royal Field Artillery, was killed in action in Belgium on October 15th 1918.

WILLIAMS ISAAC JOHN
Gunner, 'D' Battery 119th Army Brigade
Royal Field Artillery
Service No. 259655
Died 15 October 1918, age 21
Buried Harlebeke New British Cemetery, Belgium

Isaac, born in Wattsville in 1897, was the son of John and Isabella Jane Williams, (nee Symonds).
In 1901 they lived in Llanover Terrace, Abercarn with Isabella's family.
They later moved to 41 Islwyn Street, Wattsville, where Isaac was living when he enlisted in 'D' Battery, Royal Field Artillery, 119th Brigade, serving as Gunner 259655.
The 119th Brigade, originally the Welsh Bantam Brigade, was an infantry brigade formation during WWI.
Part of Lord Kitchener's 'New Armies', it served in the 40th Division on the Western Front.
Isaac was killed in action on October 15th 1918 and is buried in Harlebeke New

British Cemetery, Belgium.
His brother Edward, Welsh Regiment, was missing presumed dead at Gaza on April 26th 1917.

WILLIAMS OSWALD MORGAN
Second Lieutenant, 'B' Company
16th (Cardiff City) Battalion
Welsh Regiment
Died 9 April 1916, age 21
Remembered Loos Memorial, France

Oswald was born in Pontymister in 1893, the son of Edwin and Mary Williams.
In 1901, the family lived at the School House, Pontymister as Edwin was the head teacher at the Board School.
Oswald was educated at Llandovery College from 1908 until 1912, where he was Senior Prefect and Captain of the School. On leaving Llandovery, Oswald entered St John's College, Oxford, where he graduated with First Class Honours Moderations in Mathematics in 1913.
He enlisted into the Army in 1914, and was commissioned into 16th (Cardiff City) Battalion, Welsh Regiment in early 1915. The Battalion was attached to 114 Brigade, 38th (Welsh) Division, and moved to France during December 1915, taking up positions near Armentieres. In the April of 1916, Oswald was serving with 'B' Company of his Battalion at Givenchy, when on April 9th a raid was made on a German machine-gun emplacement.
As they attempted to place a 'Bangalore Torpedo' in the enemy wire, a bomb was thrown from the German trenches killing him. He was just 21 years old, and his body was never found.
Oswald is commemorated on the Loos Memorial, France.
He is remembered on the family grave at Risca Old Cemetery, Cromwell Road, Risca.

WILLIAMS THOMAS JOHN
Private, 1st Battalion
South Wales Borderers
Service No. 11764
Died 26 November 1914
Buried Bailleul Community Cemetery, France

Thomas was born in Cross Keys, the son of Emmanuel Williams.
He enlisted in Newport in 1st Battalion South Wales Borderers, serving as Private 11764.
The 1st Battalion South Wales Borderers played a massive part in the action to recapture Gheluvelt at the end of October 1914.
Thomas arrived in France on November 13th to join the Battalion who were in Zillebeke. Due to the large numbers of the draft of men they were ordered to remain at Brigade HQ until the next day.

After time at Outtersteene, they went into the trenches at Kemmel relieving the 9th Lancers and 18th Hussars.

Thomas was injured and died of his wounds at No 8 Clearing Hospital on November 26th. He is buried in Bailleul Communal Cemetery, France.

WILLIAMS WILLIAM JAMES
PRIVATE, 1ST BATTALION
WELSH REGIMENT
SERVICE NO. 7966
DIED 30 MAY 1915, AGE 31
BURIED BOULOGNE EASTERN CEMETERY, FRANCE

Known as James, he was born in Risca on August 11th 1883 to William and Matilda Williams.
The family moved shortly after to 25 Glamorgan Street, Aberdare where William was employed in the local pit.
By 1901 they moved to 13 Glamorgan Street and James was also now working in the pit.
In September 1901 he attested to the 3rd Battalion Welsh Regiment for a period of 6 years.
The records describe him as 5ft 4 1/2ins tall, weighed 9 stone 1 lb and had a 34ins chest. He had a fair complexion, dark blue eyes and dark brown hair.
He was also recorded as having a long narrow scar under his right shoulder blade and a small scar under left eye.
James married Amelia Davies in 1906 and by 1911 they had two children, Emily Jane and Amelia, living in 21 Glamorgan Street. They later had two more children, William James and Matilda Annie.
He enlisted in Aberdare into the 2nd Battalion Welsh Regiment.
His medal index card shows that James landed in France with the 2nd Battalion on August 13th 1914. That implies he was either a serving soldier of the regular army or was a reservist who had been recalled on 4-5 August.
He transferred to the 1st Battalion, Welsh Regiment and was serving with them when he was admitted to No. 11 General Hospital.
He died of his wounds on May 30th 1915 and was buried in Boulogne Eastern Cemetery, France.

WINSTONE WILLIAM JAMES
PRIVATE, 7TH BATTALION
ROYAL FUSILIERS
SERVICE NO. PS/9961
DIED 14 OCTOBER 1917, AGE 20
BURIED RISCA OLD CEMETERY, RISCA, WALES

William, son of William and Mary Ann Winstone, (nee Phillips), was born January 27th 1897 in Risca.
One of six children, William lived initially at 27 Danygraig Cottages before moving to the Copper Works, Risca. He was living here, when on November 10th 1909, he

moved from Danygraig Council School and was admitted to Pontywaun County School, leaving in the summer of 1913.
By 1911, the family had moved to 15 Danygraig Cottages, Risca.
William, a student, enlisted on November 29th 1915 into the Royal Fusiliers being sent to the Army Reserve the following day.
He was posted to the 29th Reserve Battalion on December 14th 1915, later transferring to the 7th Battalion serving as Private PS/9961.
William went abroad with the 7th Battalion and landed at Le Havre on July 24th 1916. There they joined the 190th Brigade, 63rd (Royal Naval) Division.
They were involved at the Battle of the Ancre in 1916, and during early 1917, the Operations on the Ancre and the Second Battle of the Scarpe.
His records show he had contracted Tubercular Disease of the Lungs which originated in 1916 as a cough whilst in Etaples, France. William was discharged on May 11th 1917 from 2nd Southern General Hospital, Bristol, as no longer physically fit for War Service.
He was awarded the Silver War Badge, number 183155 on May 22nd 1917. This badge was issued in the UK and the British Empire to service personnel who had been honourably discharged due to wounds or sickness from military service in World War 1.
He was admitted to Beechwood Hospital, Newport on October 3rd. William died on October 14th 1917 and was buried in Risca Old Cemetery, Cromwell Road, Risca.
He is remembered on the Bethany Church and Pontywaun County School Memorials.

ROLL OF HONOUR
MEMORIALS

Cross Keys and Pontywain

Gladstone Street, Primitive Methodist Church

> This tablet is erected in honour to those of this Church & School who served in THE GREAT WAR. And to the Sacred Memory of
> Alf William Bressington. Robert Brayshaw.
> A. William Hartshorn. Thomas James.
> Arthur John Rawlings.
> Who made the supreme sacrifice.
> "Greater love hath no man than this, that a man lay down his life for his friends."

This is now housed in the Cemetery Chapel at Risca Old Cemetery, Cromwell Road, Risca.

Bressington, Alfred William
Brayshaw,* Robert
Hartshorn, Arthur William
James, Thomas
Rawlings, Arthur John

* No further information can be found linking this man to the Risca area.

Hope Baptist Church

Sited in Hope Baptist Church, High Street, Cross Keys

Brown, Oliver
Dollery, Frank
Evans, William Jones
Lott, Willie
McGregor, Charles

Pontywaun Wesleyan Church & School

"So they passed over, & the trumpet sounded for them on the other side." Bunyan

Edwin Budgett.	Mar 18, 1917.	Henry Haynes.	Sep. 8, 1918.
Richard Morris.	Aug. 1, 1917.	Arthur Edwards.	May 30, 1918.
James Morris.	Jun 22, 1918.	Willie Green.	Oct 22, 1918.
Abner Lewis.	May 22, 1918.	Willie Webb.	Sep 18, 1918.
Reggie Gill.	Nov 11, 1918.	Herbert Robbins.	Oct. 27, 1918.
Joseph Godden.	Mar 25, 1918.	Herbert King.	Sep 8, 1918.

This is now housed in Cross Keys Methodist Church, High Street, Cross Keys.

Budgett, Edwin
Edwards, Arthur
Gill, Reggie
Godden, Joseph
Green, Willie
Haynes, Henry
King, Herbert
Lewis, Abner
Morris, James
Morris, Richard
Robbins, Herbert
Webb, Willie

St Catherine's Church

> St. Catherine's Church,
> Crosskeys.
>
> 1914 – 1918 WAR
>
> W. Attwell   L. Evans
> S. J. Carter   F. Leonard
> W. Chick   W. Pugh
> A. Edwards   J. Rose
>   T. Warren
>
> 1939 – 1945 WAR
> Douglas Betty
> Courtenay Purnell
> David Daniel Thomas, Priest.

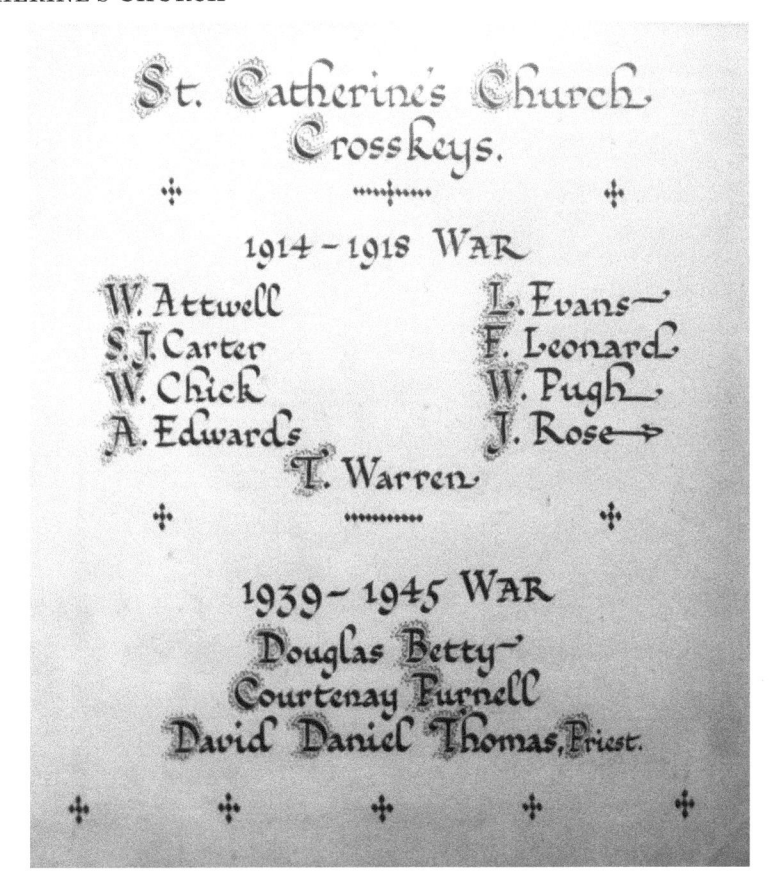

This is now housed in St Mary's Church, Church Road, Risca.

Attwell, William
Carter, Simeon John
Chick, William
Edwards, Arthur
Evans,* L
Leonard, Frederick
Pugh,* W
Rose, John
Warren,* T

* No further information can be found on these names.

Trinity Chapel

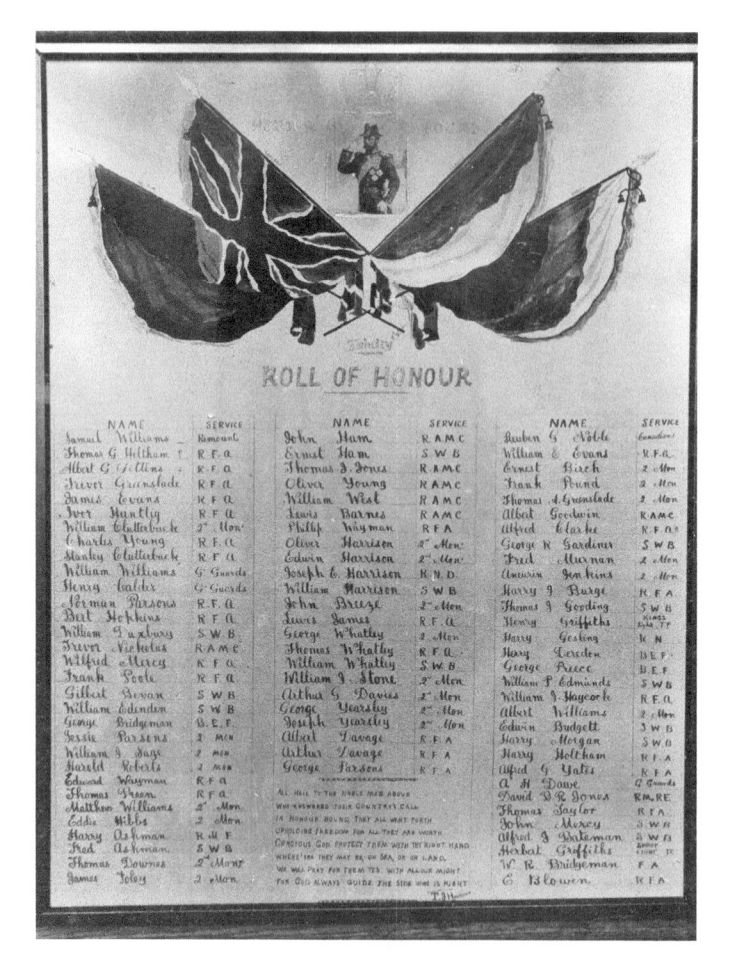

This roll of honour was originally in Trinity Church, Pontywain, Cross Keys.

Budgett, Edwin
Davies, Arthur George
Holtham, Thomas George
Jenkins, Aneurin
Nicholas, Trevor
Sage, William James
West, William

Risca and Pontymister

Bethany Baptist Church

Sited in Bethany Baptist Church, Tredegar Street, Risca

Baker, George
Booth, Lyndon
Coulson, Andrew
Dobson, William
Davies, Oswald
Dark,** Ernest
Ellis, Fred
Griffith, John
Hopkins, Ira
Hall, Thomas
Hiley, Anthony
James, Jarvis
James, Noah
Jenkins, Albert
Jones, Ralph
Knight, Bert
Knight, James

Mayberry, Courtney
Morgan, William
Morgan, Alfred
Morris, Edgar
Parkins, Walter L
Prothero, Willie
Rallinson,*** Bernard
Richards, Garfield
Richards, George
Robinson, Frederick
Robins, George
Welch, Ernest
Watts, Herbert
Wilde, Rex
Wilcox,* Raymond
Winstone, Willie

* *No further information can be found on this name.*
** Should be spelt Dart / *** should be spelt Rallison.

Ebenezer Primitive Methodist Church

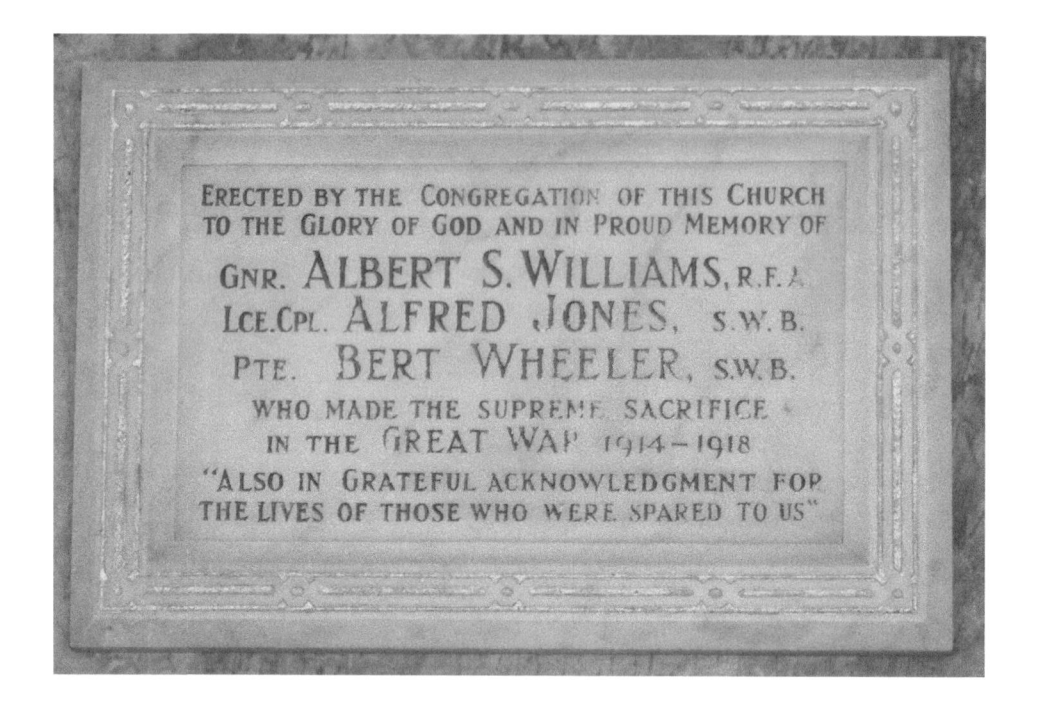

> ERECTED BY THE CONGREGATION OF THIS CHURCH TO THE GLORY OF GOD AND IN PROUD MEMORY OF
> GNR. ALBERT S. WILLIAMS, R.F.A.
> LCE.CPL. ALFRED JONES, S.W.B.
> PTE. BERT WHEELER, S.W.B.
> WHO MADE THE SUPREME SACRIFICE IN THE GREAT WAR 1914–1918
> "ALSO IN GRATEFUL ACKNOWLEDGMENT FOR THE LIVES OF THOSE WHO WERE SPARED TO US"

This is now housed in the Cemetery Chapel at Risca Old Cemetery, Cromwell Road, Risca.

Jones, Alfred
Wheeler, Bert
Williams, Albert Stanley

Miner's Memorial

Sited at the War Memorial, St Mary Street, Risca.

To the
Sacred and Everlasting
Memory of the Men who left
the Risca Collieries and District
to serve their King and Country
in the Great War 1914-1919

**"Greater love hath no Man than this.
That a Man lay down his life for you"**

*Erected by the
Risca Collieries Workmen.*

Moriah Baptist Church

THE GREAT WAR 1914 – 1918.

LT E.G. SALATHIEL. S.W.B.
SERGT J. BOOTH. W.G.
SERGT A.J. COOK. S.W.B.
CPL D.G. THOMAS. M.M. WELCH
L/C C. DOWNS. S.W.B.
L/C S. EVANS. S.W.B.
SIG J. BANFIELD. R.N.V.R.
PTE E. HART. R.F.A.

PTE H.G. HAINES. R.W.F.
PTE H.J. HATHERALL. S.W.B.
PTE A.L. JAMES. R.F.
PTE J. MORGAN. R.B.
GNR C. POWELL. R.F.A.
PTE W.H. ROBERTS. R.E.
DVR H. TUTTON. R.E.
PTE P.E. WATTS. S.W.B.

PTE C. GIBBS. K.L.
GREATER LOVE HATH NO MAN THAN THIS,
THAT A MAN LAY DOWN HIS LIFE FOR HIS FRIENDS.

Sited in Moriah Baptist Church, Tredegar Street, Risca.

Banfield, James
Booth, John
Cook, Andrew J
Downs,* Charles
Evans, Stanley
Gibbs, Charles
Haines,** Henry G
Hart, Ernest
Hatherall, Henry J

James, Arthur L
Morgan, James
Powell, Charles
Roberts, William H
Salathiel, Ewart G
Thomas, David G
Tutton, Harry
Watts, Percy E

* Spelt Downes on most other records.
** Spelt Haynes on other records.

Pontywaun County School

> TO THE MEMORY
> OF
> JOHN W. TAYLOR ASSISTANT MASTER
> AND OF
>
> JAMES BANFIELD   HOWARD JOHNSON
> FRED CAWLEY   COBDEN JONES
> CYRIL CLISSOLD   RALPH JONES
> NOEL T. DANIEL   SAMUEL LLEWELYN
> DAVID DART   ALBERT MELLISH
> J. EMLYN DAVIES   WILLIAM MORGAN M.C.
> REGINALD DAVIES   ZEPHANIAH ORMAN
> WILLIAM DOBSON   DAVID F. ROWLANDS
> W. JONES-EVANS   EWART G. SALATHIEL
> WILLIAM H. HARPER   VICTOR TYLER
> LESLIE A. JAMES   OSWALD M. WILLIAMS
> ARCHIBALD JELF   WILLIAM WINSTONE
> EDWIN W. JENKINS
>
> WHO DIED IN THE GREAT WAR 1914 — 1918
> THAT WE MIGHT LIVE IN PEACE AND SAFETY

Sited at the junction of Station Road and Tredegar Street, Risca

Banfield, James	Johnson, Howard
Cawley, Fred	Jones, Cobden
Clissold, Cyril J	Jones, Ralph
Daniel, Noel T	Llewelyn, Samuel
Dart, , David	Mellish, Albert
Davies, John Emlyn	Morgan, William
Davies, Reginald	Orman, Zephaniah
Dobson, William	Rowlands, David F
Evans, William J	Salathiel, Ewart G
Harper, William H	Taylor, John W
James, Leslie A	Tyler, Victor
Jelf, Archibald	Williams, Oswald M
Jenkins, Edwin Willard	Winstone, William J

Risca Workingmen's Club

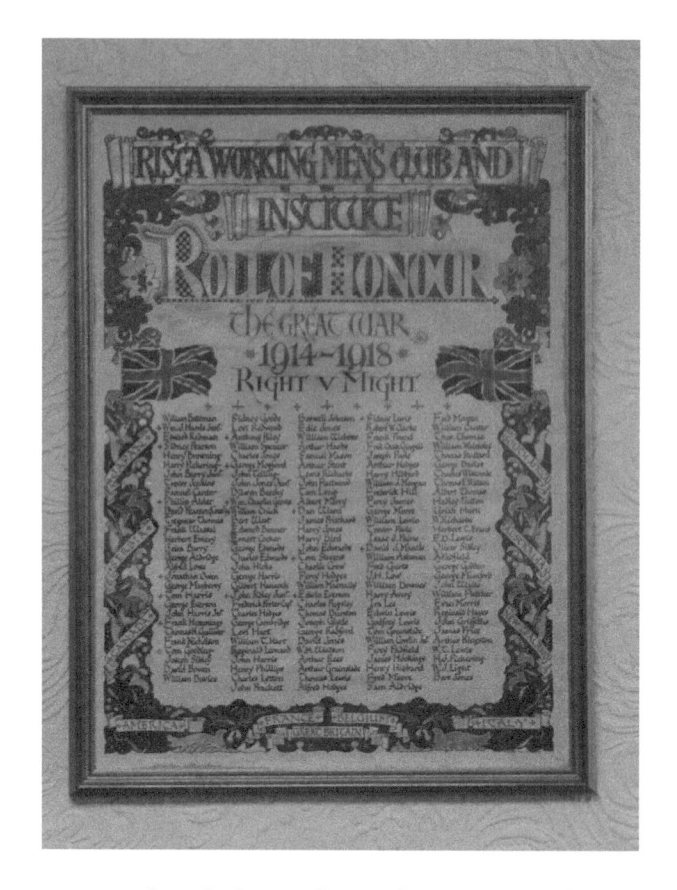

*Sited in the bar at the Workingmen's Club,
St Mary Street, Risca.*

Alder, Phillip
Chick, William
Everson, Edwin
Geeves, William C
Gooding, Tom
Hards, William J
Harris, Tom
Hemmings, Frank
Hiley, Anthony

Lewis, Sidney
Mantle, David J
Mogford, George
Owen, Jonathan
Pearson, Sidney
Sibley, John
Stevens, Tom
Ward,* Dan

* No further information can be found on this name.

St John's Church

> KILLED IN ACTION
> 1914-1918
>
> Bateman, Jarvis
> Bryant, George
> Cockell, John. H.
> Harper, William
> Roberts, Albert
> Wilcox, Raymond
> Johnson, Howard — Died on active service

These names commemorate members of the Wesley Chapel, Risca, later known as St. John's Methodist Church. It is believed this book has now been lost.

Bateman, Jarvis
Bryant, George
Cockell, John H
Harper, William

Johnson, Howard
Roberts,* Albert
Wilcox,* Raymond

* No further information can be found on these names.

St Margaret's Church

Sited in St Margaret's Church, Commercial Street, Pontymister.

Coles, William John
Everson, William
Hann, Frank
Jay, James
Knight, Bertram
Owen, Prosser
Rallison, Bernard
Rallison, Victor
White, Edwin

St Mary's Church

Sited in St Mary's Church, Church Road, Risca.

Bridge, William C
Clissold, Cyril James
Hemmings, Frank
Leonard, Frederick W
Mellish, Albert
Pritchard, Clarence H
Prout, Charles
Watkins, Herbert

I'R FYDDYN FECHGYN GWALIA!

Cas gwr nid cas ganddo elyn ei wlad.

CYMRU AM BYTH!

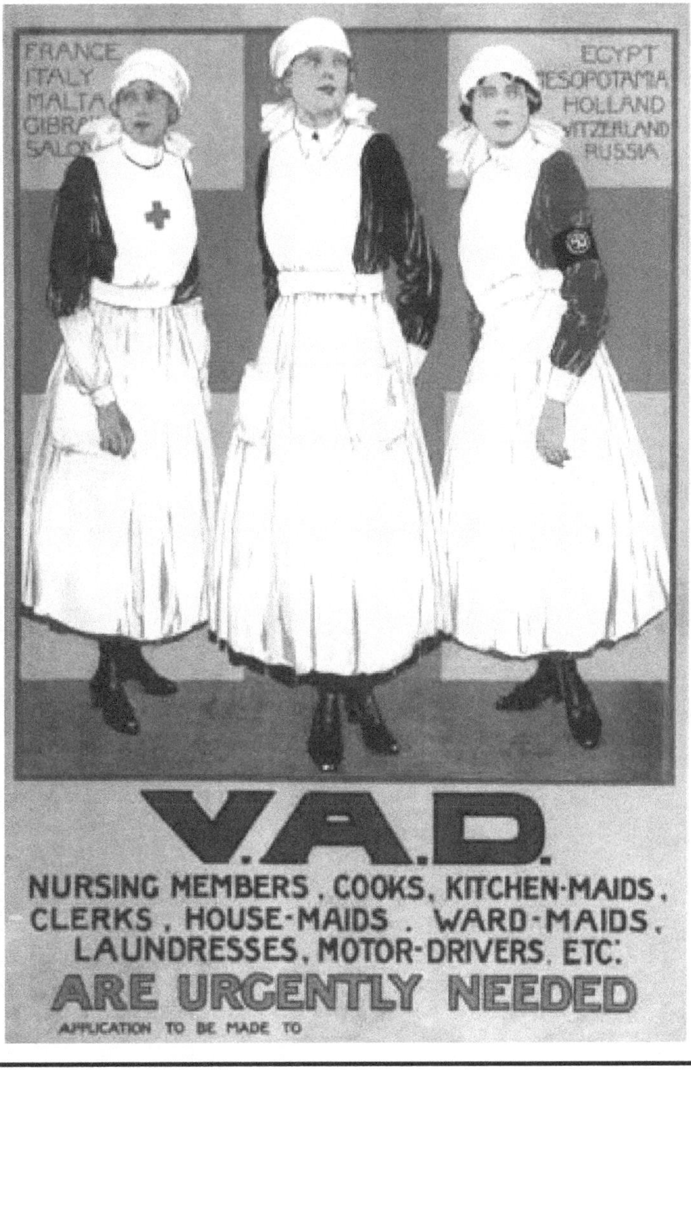
FRANCE
ITALY
MALTA
EGYPT
HOLLAND
RUSSIA
V.A.D.
NURSING MEMBERS, COOKS, KITCHEN-MAIDS,
CLERKS, HOUSE-MAIDS. WARD-MAIDS,
LAUNDRESSES, MOTOR-DRIVERS, ETC.
ARE URGENTLY NEEDED
APPLICATION TO BE MADE TO

Are YOU fond of Cycling?

IF SO

WHY NOT CYCLE FOR THE KING?

RECRUITS WANTED

By the S. Midland Divisional Cyclist Company

(Must be 19, and willing to serve abroad).

CYCLES PROVIDED. Uniform and Clothing issued on enlistment.

Application in person or by letter to Cyclists, The Barracks, Gloucester.

BAD TEETH NO BAR.